UTB 3448

W0405890

Eine Arbeitsgemeinschaft der Verlage

Böhlau Verlag · Wien · Köln · Weimar
Verlag Barbara Budrich · Opladen · Farmington Hills
facultas.wuv · Wien
Wilhelm Fink · München
A. Francke Verlag · Tübingen und Basel
Haupt Verlag · Bern · Stuttgart · Wien
Julius Klinkhardt Verlagsbuchhandlung · Bad Heilbrunn
Mohr Siebeck · Tübingen
Nomos Verlagsgesellschaft · Baden-Baden
Orell Füssli Verlag · Zürich
Ernst Reinhardt Verlag · München · Basel
Ferdinand Schöningh · Paderborn · München · Wien · Zürich
Eugen Ulmer Verlag · Stuttgart
UVK Verlagsgesellschaft · Konstanz, mit UVK/Lucius · München
Vandenhoeck & Ruprecht · Göttingen
vdf Hochschulverlag AG an der ETH Zürich

StandardWissen Lehramt

Die Bände zur Didaktik des Englischen werden herausgegeben von Engelbert Thaler

Bislang sind erschienen in der Reihe:

Mediendidaktik Deutsch von A. Barsch (UTB 2808)
Verhaltensstörungen und Lernschwierigkeiten von N. Berger/W. Schneider (UTB 3470)
Sprachbetrachtung und Grammatikunterricht von U. Bredel (UTB 2890)
Didaktik des Ökonomie- und Politikunterrichts von T. Engartner (UTB 3318)
Texte schreiben von M. Fix (UTB 2809)
Texte lesen von Ch. Garbe u.a. (UTB 3110)
Teaching Grammar von J.-U. Keßler/A. Plesser (UTB 3448)
Deutsch als Zweitsprache von G. Kniffka/G. Siebert-Ott (UTB 2891)
Lese- und Rechtschreiberwerb von P. Marx (UTB 2946)
Task-Supported Language Learning von A. Müller-Hartmann/M. Schocker-von Ditfurth (UTB 3336)
Sprachdidaktik Deutsch von J. Ossner (UTB 2807)
Orthographie von J. Ossner (UTB 3329)
Teaching English Literature von E. Thaler (UTB 2897)
Mündliche Kommunikation in der Schule von R. W. Wagner (UTB 2810)
Kinder- und Jugendliteratur von G. Weinkauf/G. v. Glasenapp (UTB 3345)
Elternhaus und Schule von E. Wild/F. Lorenz (UTB 3418)
Emotion, Motivation und selbstreguliertes Lernen von T. Götz, u.A. (UTB 3481)

Ergänzend:

Lesesozialisation. Arbeitsbuch von Ch. Garbe u.a. (UTB 8398)

Jörg-U. Kessler / Anja Plesser

Teaching Grammar

Ferdinand Schöningh

Die Autoren:

Jörg-U. Keßler ist Dekan der Fakultät II und Professor für englische Sprache und ihre Didaktik an der Pädagogischen Hochschule Ludwigsburg. Nach seinem Lehramtsstudium und Referendariat (Englisch und Geographie für das Lehramt an Gymnasien) arbeitete er viele Jahre an einer Realschule mit bilingualem Zug in Nordrhein-Westfalen. Während seiner Abordnung an die Universität Paderborn promovierte er bei Manfred Pienemann im Bereich des schulischen Zweitsprachenerwerbs. Als *Visiting Research Fellow* an der School of Education, Communication and Language Sciences der Newcastle University forschte er zum impliziten und expliziten Grammatikerwerb. Seine Forschungs- und Publikationsschwerpunkte liegen in den Bereichen Zweitsprachenerwerbsforschung, Sprachstandsdiagnose sowie bilingualem Lehren und Lernen. Ein zentrales Anliegen, das diese Forschungsbereiche verbindet, ist die Analyse von Lernersprache mit dem Ziel eines lernerorientierten Fremdsprachenunterrichts quer durch alle Schulformen.

Anja Plesser ist seit 2008 an der Universität Paderborn am Lehrstuhl von Manfred Pienemann und dem Zentrum für Sprachlehre (ZfS) tätig. Zuvor studierte sie an der dortigen Universität und der Universidad de Zaragoza, Spanien, Lehramt für die Sekundarstufen II und I für die Fächer Englisch und Spanisch. Für ihre Abschlussarbeit im Bereich der Zweitspracherwerbsforschung erhielt sie den Preis der Sprachwerkstatt für hervorragende fachwissenschaftliche Abschlussarbeiten.
Ihr von Manfred Pienemann betreutes Promotionsprojekt befasst sich mit der Psycholinguistik des Zweitspracherwerbs; neben universellen Prinzipien des Zweitspracherwerbs und Sprachprozessierung forscht sie in diesem Zusammenhang zu sprachspezifischen Aspekten für Englisch und Spanisch als Zweitsprachen. In 2009 erhielt sie für ein Projekt zum Spanischerwerb den Forschungspreis der DGS-Stiftung (gemeinsam mit Anke Lenzing, M.A.).
Sie lehrt sowohl im Bereich der Englischen Sprachwissenschaft als auch der Didaktik der englischen Sprache. Ihre Schwerpunkte liegen hier neben der Zweitspracherwerbsforschung selbst in wissenschaftlich fundierter Sprachstandsdiagnostik.

Bibliografische Information der Deutschen Nationalbibliothek

Die Deutsche Nationalbibliothek verzeichnet diese Publikation in der Deutschen Nationalbibliografie; detaillierte bibliografische Daten sind im Internet über http://dnb.d-nb.de abrufbar.

© 2011 Verlag Ferdinand Schöningh, Paderborn
Verlag Ferdinand Schöningh GmbH & Co. KG, Jühenplatz 1, D-33098 Paderborn

Internet: www.schoeningh.de

Das Werk, einschließlich aller seiner Teile, ist urheberrechtlich geschützt. Jede Verwertung außerhalb der engen Grenzen des Urheberrechtsgesetzes ist ohne Zustimmung des Verlages unzulässig und strafbar. Das gilt insbesondere für Vervielfältigungen, Übersetzungen, Mikroverfilmungen und die Einspeicherung und Verarbeitung in elektronischen Systemen.

Printed in Germany
Einbandgestaltung: Atelier Reichert, Stuttgart auf Grundlage eines Entwurfes von Alexandra Brand und Judith Karwelies
Layout: Alexandra Brand und Judith Karwelies

UTB-Bestellnummer: ISBN 978-3-8252-3448-5

Grammar is the structural foundation of our ability to express ourselves. The more we are aware of how it works, the more we can monitor the meaning and effectiveness of the way we and others use language. It can help foster precision, detect ambiguity, and exploit the richness of expression available in English. And it can help everyone--not only teachers of English, but teachers of anything, for all teaching is ultimately a matter of getting to grips with meaning.

(David Crystal 2004a: 26)

To Sarah and Hannah
To Harald and Ulrike

Table of Contents

Part III: Grammar Teaching in the EFL Classroom

Part IV: Service Section

List of abbreviations:

CEFR	Common European Framework
CLIL	Content and Language Integrated Learning
CLT	Communicative Language Teaching
CR	Consciousness Raising
EC	Emergence Criterion
EFL	English as a Foreign Language
ESL	English as a Second Language
FonF	Focus on Form
IE	Input Enhancement
IL	Interlanguage
L1	First Language
L2	Second Language (can also be a foreign language only learned in a classroom setting)
LFG	Lexical Functional Grammar
LTM	Long-Term Memory
MSH	Mode Steadiness Hypothesis
NP	Noun Phrase
NS	Native Speaker
NNS	Non-native speaker
NUM	Number
PT	Processability Theory
RP	Rapid Profile
SLA	Second Language Acquisition
STM	Short-term memory
SVO	Subject-Verb-Object
TBLT	Task-based Language Teaching
TESL	Teaching English as a Second Language
TH	Teachability Hypothesis
TL	Target Language
UG	Universal Grammar

1 Introduction

Although teaching grammar in the EFL classroom is likely to become an important every day activity for future teachers of English, it is often regarded with apprehension: all too often, grammar is viewed in a negative way among students and, unfortunately, sometimes by teachers as well. This may be due to the fact that the study of grammar is often considered to be a boring necessity which distracts the learner from the seemingly more important goals of EFL teaching such as the furtherance of communicative skills. What we need to admit, however, is that even in the communicative language classroom the teaching of grammar does, and should, play an important role. Communication without grammar would not be feasible at all.

The stereotypical image of grammar in the EFL classroom is often based on traditional beliefs about grammar itself and traditional ways of teaching grammar. This, in turn, is perpetuated by many current textbooks, which neglect decisive insights from research in such areas as second language acquisition, psycholinguistics and cognitive neuroscience.

The present volume is not a grammar book that describes and/or explains English grammar to students of English. It does not focus on grammatical categories or functions or provide rules about how sentences can or cannot be organised. What it does is propose new attitudes and approaches to the actual teaching of grammar in the EFL classroom.

This book is written for readers who are new to the field of teaching grammar. It can be used both in seminars at universities and/or teacher-training centres as well as for self-study purposes. It is specifically designed to query some "common" beliefs about grammar and its teaching. It looks at the question of why grammar should be taught from a learner-centred perspective. In other words: by addressing some of the most common misunderstandings about how grammar is learned, this book will provide an introduction to an SLA-based approach to grammar teaching based on major empirical findings in international studies.

The introduction to grammar teaching approaches in the first part of the book is followed, in the second part, by ways in which the insights we have gained from SLA, can be converted into ideas for practical application in the classroom. First, we introduce some current approaches to classroom-based grammar teaching. This is followed by a section on "Grammar Teaching in the EFL Classroom" which will provide the reader with ideas of how to apply SLA Theory to actual and successful classroom practice.

Successful grammar teaching relies on valid and reliable ways to diagnose learners' needs as well as learner progress. This is why the final section of the book addresses itself to different ways of how to assess grammatical knowledge in the classroom. This section also shows how grammar teaching can be made far more beneficial when it is done on a diagnostic basis.

The book is completed by an intensive study section integrated into each of the chapters. Additionally, this study section does not only provide a wide range of study questions and suggestions for further reading at the end of each chapter. It also includes a glossary of technical terms from the field of grammar teaching at the end of the book.

Background | I

2 Basis – Grammar: What?

This chapter lays the foundation of our approach to grammar teaching. We are aware that our approach may not be fully compatible with mainstream ideas of grammar and its teaching. However, the SLA-based approach taken throughout the book is well substantiated by empirical research. It will help (future) language teachers as well as their learners to develop a deeper understanding of the underlying processes of any foreign language acquisition, either in natural or in instructed settings. In order to understand in what way our approach to grammar teaching is innovative it is essential to realise the following two important facts:

SLA-based approach

- There is no such thing as *the* grammar of a language
- There have been many competing approaches to grammar

In the first part of chapter 2 we will discuss the role of grammar as such. Our point of departure is a critical look at so-called "Standard English". We will show that there actually is no such thing as Standard English – especially not the one and only standard that can be taken as the foundation of any grammar teaching in instructed foreign language acquisition.

This conceptualisation of different kinds of *Standard Englishes* will then lead us into a critical review of common beliefs about grammar teaching. It will become clear that there are quite a few grammar teaching myths to be found both in the minds of language users as well as in the minds of language teachers. Anyone concerned with language teaching carries his/her own myths about grammar. Being familiar with (some of) those myths may make us aware that teaching grammar is a complex issue that requires a precise knowledge of what is going on in a learner's mind when he or she acquires a new language.

grammar teaching myths

This leads us to the question of what grammar actually is and also what it is not. We will address that question in the present chapter. A differentiated approach towards what grammar is will help the reader to first of all make up his/her mind about the importance of grammar teaching and – at the same time – may contribute to finding a more learner-centred way of teaching grammar in the EFL classroom.

Knowing what grammar is (not) we will then challenge some of the grammar teaching myths (cf. Larsen-Freeman 1997) as well as the common beliefs about grammar and explain from a developmental point of view (Pienemann 1998, Di Biase 2002 and 2008, Keßler 2008a) why those myths are rather counter-productive in grammar teaching. We will address some of the most common problems in traditional grammar teaching and explain why they are problematic. After having provided a more detailed academic basis of how instructed foreign language learning takes place (cf. chapter 5) we will come back to those problems and show how they can be solved in the language classroom.

Part I of this book will be closed by discussing the question as to whether and why grammar should be taught in the foreign language classroom. It will become clear that grammar teaching is vital to instructed SLA. However, this book also includes at least one approach to language teaching that successfully refrains from teaching grammar and yet achieves highly efficient language users. This immersion approach will be introduced in chapter 13 of our book.

grammar teaching vital to instructed SLA

The last part of this chapter addresses the fact that there have been plenty of competing approaches to grammar. We will take a look at the most common ways of presenting grammar. There are different ways of dealing with grammar. The following three approaches are the most common ones:

competing approaches to grammar

- Prescriptive Grammars
- Descriptive Grammars
- Pedagogical Grammars

Additionally, and in line with the approach to grammar (teaching) taken in this book we will introduce a fourth concept of grammar. This one considers what is going on in the mind of a learner when dealing with a foreign language. It is most learner-centred and draws from SLA research. We call this approach an *Interlanguage Approach* to grammar. Whereas the first three approaches mentioned above will only be briefly described we will lay more emphasis on explaining the *Interlanguage Approach* and on showing its relevance for the EFL classroom.

Interlanguage Approach

In this chapter we will take a closer look at grammar and its importance for the language classroom and therefore, of course, also for language teachers and students of language. In the light of David Crystal's quotation used at the very beginning of our book, grammar may even be important for any teacher, not just

Figure 1:
"Grammar explained"; taken from: Crystal (2004b: 9; Cartoon by Edward McLachlan)

the language teacher, as without grammar no one would be capable of "getting to grips with meaning" (Crystal 2004a: 26). However, grammar is a rather complex concept and – as illustrated in the Cartoon above – we often find language learners who are not too much bothered with explanations about grammar.

Before we discuss grammar and its teaching in more detail it might be useful to consider some basic issues about language standards. Although large parts of our book actually refer to teaching grammar without reference to a particular foreign language and can thus be applied to any foreign language grammar, we focus on teaching English grammar to foreign language learners. This is why we will first consider what Standard English might be.

Definitions of Grammar: Standard English?

Yesterday, I toll my dad, "Buy chocolate kine now, bumbye somebody going egg our house you know, cuz you so chang." He sed, "Sucking kine mo' bettah cuz lass mo' long. Da kid going appreciate cuz..."
(Tonouchi 2001, cited in Yule 2006: 194)

Farrokh gripped the two edges of the table as of he wanted to break it in two. „I asked already," he bellowed. „I ask and I ASK. But no reply. What I can do? Mr Bommgarter, pliss, go speak to him in his language – ask him what he want? Why he sit in the Café de Paris when he have no money for food. for tea? Why

> he not go? When he get up and go? Please spick, Mr Bommgarter, and tell him GO."
> (Anita Desai[1] 1988, cited in Kohli 1989: 1322; emphasis added)

Looking at the examples above, we can state that talking about "English Grammar" is not as easy as it might look at first sight. The issue raised in the examples is that one has to consider what exactly one means when talking about English. The first example above by Tonouchi is an account of "Trick-O-Treat" in Hawai'i (Yule 2006: 194), the other example provides some insight into literature published in Indian English. The list of regional varieties of English is long – we are all familiar with British, Canadian, American, and Australian English, but of course there are plenty of other regional varieties of English (Crystal 2002, Trudgill & Hannah 2002). Crystal (2002:5f) presents a list of 75 countries (from American Samoa to Zimbabwe) where English is an official or semi-official language.

When teaching English grammar we have to be aware that in different regions people speak different *Englishes*. This can even be found within one nation – the English spoken in London is rather different from that spoken in Newcastle; in the US we know Ebonics as one of the varieties spoken by Afro-Americans. This is why linguists distinguish between different accents and dialects of a language. While different accents are distinguished just in terms of phonology, a dialect is characterized also by a different grammar and lexicon (cf. Yule 2006).

different *Englishes*

accents and dialects

If we take a closer look at the example of Indian English above, some readers might consider the examples to be ungrammatical. From a linguistic point of view, however, these examples are well-formed in terms of Indian English grammar. Kohli, a literature professor from India, explains Indian English as follows:

> Where previously the language came to us from direct contact with native users, it has now taken on a life of its own and became Indianized. Differences between the sounds and vocabularies of British English and Indian English are striking. They could have easily been explained as historical accidents had there not been

[1] Anita Desai is an award-winning author writing her literature in Indian English. She is the John E. Burchard Professor of Writing at Massachusetts Institute of Technology, Cambridge, MA. For further details see: http://www.contemporarywriters.com/authors/?p=auth124 (24/08/2009).

> also **significant differences of grammar**. And cultural differences between us and native users of English lead to a variety of differences in modes of expressions also. [...]
> What I would like to suggest is that Indian English has emerged in the amorphous yet nevertheless distinctive form it now takes on account of two conflicting principles of language change. One is the process of dialect-formation – the process by which language is simplified and is enriched when it is forced to reflect the realities of an alien culture; the other process is pidginization, whereby the language is simplified and certain linguistic distinctions are dropped. The dialect formation process enriches the body of international English; pidginization generalizes subtleties and constricts our ability to use it more sensitively.
> (Kohli, 1989: 1332; emphasis JK/AP)

In a similar vain, Bhabha (1997) compares different English-speaking works by Afro-American and Indian writers and looks at the different linguistic forms and their functions within literature.

Concerning Indian English, Trudgill & Hannah (2002: 129) point out that there is "no general agreement as to whether the standard should strictly be EngEng or whether IndEng forms (especially in grammar) which are used by the majority of educated speakers and can also be found in newspapers should be accepted in the Indian standard. So, what do we mean when we talk about English? Most teachers refer to the grammar of "Standard English". Again, different standards can be distinguished: on the one hand there are national standards, on the other hand – in particular in the English language – there are also world standards. According to Crystal (2004b: 16ff) any definition of Standard English (SE) even within an English-speaking country is not easy as a range of factors are involved[2]:

a. SE is a variety of English used in a country – a distinctive combination of linguistic features.
b. SE is the variety of English that carries most prestige within a country.
c. Although SE is widely understood, it is not widely produced in speech. This is a very important point. Only a minority of people within a country actually use it when they talk.
d. The linguistic features of SE are chiefly matters of grammar and orthography

[2] The following list is adapted from Crystal (2004: 16f).

Standard English = minority variety

Taking these factors into consideration it is evident that any Standard English defined according to the features listed above is a minority variety. If a definition of "Standard English" within a country is complicated a definition of a world standard of English is even more difficult. Although English-speaking international newspapers may pretend that there is something like a "World Standard English" any closer look at the English spoken in various countries where English is spoken as a first language reveals again various varieties (cf. Trudgill & Hannah 2002, Crystal 2004b). Various versions of English can be distinguished according to:

e. spelling (e.g. BE: theatre vs. AE: theatre)
f. regional vocabulary (e.g. BE: red pepper vs. AUE: capsicum)
g. pronunciation (compare BE: tomato vs. AE: tomato)
h. syntax
i. morphology
j. discourse

Although we might assume a World Standard English in written language, even English-speaking literature might need to be translated from one English into another. One example is the famous story of Harry Potter: the (British) English original first volume of Harry Potter is called *Harry Potter and the Philosopher's Stone*[3]; its translation into American English is called *Harry Potter and the Sorcerer's Stone*[4]. In the British version, Harry wears a *jumper*, in the American version he wears a *sweater*.

All issues raised in this section demonstrate that it is important to consider what the term Standard English actually means. However, it remains a controversial issue to fully identify what standard we are referring to when we talk about Standard English – either within a country or across national borders. Crystal (2004b: 19) even predicts "a tridialectal future":

A tridialectal future

Wherever World Standard English eventually comes from, a new **bidialectism** (the ability to use two dialects of a language)

3 The British version is published by Bloomsbury Publishing (London).
4 The American version is published by Scholastic Inc. (New York).

is sure to emerge. And because many people are already bidialectal (knowing their national standard and a regional dialect), the future is likely to be a **tridialectical** one.
- At home or with friends, we will use a variety of English influenced by the dialect of the region where we live.
- Travelling around the country, for work or for tourism, British people (for example) will use British Standard English.
- Travelling around the world, we will talk together using World Standard English.

Whenever we teach grammar we have to be aware of the different standards. Even if a certain expression or structure is not listed in a particular grammar book one must not be sure that this structure does not exist in some standard variety of that language (cf. the examples of Indian English at the beginning of this chapter) With Cheshire (1991: 7) we understand that the considerable number of different English standards may be problematic for the choice of a suitable teaching model. We suggest that any such choice must not neglect the existence of alternative versions of Standard English. In the closing section of this chapter we will introduce various approaches to grammar; a prescriptive grammar might consider something to be ungrammatical that a descriptive grammar actually accepts as grammatical. For further detail refer to pages 37-45.

What does grammar mean to you?

The title of this book, "Teaching Grammar" suggests that its primary focus is on explanations and hints about how to teach the structural components of language. This, however, suggests that we assume grammar to be teachable. An even more basic prerequisite for teaching grammar at all would be that we all know what 'grammar' is. But is this actually the case? Before you start working with this book, the following task might help you to make up your mind on what 'teaching grammar' actually means.

Please answer each of the following questions *spontaneously*.
- What is grammar?

- Is grammar teachable? Explain your answer.
- If so, should grammar be taught explicitly? Explain your answer.

In some of our seminars we asked our students to spontaneously come up with their ideas about grammar and its teaching. The following table is a selection of future teachers' views of teaching grammar. Some of these statements may be similar to your answers given above, and some may be different. Subsequently, the most common beliefs among language teachers as regards teaching grammar are addressed in more detail.

What is grammar?	**Is grammar teachable?**	**If so, should grammar be taught explicitly?**
It is basically a term for the rules that govern how the words and the language should be used. Every language has its own structure and grammar.	In fact, grammar has to be taught. At a certain level of language knowledge grammar cannot be learned through conversation anymore (although, of course, a certain feeling for the language is still of importance).	Learners do better when they discover the language and its structures independently. Learning rules by heart is usually not very effective.
Grammar is another word for the rules governing the use of a language, including morphology and syntax for example.	In general, grammar consists of basic rules and is thus teachable.	Yes.
A fixed set of rules.	Yes, of course.	Yes, although communication should be most important in the L2 classroom.
The rules of a language that one needs to know to be able to use that particular language correctly.	Grammar is teachable, as the rules can be learned. Still, I think that it isn't enough to know the 'rules' by heart, but to make it into something that can be used without thinking about it. This again is only possible if the students have enough time to use the language they are supposed to learn properly.	Yes, I think that grammar should be taught explicitly, because I'm sure that students need to learn the 'rules' before they are able to use them without thinking about it. I think that especially the basic rules of a foreign language should be taught explicitly, as I don't see the chance to develop language skills otherwise.

What is grammar?	Is grammar teachable?	If so, should grammar be taught explicitly?
A fixed system of structural rules underlying each language.	The rules are teachable, yes. However, Children do not need to be taught grammar either. They would not know what to do with 'rules'; they just start using the language at some point in time.	I don't think it should be taught, as the mother tongue is acquired naturally, too. It is the same brain that learns the L2.
Grammar is the system of a language. It is also a field of linguistics that involves all the various things that make up the rules of language. The rules of grammar create meaning.	Yes, grammar is teachable. It is necessary in order to teach the use of a language and to be able to understand and reflect on a language. Of course it isn't always easy to teach grammar because most pupils feel bored when confronted with grammar. They often reject the learning and practising of grammar, which makes it very difficult to teach it properly.	First of all, the teacher needs to be aware of the fact that most the pupils will reject the learning of grammar. In order to improve this it is the teacher'a responsibility to make the topic of grammar more interesting. The pupil should get the feeling that grammar is an important and necessary component for learning a language.
Grammar is the structure of a language. The grammar tells us how to "use" a language.	Yes, because it consists of fixed rules (in most cases).	Yes. The pupils need certain grammar-skills as a solid foundation.
Grammar contains the structural aspects of language like word order and flections.	Yes it is, because there is a structure, meaning that it is not arbitrary.	Yes, it should. Students should be aware of these structures.
Grammar is a rational system of a language which provides students with certain rules in order to use and analyse a language.	Grammar is teachable, because it is a system which can be taught in sequences. You can build up grammar knowledge by starting at the very basics. In a second step you can add more detailed information. In time students get a complex overview.	I believe that it has to be taught explicitly, because otherwise it is simply impossible for students to get a complex overview of the target language.
Rules for language; rules for syntax, morphology, lexis, semantics, phonetics, phonology.	If rules are teachable and grammar consists of rules, grammar must be teachable.	Yes, grammar should be taught explicitly, because it forms the basis of a language.

Table 1: Future teachers' views on grammar and its teaching

According to the above selection of future teachers' views of grammar and its teaching, the apparently most 'common' view is that the structural basis of language is generally seen as a fixed set of rules and regulations that has to be (and can be) taught. Even though the structural properties of a language appear to be rather fixed at first glance, this static view of linguistic systems does not correspond to one of each language's most important features: dynamicity. Languages, and thus their grammars, are constantly subject to change, as historical linguistics illustrates (see Brinton 2006). Languages are, in fact, dynamic because its use is: "[...] grammar(ing) is one of the dynamic linguistic processes of pattern formulation in language, which can be used by humans for making meaning in context-appropriate ways." (Larsen-Freeman 2003: 142) Languages change, because the respective speech community(-ies) change. This may, at first sight, be bad news for teachers as this implies that they do not know enough (about) grammar. However, just like linguists (future) language teachers

languages and its grammars: A fixed set of rules?

teachers have to know everything about the L2 grammar

> have to accommodate the changing nature of language. For example, most grammar books make clear the fact that progressive aspect is not used with stative verbs; therefore, the following would be ungrammatical: (5) "I am wanting a new car." For some English speakers, the sentence is not ungrammatical, and even those who find it so would be more inclined to accept progressive aspect when it co-occurs with perfective aspect, as in : (6) "I have been wanting a new car" (for some time now).
>
> (Larsen-Freemann 1995: 5)

In terms of foreign language teaching, the belief that grammar is a fixed set of rules implies, at first glance, that the L2 grammatical system builds a 'natural' guideline for the order of introducing linguistic structures in the L2 classroom. That is to say, classroom activities can be designed on the basis of how the language is structurally organised. This, in turn, implies a very strong idea as to how language learning works: learners learn what teachers teach. In fact, this sounds very appealing and true, as in formal SLA it is the foreign language teacher who provides L2 learners with input and feedback. Accordingly, learners should acquire those TL structures which the teacher presents. Every (future) teacher, however, will have come across students who 'forgot' the 3rd-SG-s – despite repetitive explanations plus numerous oppor-

do learners learn what teachers teach?

tunities to practise its use. In the language classroom, there are various grammatical structures like the English 3rd-SG-s the learners seem to use or fall short of using more or less independently of what they have been taught so far. Why? Does this observation render teaching grammar redundant? As will be shown in this book, teaching grammar is not redundant. In fact, instruction is beneficial and conducive to the learner's acquisition process. The potential effectiveness of teaching grammatical structures, however, depends on the cognitive prerequisites of the L2 learners (see chapter 7).

Practice makes perfect. Doesn't it?

Given that L2 learners fail to produce the, e.g. 3rd-person-singular-s (henceforward: 3rdSG-s), for instance, even though it has been introduced and explained in class, the teacher should offer classroom activities that promote its use, because practice makes perfect or does it not? This can be observed when children learn to ride a bike, swim or as adults learn to drive a car. Learning how to use a TL structure automatically does, indeed, require a certain amount of practice. However, practice does not necessarily result in the learners' acquisition of a particular structure (Pienemann 1995; see chapter 6 and 7).

errors should be eradicated

If language use is dynamic, as was clarified above, why should language learning be static? This would rule out the human mind's capability of being active and creative. Even though first language acquisition and SLA are not the same, they share one phenomenon, namely that individuals can, basically, produce an infinite number of sentences on the basis of limited input[5]. Language learners can do a lot more than simply parrot grammatical structures. However, when learners produce spontaneous spoken or written output which is not simply repetitive in nature, they make mistakes. This leads us to another common belief in teaching grammar, namely that errors should be eradicated. As is commonly observed by ESL teachers, omission of the 3rd-SG-s, for example, is a very frequent 'mistake' among L2 learners. This very morpheme is, actually, not only a little 's' to be attached to a verb in 3rd person, but a complex ESL structure which is acquired rather late. Correcting this inaccuracy straight away does not result in the learner acquiring it. On the contrary, to insist on the learner 'concentrating and paying attention" to what s/he says in

5 See "*Poverty of the Stimulus*"-argument (Chomsky 1965).

order to promote the accurate production of the 3rd-SG-s to be produced can have a harmful effect on the SLA process. The fact that numerous ESL learners have 'problems' with the 3rd-SG-s suggests that this error is systematic in nature. As Pienemann summarises

> the error is an indicator of the creative and constructive use of the [L2]. This is a concept that some language teachers might find difficult to accept because there appears to be a contradiction in terms. Errors are normally seen as something negative and a bad learning behaviour and not as creative language use. It is interesting to note that even in language behaviour which contains errors, learners are behaving in a systematic rule-governed way. For example, learners who say "goed" for "went" are showing that they have acquired the regular past tense, but not yet the irregular. They are following a rule.
>
> (Pienemann 1995: 5)

The treatment of errors (see Chapter 7) along with explicit grammar teaching has been a hotly debated issue ever since. Whereas some think errors should be avoided or corrected at all costs, others put sole emphasis on meaningful interaction in the L2 classroom. Classroom activities in the early Stages of Communicative Language Teaching were carried out on the absolute premise of getting meaning across without any focus on grammar. This rather radical way of leaving errors uncorrected can result in learners developing a simplified mental representation of the target grammar. A case in point which we will refer to later on (see Chapter 5) in detail is the omission of the copula 'to be'. Needless to say, the purpose of language is to communicate and at face value there is no need to focus on grammatical structures as long as the speaker gets her/his message across. But language forms correspond to a function, which implies that they are not redundant in nature. Therefore, it may fulfil the communicative purpose to say "*Me John. You Mary?", in an informal situation. On the other hand, it seems rather inappropriate as a foreign superior of a multinational company to introduce a new employee to the personnel by saying "*This new colleague John."

no error correction at all

meaning before accuracy

To prevent L2 learners from developing simplified versions of the L2, pedagogical intervention in terms of teaching grammar is useful (see Chapter 7). However, as was briefly sketched above, learners do not necessarily learn what teachers teach. In order to provide valuable support for the L2 learner, teachers should know about how language learning works in the learner's mind. Coming back to the title of this book, the good news is that both the terms 'teaching' and 'grammar', have somewhat different meanings from those one might traditionally be used to. Grammar is neither nebulous nor a dogmatic system of unchangeable rules that has to be learned before it can be used. The unfolding of the L2 grammar follows certain cognitive 'principles', as it were, which will be presented in this book. The issue of' 'teaching' grammar will also be addressed, on the basis of which the reader will learn about language learning. At the end of this book, we will have a look at the above beliefs on 'teaching grammar' and either complement, confirm or re-evaluate them. Now, let us first discuss some common problems and grammar myths in traditional grammar teaching before concluding this section of Chapter 2, by taking a closer look at the question why to teach grammar at all. By challenging the grammar teaching myths we make a case for grammar teaching right at the beginning of this book. This does not necessarily, however, imply that teachers ought to stick exclusively to traditional approach to grammar teaching. We rather aim at encouraging (future) teachers to apply a more learner- and learning-centred approach to grammar teaching, based on international empirical findings in SLA and Applied Linguistics. The *Interlanguage Approach* as put forward here combines recent research findings with classroom practice.

> It is necessary to know grammar, and it is better to write grammatically than not, but it is well to remember that grammar is common speech formulated.
> Usage is the only test.
> (William Somerset Maugham, The Summing Up, 1938)

Grammar Myths

> I'd like to explain what I call "The Final -*S* Problem." For a lot of teachers, it goes like this: "I teach my students when to use a final -*s*, and they can do it fine in a controlled exercise, but then

when they talk or write freely, they go and make final -s errors!" Whereupon the teacher throws up his or her hands in despair and determines that teaching grammar does no good because there is no immediate transfer to internalized language.

(Azar 2009)[6]

The observation described by Azar (2009) has probably been made by every teacher of English in every EFL classroom. Teaching grammar does not necessarily lead to the effect of understanding and acquiring the underlying grammar rules. How come those learners are actually able to state the rule of when or how to use third person singular-s (3rd –SG-s) but are not able to produce it in spontaneous language production? In this section we will explore some common problems of traditional grammar teaching. We will not yet discuss what can be done to overcome those problems as we feel that the reader first ought to be familiar with internal processes of language production. Once we have introduced the interface between Second Language Acquisition Research and Grammar Teaching in part II of this book we will revisit this section and provide answers that show how the problems of traditional grammar teaching can be addressed in the modern foreign language classroom.

ancient languages

Traditional grammar teaching (also see chapter 3 of this book) was based on the ideas of ancient Greek and Latin. This teaching approach is widely concerned with teaching how a language "works". Teachers who follow the traditional approaches to grammar teaching teach their learners the established grammatical concepts, categories and descriptions based on those ancient languages and adapt them to the modern language classroom (Yule 2006). However, this approach rather leads to learning about the target language rather than learning the target language itself (Larsen-Freeman 2000). In other words there are many language learners who are taught in a tradition of rather knowing about the rules of a language than knowing (and apply-

knowing about the rules vs. knowing the rules

6 This quotation is taken from Teacher Talk, a blog at azar.grammar.com (for the full article see: http://www.azargrammar.com/teacherTalk/blog/2009/04/final-s-problem-does-teaching-grammar.html. 26/08/2009).

ing) those rules in spontaneous language production (cf. Crystal 2004, Cowan 2008).

implicit/explicit dichotomy

The problem of knowing about the rules of a language rather than knowing the rules is related to the so-called "implicit/explicit dichotomy" (DeKeyser 2003: 313). Implicit learning generally is considered to be a less conscious form of learning, whereas explicit learning rather involves the use of strategies and mnemo-techniques by the learner. Implicit and explicit learning must not be confused with another dichotomy often found in instructional settings of foreign language acquisition, namely the concepts of inductive and deductive learning. DeKeyser (2003) points out that these concepts are often confused even in second language literature. In inductive learning the teacher first presents a couple of examples and the learners are supposed to discover the rules from the examples. This inductive approach to grammar teaching, however, is not an implicit but an explicit one. Inductive and implicit learning of language rules hardly ever takes place in foreign language but is rather a feature of first language acquisition as it is learning from the full and rich input of the target language without any providing of grammar rules. DeKeyser (2003: 314) illustrates the inductive/deductive and implicit/explicit dimensions of language acquisition as follows:

inductive/ deductive learning

	Deductive	Inductive
Explicit	Traditional teaching	Rule discovery
Implicit	Using parameters	Learning L1 from input

acquiring or Learning a language?

Teaching grammar rules exclusively in an explicit way often leads to knowing about the rules. Knowing about the rules, however, does not prevent the learners from not applying the very rule they are quite happily ready to state – this is exactly what Azar (2009) is referring to in her example quoted above.

Many Applied Linguists as well as SLA researchers have denied that traditional grammar teaching leads to hardly any positive effect for the language competence of the learners. In the early days of SLA research Krashen (1985) came up with his Input Hypothesis. This hypothesis states that there are two independ-

Input Hypothesis

ent processes of language learning: acquisition and learning. Whereas acquisition is "a subconscious process identical in all important ways to the process that children utilize in acquiring their native language" (Krashen 1985: 1) learning is "a conscious process that results in 'knowing about a language'" (Cowan 2008: 29). Following the non-interface position there is no relationship between learned and acquired knowledge. In other words learned knowledge can never be transferred into acquired knowledge (cf. Doughty 2003, Cowan 2008). Krashen suggests that any grammar teaching would only result in learning (= knowing about language) and thus be useless as the learners would not be able to apply the learned rules in spontaneous production. Rather than teaching grammar Krashen & Terrel (1983) suggested the Natural Approach to language teaching, which neglects the teaching of (explicit) grammar. Their approach relied on the idea of comprehensible input, a concept that was to help the learners to discover second language rules in an implicit manner. According to Krashen comprehensible input approximates best to acquiring a language as the processes involved are implicit. The best way of enhancing classroom-based foreign language acquisition would be the provision of comprehensible input using the formula of "i + 1" In Krashen's eyes, any input that was slightly above the learners' current state would be a challenging yet comprehensible input and thus lead to best results in the foreign language classroom.

comprehensible input

i + 1

Krashen's approach has been criticised by many SLA researchers for various reasons:

critique against Krashen

- One reason was the lack of empirical evidence in Krashen's hypotheses.
- McLaughlin (1987) criticised the fact that the distinction between acquisition and learning was weak because Krashen did not provide a clear definition of the two terms (cf. Cowan 2008:30 who characterises these two terms as the "cornerstone of Krashen's theory).
- Another strand of criticism Krashen had to face was the fact that he had not precisely defined what different Stages of acquisition would look like. This deficit makes it impossible to decide how comprehensible input could be provided according to the "i + 1" formula.

- Issidorides and Hulstijn (1992) showed that input modification which results in syntactic simplifications that may lead to learning problems in language production has no effect on comprehension (cf. Pienemann 1998). In other words comprehensible input is an important yet not sufficient factor in instructed foreign language learning as it does not necessarily lead to comprehensible output.
- Finally, many SLA researchers who are also concerned with instructed acquisition (e.g. Ellis 1985, 1989) refuted the strict distinction between acquisition and learning as introduced by Krashen, as the underlying processes in the minds of the learners have actually been found to be very similar (cf. Pienemann 1998). Today, in most publications acquisition and learning are used synonymously.

Despite all the criticism of Krashen's approach he was definitively right to point out the problem that knowing about language rather than knowing the language occurs in many instructed settings. So why do so many students tend to rather know about the rules but are not able to apply them? This must have to do something with traditional grammar teaching.

What's wrong with traditional grammar teaching?

> [...] meaningful verbal communication is not possible without grammatical knowledge, and that if the goal of language learning is communicative competence, then the language-teaching syllabus must integrate aspects of both grammar and function
> Rutherford (1988: 232)

theoretically and empirically unmotivated

Traditional grammar teaching is far too often concerned with teaching the learners rules. Textbook grammars and teachers very often are more concerned with linguistic forms rather than their function. Furthermore, many of them are not familiar with the natural route of development of grammatical structures in the mind of the learners (for details see chapter 7) but present grammatical structures in an order that randomly draws from the developmental hierarchy. In other words many textbook grammars and syllabi contain too many structures that are neither theoretically nor empirically motivated (Long 2005).

Another basic problem is that in traditional grammar teaching learners are confronted with one structure to be learned at a time. This is meant to be supportive as the learners then have to deal only with a limited amount of new structure. However, learning one structure at a time is not what one would find in any natural learning environment (cf. Lightbown & Spada 2003, Long 2005). Learning one structure at a time very often rather complicates the learning process because many grammatical structures are inter-dependent. One quite popular approach based on the idea of teaching one structure at a time is the so-called P-P-P model (Willis & Willis 1996, Richards & Rodgers 2006). This model has played a major role in teacher training. The basic idea is to first (P)resent a grammatical structure in a context, then (P)ractice this structure in a strictly controlled manner and eventually (P)roduce it in a freer phase. Though this method of grammar teaching "offers to the novice teacher the reassurance of a detailed set of sequential steps to follow in the classroom" (Richards & Rodgers 2006: 246), the P-P-P sequence has been criticised for not being in line with basic principles of SLA. As we will discuss in detail in part II of this book, SLA research has demonstrated that

learning one structure at a time

- focusing on one structure at a time does not lead to successful foreign language learning (Long 2005)
- learners will not necessarily learn what is presented to them in exactly that sequence (e.g. Pienemann 1989 and 1998, Skehan 1996)

In traditional grammar teaching form is considered to be more important than meaning. This is another problem of traditional grammar teaching as the teaching of isolated structures is not meaningful. Teaching a structure in a non-meaningful way may lead to an imitation of the structure by the learner rather than to learning how to apply the underlying rules in real communication. Without knowing how to apply the rule in meaningful ways the learners will then not be in a position to transfer the imitated structure to new contexts. Larsen-Freeman (2001: 251) accounts for this fact in the following way:

form before meaning

> Grammar is about form and one way to teach form is to give students rules; however, grammar is much more than form, and its teaching is ill served if students are simply given rules.
>
> Larsen-Freeman (2001: 251)

We have listed and explained a few problems with traditional grammar teaching in this section. Many of the problems listed and briefly discussed in this chapter are far from being new or unheard of. Bialystock (1988: 40) already pointed out that "Rules memorised as routines and recited verbatim may indicate nothing about the learner's knowledge if that rule has no meaning for the learner." Nevertheless, even today we still find plenty of rather traditional approaches to grammar teaching. This kind of instruction is not as beneficial as teachers intend and does not account for the individual learner within the foreign language classroom. Yet, with Doughty (1991) we believe that "instruction does make a difference"; however, it needs to be based on a sound understanding of basic findings of SLA research. In chapter 7 of this book we will discuss those findings and their impact on grammar teaching in detail. Now we will conclude this chapter by exploring the question as why it is necessary to teach grammar at all?

Further Reading

Crystal, D. (2002): The English Language. London: Penguin Books.

Crystal, D. (2004): Rediscover Grammar. 3rd Edition. Harlow: Pearson and Longman.

Doughty, C. (2003): "Instructed SLA: Constraints, Compensation, and Enhancement." In: Doughty, C. & M. Long (eds.); pp. 256-310.

Krashen, S. (1985): The Input Hypothesis: Issues and Implications. London: Longman.

Trudgill, P. & J. Hannah (2002): International English: A Guide to the Varieties of Standard English. 4th Edition. London: Edward Arnold.

Why teach grammar?

> Basic English Course
> 20 lessons
> We teach you how to speak
> so there's not much grammar.
>
> English ... has a grammar of great simplicity and flexibility.
>
> Crystal (2002: 21)

Why bother with teaching grammar? In the previous sections we have discussed some grammar teaching myths and also pointed out some common problems in traditional grammar teaching. We have also pointed out that instruction does make a difference (cf. Doughty 2001) Looking at the quotations above one might get the impression that grammar teaching is one of the less important aspects of language teaching. However, a look at any foreign language classroom makes it very clear: grammar does play a major role in instructed foreign language acquisition. Grammar is widely explained in students' textbooks. This is meant to be helpful but may not always as helpful as intended by the textbook authors. First of all textbooks often provide misleading and/or oversimplified or even wrong accounts of the target language (Cowan 2008). Unfortunately, the approach taken by most textbooks when explaining grammar is rather prescriptive and does not take into account that there are various versions of Standard English (cf. the discussion above). Furthermore textbooks very often do not consider what is going on in a learner's mind when the learner is acquiring a foreign language.

grammar in textbooks

Knowing about the grammar of a given language puts the learner into a position produce meaningful utterances and thus participate in communication. From an SLA perspective it is essential to be able to arrange morphemes and words of a foreign language in a meaningful way (Cowan 2008). Mere exposure to a foreign language may not be sufficient for learners to acquire the target language – especially if the learner has hardly any access to input beyond the classroom.

is exposure enough to acquire a foreign language?

Having stated the alleged lack of grammar in language courses and its simplicity on the one hand and the importance grammar plays in foreign language instruction on the other, we will now address the question of why we should teach grammar at all in the (foreign) language classroom.

language awareness

One good reason for teaching grammar in the foreign language classroom is to raise the learner's consciousness about certain rules of the target language that otherwise would take a lot of time to notice in a natural setting of SLA. Teaching grammar can accelerate the intake of grammar rules into the learner's Interlanguage. We will get back to this in chapter 6 of this book.

Another reason for teaching grammar in the foreign language classroom is that (the English) language consists of numerous exceptions to the rules of grammar. Recent grammar books often contain more than 700 pages (e.g. Cowan 2008) either prescribing or describing the grammar rules and their exceptions in a language. The standard volume of reference for English grammar is still the one by Quirk et al. (1985). On more than 1,700 pages the authors provide detailed insight into the English grammar. Teaching grammar can thus enhance the efficiency of language learning as a guideline to the rules and their exceptions in a language and may help learners to produce language. We will show later in this book that this is not always true as there is an important difference between knowing a rule/exception and actually applying it (cf. chapter 9 of this book).

efficiency of language learning

spoken vs. written language

Teaching grammar is also important to provide learners with background information about the differences between spoken and written language. According to Crystal (2002: 24) many people consider only written language important enough to bother about grammar. The most obvious difference between any piece of spoken and written language is the fact that written language always provides some kind of a final and thus polished version of what a person wants to communicate. There is much more thinking time when writing than there is for spontaneous oral language production. This may lead to different approaches to grammar even by native speakers of a language. Crystal (2002: 24 assures his readers "that the first draft of this paragraph looked very different from the final one." Actually the same is true for the passage you are reading right now in this book. Furthermore, spoken language is subject to quicker changes than written language. In other words, structures that are considered to be ungrammatical in writing may be considered to be acceptable in speaking by the same person (e.g. *I wonder if it will start raining, soon*).

In an above section we explained that there are a number of linguists (e.g. Dulay & Burt 1973, Krashen 1985) who are making a case against grammar teaching and argue that grammar teaching will lead to "knowing about the rules of a language" rather than "knowing the rules" in such a way as to be able to apply them (cf. Crystal 2002 and 2004, Cowan 2008). In 1973 Dulay & Burt published a paper asking the following question: "Should we teach children syntax?"

explicit grammar teaching

It is obviously true that mere explicit grammar teaching as can be found in various historical approaches to grammar teaching does not lead to long-lasting effects of knowing grammar (for details see chapter 9 of this book). Unfortunately many textbooks even to date still stick to rather traditional explicit ways of presenting and teaching grammar. Explicit approaches to grammar teaching have been criticised as not being sustainable enough in language learning as they often neglect meaning. Long (1991) has distinguished between **focus-on-formS** which is primarily concerned with "the accumulation of individual language elements" (Doughty & Williams 1998: 3) and **focus-on-form** (see chapter 11 for more detail) which "entails a prerequisite engagement in meaning before attention to linguistic features can be expected to be effective" (Doughty & Williams 1998: 3). In chapter 5 of this book we will return in more detail to an SLA-driven account of grammar and its teaching after having briefly summarised selected historical approaches to grammar teaching in chapter 3.

We have seen that why we should teach grammar is not an easy question to answer. Throughout the following chapters of this book we will even become aware that *teaching* grammar may be far less successful than *studying* grammar. However, let us conclude this section by summing up some good reasons for teaching grammar:

reasons for grammar teaching

- Any use of language (spoken or written) *is* grammar; grammar can be seen as the backbone not only of language but even of literature: without being able to change the syntax we would always have to stick to the same sentence pattern and thus make communication rather monotonous.

- If Grammar simply is there, we want to master it (cf. Crystal 2004b); teaching grammar can support this mastering.
- Grammar is a system of finite rules that can generate an infinite number of utterances; teaching grammar can help us understand that system in more detail and put learners into the position of having a choice between different ways of expressing something
- Quite a number of grammar rules can be transferred from one language into another; teaching grammar concepts (e.g. nouns, verbs, number, gender, tenses, aspect, etc.) in both the first as well as in a foreign language supports successful language use by native and non-native speakers

Throughout this book we take an approach towards teaching grammar that is inspired by and based on findings from SLA research (e.g. Pienemann 1998, Doughty 2003, DeKeyser 2003).

focus on Learner Grammars

This implies a focus on Learner Grammars; in the following section of this chapter we will explain the concept of Learner Grammars after having briefly reminded the reader about different kinds of grammars. The *Interlanguage Approach* to grammar teaching as promoted in this book accounts best for Learner Grammars. In doing so, it contributes to a learner-centred approach to grammar and its teaching and thus it supports both teachers and language learners.

Further Reading:

Cowan, R. (2008): The Teacher's Grammar of English. A course book and reference guide. Cambridge: Cambridge University Press.

Krashen, S. (1985): The Input Hypothesis: Issues and Implications. London: Longman.

Doughty, C. (2003): "Instructed SLA: Constraints, Compensation, and Enhancement." In: Doughty, C. & M. Long (eds.): The Handbook of Second Language Acquisition. Malden, MA: Blackwell; pp. 256-310.

Representations of Grammar

In the previous chapter we tackled grammar in a rather general way. We have collected some common beliefs about grammar and its teaching and also made a point for grammar teaching. In this chapter we will now take a closer look at different kinds of grammars. In the introductory part of this chapter we explained that we will briefly look at three common types of grammar, namely:

- Prescriptive Grammars
- Descriptive Grammars
- Pedagogical Grammars

The main focus of this book, however, is put on an *Interlanguage Approach* to grammar and grammar teaching. This approach considers the rather natural development of a second language grammar in the mind of the learner. This chapter will therefore be concluded by a more detailed discussion of the notion of

- Learner Grammars.

Before we start to get deeper into the matter, let us have a quick mental exercise: language teaching in general and grammar teaching in particular deal with "errors"; many teachers make strong efforts to eradicate their learners' errors – especially grammar errors – as soon as they occur. Grammars are therefore mental constructs that are supposed to help learners not to make errors. But: what actually is an error? A little dictionary survey (cf. Ko, 2005) provides some insight: errors

An error is:

- 🕮 an act that through ignorance, deficiency, or accident departs from or fails to achieve what should be done. (Meriam-Webster Dictionary)
- 🕮 something that you have done which is considered to be incorrect or wrong, or which should not have been done. (Cobuild English Dictionary)
- 🕮 a mistake. (dictionary.com)

INFOBOX: Defining Grammar

Crystal, 1987:88

"'It is difficult to capture the central role played by grammar in the structure of language, other than by using a metaphor such as 'framework' or 'skeleton'. ..... Two steps can usually be distinguished in the study of grammar. The first step is to identify units in the stream of speech (or writing or signing) units such as 'word' and 'sentence'. The second step is to analyse the patterns into which these units fall, and the relationships of meaning that these patterns convey.

Depending upon which units we recognize at the beginning of the study, so the definition of grammar alters. Most approaches begin by recognising the 'sentence', and grammar is thus most widely defined as 'the study of sentence structure'. A grammar of a language, from this point of view, is an account of the language's possible sentence structures, organized according to certain general principles."

J. C. Richards, J.C., Platt J. and Platt H., 1992:161

"'A description of the structure of a language and the way in which linguistic units such as words and phrases are combined to produce sentences in the language. It usually takes into account the meanings and functions these sentences have in the overall system of the language. It may or may not include the description of the sounds of a language."

Batstone, 1994b:4

"At its heart, then, grammar consists of two fundamental ingredients – syntax and morphology – and together they help us to identify grammatical forms which serve to enhance and sharpen the expression of meaning."

Brown, 1994b:347

"Grammar is a system of rules governing the conventional arrangement and relationship of words in a sentence."

Lock, 1996:4

"Grammar includes two aspects:
1. the arrangements of words and
2. the internal structure of words."

Larsen-Freeman, 2003:142
"...grammar(ing) is one of the dynamic linguistic processes of pattern formulation in language, which can be used by humans for making meaning in context-appropriate ways."

David Crystal, "In Word and Deed," ***TES Teacher*****, April 30, 2004**
"Grammar is the structural foundation of our ability to express ourselves. The more we are aware of how it works, the more we can monitor the meaning and effectiveness of the way we and others use language. It can help foster precision, detect ambiguity, and exploit the richness of expression available in English. And it can help everyone – not only teachers of [foreign languages], but teachers of anything, for all teaching is ultimately a matter of getting to grips with meaning.

Prescriptive Grammar

A Prescriptive Grammar is a set of rules about the structure of a particular language; prescriptive grammarians present grammar in the way that it should be used. This concept, therefore, forms the basis of the standardization of languages, e.g. Standard English. The so created 'prescribed' evaluation basis for correct and incorrect language use, on the one hand, facilitates communication between highly different dialect regions (Hughes & Trudgill 1987). If there were no Standard English forms and therefore no limit to the variation permissible, speech and writing would inevitably diverge much more from the target language. On the other hand, it degrades dialectal variation which is an essential feature of every language as a dynamic system. Prescriptive linguists consider the syntax and morphology of a language as crucial and do not focus on non-standard English.

In terms of SLA, Prescriptive Grammars set certain orientation patterns for the learners' linguistic behaviour. Prescriptive Grammars can thus provide L2 learners with a guideline to speak and write homogeneously in that they can modify their output toward a narrower range of the standard version of the target language, e.g. American English and British English. Due to prescriptivism, standard varieties are therefore accessible to all learners and thus language learning and teaching must include the development of knowledge *about* the target language (Odlin 1994), i.e. metalinguistic knowledge.

However, prescriptive grammarians are "involved in making social judgments and about the effects and validity of particular language uses" (Brumfit & Roberts 1983: 14), and thus ignore the social and historical value of linguistic varieties.

Descriptive Grammar

A Drescriptive Grammar provides a much more detailed and objective view of languages. Descriptive grammarians, in contrast to prescriptive grammarians, observe and describe how a particular language is actually used by its speech community (cf. Brumfit & Roberts 1983). A Descriptive Grammar accounts for syntax, morphology, phonetics, phonology, as well as semantics, and lexis. On the basis of their descriptions, descriptive grammarians deduce a rule system about the language, without evaluating its varieties. A descriptive grammar, thus, includes linguistic structures a prescriptive grammarian would ignore as being non-standard forms which are perfectly acceptable in local dialects or language variations of the standard language, such as 'ain't', which is used highly frequently in AE. Therefore, as descriptive grammarians also focus on non-standard varieties, regulations in language are considered to be various, dynamic and not fixed. Any linguistic variety consists of rules and therefore it is "grammatical according to variety X" (Hudson 1992: 28).
Example:

1. *'I done it' is in a non-standard dialect*
2. *'I did it' is incorrect in that non-standard dialect but correct in standard language*

When it comes to SLA, learners have to deal with the inherent creativity of language use (cf. Odlin 1994). A Descriptive Grammar can be used as a reference tool for teachers and learners to look up particular features of the target language. In addition, L2 Learners should be encouraged to observe their own and other learners' grammars in order to discover the different varieties of the target language gradually.

Pedagogical Grammar

The primary purpose of a Pedagogical Grammar is to "translate" what pre- and descriptive grammars of the respective target language say for the benefit of L2 learners. That is, those linguistic structures considered relevant by descriptive and prescriptive linguists are taken by teachers as a basis for teaching materials and their use in formal SLA. Pedagogical Grammar is thus "a cover term for any learner or teacher and learner-oriented description or presentation of foreign language rule complexes which has the aim of promoting and guiding learning processes in the acquisition of that language" (Dirven 1990).

In foreign language teaching, communicative activities and grammatical instructions must be balanced for the benefit of the learner. The concept of Pedagogical Grammar takes all those ideas into account (Odlin 1994). Thus, the teachers' knowledge of grammar in terms of a formal learning environment is wider than a linguists' or learners' knowledge as it includes descriptive units *and* pedagogical ideas of how learners acquire a L2. Accordingly,

> "[o]ne of the central tasks of Pedagogical Grammar is the formulation of rules, in the broad sense of the statement of language regularities. [...] To achieve optimal pedagogical rules (whatever they might be), it would be necessary to have access to (a) the best description of the language, (b) relevant psycholinguistic criteria that could determine how learners (whether considered collectively or individually) are best helped in acquisition, and (c) a means of deriving appropriate pedagogical formulations from this information."
>
> Odlin (1994: 72 and 83)

Teaching a L2 will ideally provide explanations about what constitutes the grammatical system of the target language, i.e. metalinguistic knowledge, and combine this knowledge with communicative activities.

However, the teaching of grammar does not lead to the L2 learners being able to use the respective grammatical structures spontaneously and creatively. Therefore, first and foremost, foreign language teachers should know how that a grammatical system is discovered and acquired by the learners independently, i.e. in their minds. As Pienemann put forward (1984; 1998; 2005 and elsewhere), grammatical structures cannot be acquired and used in a target-like way by the learners until they are developmentally ready for it (Pienemann 1984 and 1989).

Learner Grammars – the *Interlanguage Approach*

In this section we will take a closer look at learner grammars. We feel that this approach to grammars – though not as widespread as the grammars discussed in previous sections of chapter 2 – have a great potential for approaching grammar and its teaching from a learner-centred perspective.

Interlanguage (Selinker 1972)

Learner Grammars are based on Interlanguage development. Henceforth we will use the term Interlanguage Grammar when talking about learner grammar. The term Interlanguage was coined by Selinker (1972). It describes the state of a language that has not yet been fully developed by a learner of a second (or foreign) language who has not yet fully acquired the target language but only approximated to it. Interlanguage contains features of the target language but also "innovations" by the learner that are neither target-like nor totally in line with the learner's first language. According to Long (2003) Interlanguage is based on the theory that there are psychological structures in the mind of the language learners that are activated when they are attempting to learn a language other than their L1. In other words, while learning another language learners are on their way from the initial state of second language learning to the target language. However, in contrast to L1 acquisition, learners may not reach target language attainment in an L2 but "get stuck halfway", so to speak. Selinker (1972) called this process of getting stuck fossilization; Long (2003) suggests rather using the term stabilisation as there has not been a coherent theoretical framework to empirically support the claim of fossilization. We will discuss this phenomenon in detail in part II making a case for instruction as a potential means to prevent, at least, grammatical (i.e. morphosyntactic) and lexical (i.e. the learning of new words) stabilisation. Of course, Interlanguage development is not a linear process. Learners may slide back in their development and produce errors at a Stage of Interlanguage development that they had not made be-

Figure 2: "Man walking to the Sky" by Jonathan Borofsky; an 'unintended' representation of Interlanguage development. (taken from Schwarze 2005: 110)

fore. Figure 2 actually shows a piece of modern art by the American artist Jonathan Borofsky. He designed the "Man walking to the sky" for documenta 9 which was held in Kassel in 1992. The man walking to the sky can be seen as an illustration of the concept of learner grammars as approached in this book. The line he is walking on can be seen as the trajectory of Interlanguage development. It is a predictable path the learner walks on. However, there is no guarantee that s/he will reach the top (= target language). Furthermore, even though all learners of a foreign language do follow the same predictable path there is nothing said about the pace at which they move along the path. In other words, some learners may go through the various Interlanguage Stages much more quickly than others. If the teacher knows about the current state of Interlanguage development of the learners s/he is in a position to support each learner in the EFL classroom according to her/his individual state of the target language. In chapter 5 we will discuss selected approaches to grammar teaching that cater for the learners' Interlanguage development and can be applied in heterogeneous classrooms. In chapter 15 we will then introduce a diagnostic tool that can quickly and reliably diagnose the current state of Interlanguage development of all the learners in one EFL classroom.

mental representation

Interlanguage grammars can be considered a mental representation of grammatical knowledge at any Stage of the acquisition process (cf. Selinker 1972, Corder 1981). This mental representation of grammatical knowledge may differ from actual target language grammar. However, the structures produced by the learners are systematic and rule governed and thus predictable. Certain "errors" are produced by (almost) any learner of the target language, regardless of the learners' first language. In chapter 7 we will discuss in detail what the Interlanguage structures of English as a second language look like. We will see that all learners who learn English as a second language will start speaking English following the SVO-pattern. This is of particular interest for the EFL classroom as this is the universal pattern used by learners of typologically different L1 backgrounds. This means that no matter whether our learners grew up monolingually or with a migration background they all start – in terms of grammar – with the same hypothesis. Only later does there develop an L1-specific transfer of grammar structures into the target language. We will come back to this in chapter 6. Grammar teaching that is in line with Interlanguage development will thus support learners best in their learning process. Teachers who are familiar with this approach can analyse learner errors in a different light from the one in which this is traditionally done and can help the learners to develop their Interlanguage as closely to target language standards as possible. Some errors that occur in the process of developing their learner grammar can be disregarded by the teacher as the learner may not be ready to understand and incorporate the teacher's correction. Lightbown and Spada (2006: 16) came up with a cartoon that illustrates nicely the idea of a developing Interlanguage grammar (see figure 3).

Figure 3: Interlanguage (taken from Lightbown & Spada 2006: 16)

This cartoon illustrates the concept of mental representation of Interlanguage structures and also shows that error correction may be useless if the learner is not yet developmentally ready to grasp the correction. In this example the boy does not see the mother's correction to be a morphological one (*putted vs. put) but a semantic one (I vs. you). This is why he answers rather indignantly and repeats the error that had just been corrected by the mother. In chapter 7 we will account in detail for the different kinds of errors from an Interlanguage Grammar perspective. We will show the relevance of this approach to error correction for the EFL classroom.

Further Reading:

Long, M.H. (2003): "Stabilisation and Fossilization in Interlanguage Development." In: Doughty, C. & M. Long (eds.): The Handbook of Second Language Acquisition. Malden, MA: Blackwell; pp. 487-535.
Selinker, L. (1972): "Interlanguage." In: International Review of Applied Linguistics 10; pp. 209-231.

Study Questions:

1. Why is it important to rethink the role of "Standard English" when teaching grammar?
2. Name at least three myths about grammar teaching and discuss them in small groups.
3. List the four approaches to grammar discussed in this chapter and say how they compete with each other.

3 Historical Approaches to Grammar Teaching

This book is not a book on the history of language teaching. There have been plenty of summaries and discussions of various approaches to language teaching. Both Larsen-Freeman (2000) and Richards and Rodgers (2006) provide easy, accessible overviews of the most important approaches to the field.

However, we feel that a conclusive introduction to teaching grammar must not lack at least a brief summary of the most important historical approaches to grammar teaching. Without knowing and understanding the past it is hardly possible to understand the present and develop models for the future of grammar teaching. This is why in this chapter we will briefly introduce those historical approaches to grammar teaching that have been most influential.

Latin

Up to the present day, many people believe that any grammar teaching should be derived from Latin. There has been a renaissance of Latin as the second – sometimes even the first – foreign language to be taught at school. Many teachers, parents and learners believe that Latin is a good role model for any further foreign language learning. In the past, Latin played a major role in the development of grammar instruction. For centuries modern languages were taught according to the Latin classroom.

Foreign language teaching became a profession in its own right only just recently in the 20th century. Before that time, and of course until today, it has been subject to substantial changes. Like every other teaching methodology, teaching an L2 has always been based on the philosophy of the respective era. One could say that language teaching has changed according to 'scientific and philosophical fashion' and along with this the goal of language learning, the view of language, and the role of the L2 learner and the teacher. Up to the 20th century, language teaching lacked a well-defined theoretical scientific background, which is nowadays provided by the parallel development of linguistics and psychology as research fields. This chapter serves to give an overview of the major developments and discussions in language teaching from its traditional roots to today's trends based on a psycholinguistic theoretical foundation.

various approaches to grammar teaching

In the following sections of this chapter we will briefly discuss and question the role of Latin for modern foreign language teaching. This will be followed by an introduction to four major approaches and methods to foreign language teaching, namely:

- Grammar Translation
- Direct Method
- Audio-Lingual Method
- Communicative Language Teaching (CLT)

One might wonder why we consider the communicative approach to be one of the historical approaches to language teaching and why a book on teaching grammar actually covers the CLT approach at all. A strict application of CLT has always denied any explicit grammar focus. However, even in the so-called communicative language classroom grammar does play a role. In this chapter – and throughout the book – we are not arguing against a communicative approach to grammar teaching. We will, however, demonstrate in the following chapters that the mere focus on communication that stresses the role of message as always being more important than the role of accuracy may be a little short-sighted and may lead to a simplified (Tarzan-like) use of the target language. We will draw on the CLT approach again and again throughout the following chapters making a point for real and authentic communication, which also plays a major role in the development of a standard-oriented target language by the language learners.

Before selected approaches to language teaching are presented which were very influential in the past, three recurring key technical terms are briefly defined: 'approach', 'method' and 'technique' (see table 2; Richards & Rodgers 2006; Brown 2007). This clarification of terminology provides a better understanding of the theoretical background the presented approaches/methods/techniques are based on – and their interrelations.

Table 2 presents two major suggestions for distinguishing the terms. First, the frequently cited definitions of Anthony (1963) and secondly, the reformulations and refinements of Brown (2007) are given:

	Approach	Method	Technique
Anthony (1963)	• a set of correlative assumptions dealing with the nature of language teaching and learning • axiomatic, i.e. self-evident; obvious • describes the nature of the subject matter to be taught • within one approach, there can be many methods	• theory (ideas underlying a respective approach) is put into practice • an overall plan for the systematic presentation of language material, i.e. the choice of content & the order of its presentation • procedural • does not contradict, but is based upon the selected approach	• what actually takes place in the classroom • implementational • a particular trick, plan or scheme used to accomplish an immediate objective • must be consistent with a method • must be in line with an approach
• **Richards and Rodgers (1986; 2002)** • *Method* used as the umbrella term, which is subdivided into *approach*, *design* and *procedure*	• *Approach* • theories about the nature & structure of language • theories about language learning, in particular the psycholinguistic and cognitive processes involved	• *Design* • a syllabus model • the instructional concept drawing upon the ideas underlying the respective approach (e.g. kinds of tasks and materials) • function & form of materials • learner roles • teacher roles	• *Procedure* • what actually happens in the classroom, drawing upon the ideas underlying the respective approach and the design based on it • resources in terms of time, space, and equipment used by the teacher • interactional patterns observed in the lessons • tactics and strategies used by the teachers and learners when the method is being used
(Brown 2007)	• theoretically well-informed positions and beliefs about • (1) the nature of	• a generalized set of classroom specifications for accomplishing linguistic objectives	• exercises, activities or tasks used in a language classroom for realising lesson objectives

	language, (2) the nature of language learning, and the applicability of *both* to pedagogical settings	• concerned with linguistic subject-matter objectives, sequencing and materials • concerned with teacher and student roles and behaviours	

Table 2: adapted from Anthony (1963: 63-67), Richards and Rodgers (2006: 33) and Brown (2007: 16)

Anthony saw a hierarchical arrangement between the three concepts. "The organisational key is that techniques carry out a method which is consistent with an approach." (Anthony 1963: 63, as cited in Richards and Rodgers 2006: 19) Even though his suggestions as to the distinction and relation of the above presented terms are vital,

> [n]othing is said about [...] the role of instructional materials or the form they are expected to take. [They] fail to account for *how* an approach may be *realized* in a method, or for how method and technique are *related*

as Richards and Rodgers correctly state (2006: 20, emphasis added). According to Rodgers (2009), the term teaching 'method(ology)' implies "the notion of a systematic set of teaching practices based on a particular theory of language and language learning." Ideally, language teaching methodology should link theory and practice. That is to say, that a methodological concept requires "theories of what language is and how language is learned" (*ibid.*), namely a theory of SLA (see chapter 6). On that basis, a methodology of language teaching can be designed, including "objectives, syllabus specifications, types of activities, roles of teachers, learners [and] materials." (*ibid.*) In this regard, Richards and Rodgers suggest the umbrella term 'method' to comprise the three elements approach, design and procedure (see table 2).

In order to gain a deeper understanding of how these three concepts, either referred to as approach – method – technique or approach – design – procedure, relate to each other in foreign language teaching, we will take a closer look at the cases in point which are presented in the following. Beforehand, it should be reflected language teacher: there is no single perfect method

pointed out here there is no perfect method – a reflected language teacher should not only draw upon one approach, but alter or combine it with features of other approaches depending on the students' developmental state (see chapter 6), institutional frameworks, and group profile. However, time has shown that certain methods do not fulfil the purpose of providing an adequate, i.e. learner-centred, learning environment. In order to point out the importance of research before selecting one or more suitable methods to structure a lesson adequately, we present five of the milestones in the development of the art of language teaching – Latin as a role model, the Grammar Translation Method, the Direct Method, the Audio-Lingual Method in this chapter and Communicative Language Teaching in chapter 4.

Latin as a Role Model?

For a long time in history, Latin was the lingua franca of Europe including the British Isles. Especially in the beginning this was due to the intertwining of politics and the Catholic Church and their influence on culture and tradition. The literary records taken in England during the Early Middle Ages were largely kept in Latin, as the tradition of keeping records itself was imported with the monastic tradition of conserving historical events in chronicles[7].

In the course of history, modern languages gained importance on the British Isles. It is remarkable though, that this paradigm shift recognised French as a prestigious language first, turning the English society in a diglossic one, with French as the language of the upper classes.[8] Nonetheless, Latin and Greek remained the important languages in the scholarly field and the only ones to be formally taught in the classroom until the 13th century. This

7 Such an instance of record keeping is the *Historia Ecclesiastica Gentis Anglorum* (*Ecclesiastical History of the English People*) by Beda Venerabilis/ Venerable Bede (finished about 730 and translated into Old English in the 9th century).

8 Especially from the end of the 11th century on, when England was being reigned by French-speaking rulers until English was finally re-established from the 13th to the 15th century. There were several other waves of French importance, especially during the 17th and 18th century and after the French Revolution, when France was established as a cultural and sociopolitical role model for several European countries.

resulted in the fact that Latin was an obligatory subject for any adolescent aiming at higher education, i.e. only through high proficiency in Latin one could become a member of the world of scholars. Latin was primarily taught by oral methods; there was no emphasis on grammar whatsoever.

The dominance of the classical languages in scholarship and education even increased in the Renaissance Era, when scholars focused on classical literature and revealed the 'deficiencies' of English, especially with regard to spelling and the lexicon[9]. It was not until the Modern Age that English started to gain importance in the scholarly domains as well. Although Latin was still seen as model for other languages, especially during the Enlightenment the number of scholarly texts written in English grew. This went along with an increase in linguistic awareness accompanied by a rise of prescriptivism (see chapter 2). This wave of prescriptivism was also promoted by the 18th-century Grammarians, working on standardisation and ascertainment, which meant making both grammar and usage more systematic, removing flaws and errors, and stabilising the new purified state with the help of codification. As languages are dynamic, however, this codification process did not work out. Nonetheless, it resulted in the publication of the first dictionaries and grammar books on the English language[10], which predominantly aimed at refining and standardising the language. The notion of usage with regard to the English language gained importance during the 18th century, when it was first interpreted in a prescriptive manner (i.e. the way in which language should be used), before people turned to a rather descriptive interpretation (i.e. the way in which language is actually used) towards the end of the century. Thus, English was eventually recognised as a language with equal expressive power and abili-

9 This resulted in the famous debate about the so-called 'inkhorn terms'. These were terms predominantly borrowed from model languages like French and Latin with the objective of enlarging the English word stock, filling its alleged gaps and thus overcoming the assumed inferiority of the English language. Opponents of this practice ridiculed those terms as inkhorn terms, because they would only be used in writing by those promoting borrowings; the opponents thus considered them unnatural and inappropriate.

10 Two of the most prominent examples in this respect are the *Short Introduction to English Grammar* (1762) by Robert Lowth and Samuel Johnson's *Dictionary of the English Language* (1755).

ties, which was the result of the long-timeshift from Latin and Greek to English in the fields of scholarship and education.

The Grammar Translation Method

When the so-called 'Age of Reason' had arrived, a major paradigm shift in language teaching methodology occurred. In the 17th century, the 'father of didactics', Comenius, proposed the idea of language learning being based on pre-set rules of grammar, i.e. on introducing linguistic forms deductively. The Grammar Translation Method was born, which lasted until the mid-19th century – reflecting an educational system whose focus was logical reasoning based on rhetoric skills and, thus, aiming chiefly at educating an elite of cultivated minds. This was accomplished by the main focus of the Grammar Translation Method: to teach the students to read the literature written in the target language.

Whereas Renaissance man was a doer and an active language user whose primary need was to speak the language, people of the 17th, 18th and 19th centuries were thinkers. At that time, the view of language was that of a rather fixed system governed by logic, i.e. the structure of language being governed by a set of rules. The goal of language learning changed from mere communication towards, for example, the decoding of literary texts; this is why written language became more important than spoken language. The art of translation became therefore the central aim of teaching a foreign language. Comenius' textbook *Orbis Sensualium Pictus* was designed to teach Latin to speakers of German. The sentences are presented in such a way that the illustrated vocabulary is easily situated – to each word in the text corresponds a number, which in turn directs the reader to the object in the accompanying illustration (cf. Mason 2010). According to Comenius, there is a natural order to teaching: the teacher begins by giving examples, then moves on to give the rules, and finally asks the pupil to do exercises, to put into practice what s/he has learned. He was convinced that we learn above all through active use. At first sight, this suggests a rejection of teaching grammar. This is misleading, however, as the rules should aid and confirm usage, as stated by Comenius. Moreover, the learning process should be directed, and errors should be corrected straight away, otherwise the learner may get into bad habits. The learner, then, needs frequent opportunities to express him or herself, in situations where there is a guide who can stop her/him whenever an error occurs, and explain why the language s/he produces is incorrect. (cf. Mason 2010). Thus, in Grammar Translation providing explicit corrective feedback was one of the main tasks of the teacher.

Figure 4: Grammar Translation Method

As expressed by Richards and Rodgers (2006), the Grammar Translation Method is "a way of studying a language that approaches the language first through detailed analysis of its grammar rules, followed by application of this knowledge through the task of translating sentences and text into and out of the target language". This contrastive way of teaching the L2 linguistic skills in the learners' L1 was also to be trained. In order to amplify their L2 vocabulary, students memorised bilingual word lists as well as verb conjugations.

Unfortunately, there is hardly any attention paid to the training of listening and authentic communication in this framework. As a result, L2 learners fall short of using the target language for its primary purpose: communication. This negative effect is supported by the medium of instruction being the respective L1.

The Direct Method

Criticisms of such features as the explicit presentation of grammar rules and the sole focus on learning to read and write in the TL of the Grammar Translation Method led to the development of the Direct Method. This method is also referred to as 'Reform Method', 'Natural Method', 'Phonetic Method', 'Anti-grammatical Method'.

Here the focus was no longer on translation and memorisation of grammar rules and vocabulary, but on active use of the target language in real life situations, i.e. the spoken word became more important again. In the Direct Method, it is assumed that learners acquire an L2 the way in which they acquire an L1. This assumption was integrated in the language classroom in that the L2 was the only medium of instruction, similar to the concept of Immersion (see chapter 13). As Larsen-Freeman (2000) concisely puts it, "the Direct Method has one very basic rule: no translation is allowed." The written word is rejected in the Direct Method. However, as writing is the second mode of L2 production, this was a major disadvantage of the method. As far as vocabulary learning is concerned, the basic principle was demonstration: apart from pantomiming, teachers illustrated new terms with real-life objects or further visual materials.

Figure 5: Direct Method

The method is rather teacher-centred; therefore the lessons are characterised by intensive question-and-answer patterns between teachers and L2 learners. In this regard, both reading comprehension and pronunciation play important roles in the Direct Method. The students are asked questions referring to a particular reading passage, for example. However, in contrast to the primarily authoritative role of the teacher in the Grammar Translation Method, in the Direct Method "the teacher directs the class activities, the student role is less passive than in the Grammar-Translation Method. The teacher and the students are more like partners in the teaching/learning process." (Larsen-Freeman 2000: 28)

In a nutshell, the Direct Method led to the development of more communicative approaches to language teaching. However, some features of the Direct Method are still evident in foreign language classrooms, such as the use of visual aids or realia.

The Audio-Lingual Method

The Audio-Lingual Method (ALM)[11], which followed the Direct Method, is the first language teaching method that is based on a theoretical framework, i.e. behaviourist psychology, and was prevalent in the 1940s and 1950s. As to the view of language, the method is based on the structuralist view represented by Bloomfield. The most important aspect of this theory as far as language learning and teaching is concerned is that learning is based on stimulus-response-cycles and reinforcement. That is, once a learner produces target-like output, s/he receives positive feedback, whereas incorrect use of the target language results in negative feedback. As holds for the Direct Method, too, in audiolingualism there is no room for explicit grammar instruction and the use of the L1 is supposed to be avoided. The L1 and the L2 have to be "kept apart" from each other (Larsen-Freeman 2000: 42) so that the L1 does not hinder SLA. According to ALM principles, pattern drilling is assumed to help the learner "overcome the habits of their native language and form the new habits required to be target language speakers." Similar to the Grammar-Translation Method, the teacher is the model for correct L2 use in that s/he presents target-like versions of a sentence that the student has to repeat in parrot-like manner. In ALM, this instruction technique is also referred to as 'oral pattern drilling'. Every new language form is simply memorised by repetition. In fact, in

pattern drill

[11] ALM is also referred to as the 'Army Method' since with the outbreak of World War II there was a sudden need for numerous American servicemen all over the continents. These servicemen were to be trained in basic knowledge of the respective national language. Due to the teacher (single authority and model) – student (passive repeater) relation and the drill-character of ALM lessons, teachers could deal with the military men in large numbers.

ALM the repetition of sentence patterns is more important than the students' understanding of a particular notion.

Once memorised, according to behaviourist psychology, this learning of the L2 linguistic forms 'by heart' is supposed to enable the learner to use the respective structure spontaneously. However, in line with findings of 20th and 21st century cognitive psychologists and linguists on how (language) learning takes place in learners' minds, this formulaic use of language by no means results in the learner being able to communicate authentically in the L2.

Figure 6: Audio-Lingual Method

Further Reading

Larsen-Freeman, D. (2001). *Techniques and principles in language teaching*. Oxford: OUP.

Richards, Jack C. & Rodgers (2006). *Approaches and methods in language teaching*. Cambridge: CUP.

Study Questions

1. Why did Latin function as a role model for language teaching for several centuries?
2. Please summarise the role of grammar in the Grammar Translation Method, the Direct Method and the Audio-Lingual Method.
3. Which were the respective theoretical motivations that resulted in a varying importance of teaching grammar in the above teaching approaches?

4 Communicative Language Teaching CLT

In order to overcome the limitations of structuralism and behaviourism as manifest in the grammar focused ALM, British applied linguists developed the very influential Communicative Language Teaching (CLT) approach, which experienced its heyday in the 1970s and early 1980s (Hymes 1976; Wilkins 1976; Widdowson 1978) and is still used nowadays. CLT primarily concentrates on form-function relationships, i.e. meaning, and interaction as the instrument *and* purpose of SLA. An explicit focus on grammar is generally rejected as it is assumed to hinder authentic communication. Moreover, the focus is on fluency rather than on accuracy.

CLT is, amongst others, a response to works of the famous linguist Noam Chomsky (1957) who criticised that "the current standard structural theories[12] of language were incapable of accounting for the fundamental characteristics of language – the creativity and uniqueness of individual sentences." (Richards and Rodgers 2006: 153) That is to say, e.g. mere translation (see Grammar-Translation Method) and pattern drilling (see ALM) disregard a key feature of human language: we can generate an infinite number of sentences by ourselves. It should be noted, however, that Chomsky's view of linguistic competence differs from that implied in CLT.

CLT has a remarkably broad theoretical base and is, at the same time, the first approach which is not based on a single authoritative work prescribing a fix set of learning goals and classroom activities. According to Richards & Rodgers (2006: 161), it rather consists of a "diverse set of principles that reflect a communicative view of language and language learning and that can be used to support a wide variety of classroom procedures."

1) Language is a system for the expression of meaning.
2) The primary function of language is for interaction and communication.
3) The structure of language reflects its functional and communicative uses.
4) The primary unit of language is not merely its grammatical and structural features, but categories of functional and communicative meaning as exemplified in discourse.

(Richards &Rodgers 2006: 161)

---

[12] see, e.g. Bloomfield's works of the 1930s and 1940s

In line with CLT, the primary goal of language teaching is thus to enable the learners to communicate authentically in the TL, i.e. the social, functional dimension of language became of central importance. In order to promote genuine negotiation of meaning, CLT classroom activities should include information gaps, choice and feedback (Johnston and Morrow 1981). As coined by Hymes in the mid-1960s, the learners have to develop *communicative competence*. This term comprises four sub competences, namely grammatical competence, sociolinguistic competence, discourse competence, and strategic competence.

communicative competence

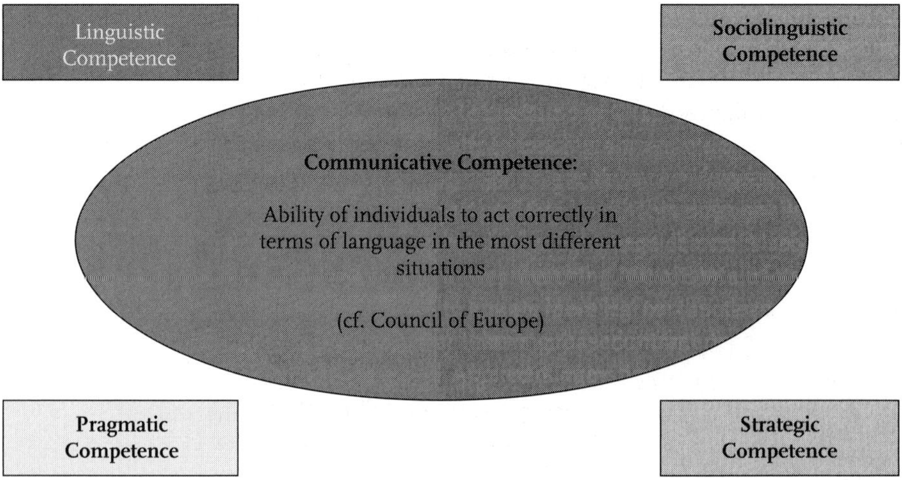

Figure 7: Communicative Competence – Sub Competences

Hans Eberhard Piepho

According to Piepho (1974 and 2001) communicative competence enables the learners to act adequately in various situations. The aim of the EFL classroom is to provide the learners with the necessary strategies to be communicatively competent speakers of the target language. Actually, the concept of communicative competence consists of four sub competences as linguistic, sociolinguistic, pragmatic, and strategic competence (cf. figure 7).

In a nutshell, Piepho (2001: 10) summarises the major goal of any communicative language teaching in the following way:

> Ziel einer jeden Etappe, Stunde, Phase, Einheit, Jahrgangskurs, Lehrgang ist es, die Schüler zur souveränen, bereitwilligen und aus der eigenen Perspektive geplanten und vollzogenen Teilnahme an der sozialen und geistigen Realität Unterricht zu befähigen.
>
> (Piepho, 2001:10)

Even though grammatical competence is part of language proficiency in CLT terms, its explicit teaching was avoided. At the time when CLT emerged, this view of teaching grammar was in line with contemporary research findings. In the early 1980s, Krashen put forward the acquisition-learning distinction, stating that L2 learners have two distinct systems when acquiring the TL. Acquisition is classified as a subconscious process and learning a conscious process. According to Krashen's view, the acquired language system requires primarily meaningful interaction and develops subconsciously, whereas the learned system is based on conscious metalinguistic knowledge, i.e. grammar rules the learner may have been taught. In his famous work *Principles and Practice in Second Language Acquisition*, he claims that

Krashen

> [SLA] occurs when comprehension of real messages occurs[.] Language acquisition does not require extensive use of conscious grammatical rules, and does not require tedious drill. [...] The best methods are therefore those that supply 'comprehensible input' [...] These methods [...] allow students to produce when they are 'ready', recognizing that improvement comes from supplying communicative and comprehensible input, and not from forcing and correcting production."
>
> (Krashen 1981: 6f.)

Even where there is grammatical inaccuracy, communication can still take place successfully (Wilkins 1974: 14). The following figure illustrates this idea. The learner on the right hand side of the figure makes a lexical error (a typical 'false friend' for L1 German learners of English). This, however, does not at all affect the communication that takes place between the two speakers. In a nutshell, one of the core ideas of the communicative approach to language teaching is the concept of message before accuracy. In other words, it is more important for the learners to acquire strategies that supports their ability to convey the meaning of what they want

message before accuracy

to express. This may then lead to some problems in terms of accuracy but this is considered to be of less importance. Error correction (at least in spoken language) can then be far less strict.

As we will see in a later chapter of this book the approach to grammar teaching taken throughout this book will also draw from this concept.

Figure 8: Communicative Language Teaching

The fact that there is no focus on grammar in CLT relates to the treatment of errors in the L2 classroom. In CLT, errors were seen as part of the learning process and, as such, ignored. Early versions of CLT were right to understand errors as fundamental feature of SLA (see chapter 7), but to not give any feedback at all is hardly conducive to the SLA process. In fact, it can lead to the development of a simplified variant of the TL in the learner's mind (see chapter 8 of this book).

However, today's L2 classrooms are primarily communicative. What did change in the foreign language teaching in the past two decades is the view of teaching grammar. Contemporary linguists and applied linguists (Pienemann 1984, 1985, 1987, 1989, 1998; Long 1991; Doughty and Williams 1998; Norris and Ortega 2001 and others) conducted extensive research on the effectiveness of teaching grammar and, in general, it turned out that an adequate focus on form in the L2 classroom can be conducive to the SLA process (see chapter 11 of this book).

Principles

According to Richards & Rodgers (2006: 93f) communicative language teaching combines a variety of learning tasks and activities and make authentic communication the focus of the lessons. As early as 1984 Howatt pointed out that there is a strong and a weak approach to CLT:

learning to use English vs. using English to learn it

> There is, in a sense, a 'strong' version of the communicative approach and a 'weak' version. The weak version which has become more or less standard practice in the last ten years, stresses the importance of providing learners with opportunities to use their English for communicative purposes and, characteristically, attempts to integrate such activities into a wider program of language teaching. [...] The 'strong' version of communicative teaching, on the other hand, advances the claim that language is acquired through communication, so that it is not merely a question of activating an existing but inert knowledge of the language, but of stimulating the development of the language system itself. If the former could be described as 'learning to use' English, the latter entails 'using English to learn it'.
>
> Howatt (1984: 279)

According to Finocchiaro & Brumfit (1983: 91ff) Communicative Language Teaching comprises the following key features and principles; this list is contrasted to the principles of the Audiolingual Approach by Richards & Rodgers (2006: 156f). According to that list, in CLT:

- Meaning is paramount
- Dialogues, if used, centre around communicative functions and are normally not memorised
- Contextualisation is a basic premise
- Language learning is learning to communicate
- Effective communication is sought
- Drilling may occur, but only peripherally
- Comprehensible pronunciation is sought
- Any device that helps the learners is accepted – variety according to their age, interest, etc.
- Attempts to communicate may be encouraged from the very beginning
- Judicious use of native language is accepted where feasible
- Translation may be used where students need of benefit from it

- Reading and writing can start from first day, if desired
- The target linguistic system [i.e. the grammar, JUK/AP] will be learned best through the process of struggling to communicate
- Communicative competence is the desired goal (i.e., the ability to use the linguistic system effectively and appropriately)
- Linguistic variation is a central concept in the materials and methodology
- Sequencing is determined by any consideration of content, function, or meaning that maintains interest
- Teachers help learners in any way that motivates them to work with the language
- Language is created by the individual, often through trial and error
- Fluency and acceptable language is the primary goal: accuracy is judged not in the abstract but in context
- Students are expected to interact with other people, either through pair or group work, or their writings
- The teacher cannot know exactly what language the students will use
- Intrinsic motivation will spring from an interest in what is being communicated by the language.

communicative competence

These features point out quite neatly the differences to former approaches to language teaching as spelled out in more detail in chapter 3 of this book. The key issue of communicative language teaching is to put the learners into a position of using the target language in an efficient way in authentic contexts. This is one of the main reasons for the overwhelming success the CLT approach has had for almost 40 years now. Ever since Hymes (1972) coined the term of "communicative competence" CLT has been a success story. In Germany, Piepho introduced the term with his influential book *Kommunikative Kompetenz als übergeordnetes Lernziel im Englischunterricht*.

Techniques

Obviously, there are plenty of different techniques of teaching grammar communicatively. The choice of an appropriate technique depends on a variety of factors such as age of your learners, content, grammar structure under scrutiny and many more. In the following section we will present some techniques that have proven successful in various settings and that are in line with a communicative approach to foreign language teaching.

All our following examples are based on Thornbury (1999). Due to space limitations we can only briefly introduce some of the techniques. If you are interested in how to actually integrate those techniques into a foreign language grammar lesson, Thornbury provides a stepwise introduction to how to implement each of the techniques into a lesson.

Teaching through actions: (cf. Thornbury, 1999: 55f)
- good for beginners
- based on the Direct Method
- includes TPR features
- underlying idea: learners learn best when they are involved with learning both in a physical as well as a mental way

- *Teaching through using realia:* (cf. Thornbury, 1999: 57f)
- bring objects into the language classroom
- teach networks by showing real objects
- elicit examples for grammatical structures (e.g. simple present)

Teaching through using concordance data: (cf. Thornbury, 1999: 65f)
- use concordances to "guide the students towards discovering [...] differences by themselves" (Thornbury, 1999: 65)

Step 1

The teacher divides the class into three groups (A, B, and C), and gives each group a different set of concordance lines as shown here:

Group A: *Remember*

REMEMBER (19:26, 07.05.98)
d Yanto, thoughtfully. On the other hand, I *remember* seeing them dancing together at a ball shortly before the month's Top to Tail if you own a poodle. *Remember* to listen out for Katie and friends on Radio 2. Should yo here wasn't anyone to see me go. I *remember* thinking how white and cold her face looked, with ve food started to de-

crease in September, so *remember* to feed fish. Remember to check on them from time to tit remember being so unhappy – not ever. I *remember* being in La Scala, Milan during the war. In the early 40s her to a colliery tip about four miles away. I *remember* going to a fruit and flower market in Leeds very early one what I can do but it's all working. Oh I must *remember* to take that film out. Is that the finish of it total? All I rem (which doesn't mean there weren't any). 'I *remember* seeing pictures of a fish like that at school, but I'm damn was working in Worcester. 'I don't seem to *remember* seeing you in church, Bridget,' said Clare. The last thing ber to feed him,' so I'll just have to *remember* to bring an electric drill up and see what I can do but it's ehudi Menuhin was in town for a concert. I *remember* being rather keen on Bert when I was about fiteen.

Group B: *Forget*

FORGET (18.53, 07.05.98)
ernment last year announced that those who *forget* to flush public toilets will be fined up to US dollars. Results frothy fronds lit up by evening sun. I'll never *forget* seeing your Grandfather for the first time. I couldn't believe acting inspector over the weekend. I'll never *forget* being in hospital.
s are getting shorter it doesn't mean you can *forget* having a bit of fun in the garden. Results of your search Yo othes. For instance, if you load Windows, but *forget* to take the mouse out of the bag, you can just clip the Tosh live alone. If you are leaving the area do not *forget* to pick up any clothes that are at the cleaners, or shoes, e, where shamrock fans forget to blur. Don't *forget* to put your clocks back tomorrow night. Once the removal o our or two watching TV together. She hadn't *forgotten* going to the pictures with Vernon to see The Song of Pa y solutions found for this query M. B. I never *forget* being called by a superintendent who said: 'sergeant Bullo to add more volume of food daily. I must not *forget* to say something to the whole school about her.' Don't corr forget to bring music. 'Now eat up and don't *forget* to take your litter home with you.' If there is anything else yo

Group C: *Stop*

STOP (19.18, 07.05.98)
tense, listening. At the age of twelve, Bailey *stopped* eating meat. Although he had already taken his first mout though Anna was sure her mother had not *stopped* having baths or using perfume. Annabel was determined asthma? And it was two o'clock when they *stopped* talking, they stopped having their break! Results of your s s of Ron's hard training schedules. I finally *stopped* going to school when Charlie did, and Eva arranged for m ould appreciate it if the two gentlemen who *stopped* to help

me when I had an accident with my car on the road these last two days,' she told him when he *stopped* to greet her and ask if she had heard the brilliant spontan day I was filling up with petrol when a chap *stopped* to say he was a member of the Ferrari Owners Club and examine his reflection in the mirror. The bus *stopped* to pick up a passenger off one of the first terraced streets to the newspapers, but Mr Carter has never *stopped* believing he could solve the world's problems. But Joy defeat as gracefully as he could. Churchill *stopped* to take a cigar from the flap pocket of the one-piece siren he idea that had flitted through his mind. He stopped eating and reached across and took his wife's hand. I'd st [...]

Step 3
The teacher summarises by drawing the following timelines:

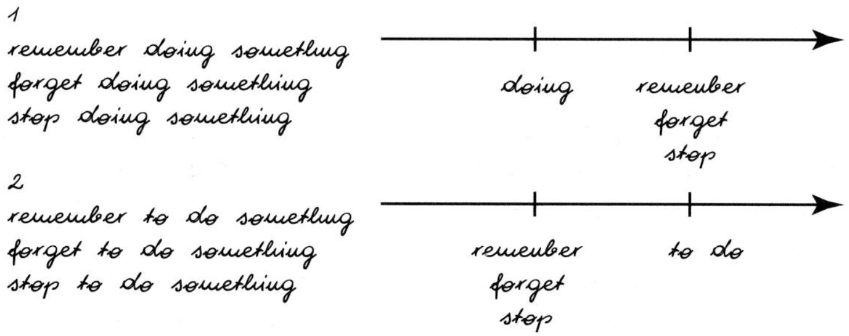

In other words, in the case of 1 the *doing* precedes the *remembering, forgetting, stopping*. In the case of 2 this sequence is reversed.

Figure 9: Example (Step 1, Groups A-C, and Step 3) taken from Thornbury (1999: 66f)

Using a scripted dialogue: (cf. Thornbury, 1999: 73f)

- choose a recorded dialogue (e.g. from the textbook)
- use this dialogue as a vehicle to introduce targeted grammar structure
- make your learners think about the content first
- let them find out regularities that lead to an implicit acquisition of the structures

Using an authentic text: (cf. Thornbury, 1999: 77ff)

- choose an authentic text that was written for a real purpose outside a (language) classroom

- tell the title of the text to your class
- continue like in the example above
- à advantage: less artificial and more motivating than textbook texts

Using student language to review ways of talking about grammar phenomena: (cf. Thornbury, 1999: 79ff)
- set a topic (e.g. the next holiday)
- students record what they say about the topic (utterance by utterance) – resembles natural conversation
- use your students text as resource for grammar analysis

A typical sequence might go like this:

ERNST (a student):	Ana, what will you do the next Easter holiday?
TEACHER:	Listen: Ana, what are you going to do this Easter?
ERNST:	Ana, what are you going to do this Easter?
TEACHER:	Good. Again. [She indicates she is going to record it.]
ERNST:	Ana, what are you going to do this Easter?
ANA (a student):	I don't know. Maybe I'll stay in the house.
TEACHER:	At home.
ANA:	I don't know. Maybe I'll stay at home.
TEACHER:	OK. [She indicates she is going to record it.]
ANA:	I don't know. Maybe I'll stay at home.
PAOLO (a student):	And you, Ernst, what are you going to do?
TEACHER:	Good. [She indicates she is going to record it.]
PAOLO:	And you, Ernst, what are you going to do?
ERNST (to teacher):	How do you say [he mimes skiing]?
TEACHER:	I'm going to go skiing.
ERNST:	I'm going to go skiing.
TEACHER:	OK. [She indicates she is going to record it.]
ERNST:	I'm going to go skiing.

etc.

This produces the following amount of recorded text:

ERNST:	Ana, what are you going to do this Easter?
ANA:	I don't know. Maybe I'll stay at home.
PAOLO:	And you, Ernst, what are you going to do?
ERNST:	I'm going to go skiing.

Ana, what are you going to do this Easter?

I don't know. Maybe I'll stay in town.

She asks the learners to identify the different forms and to offer an explanation of their use in this context. For example, she guides them to the rule of thumb that *going to* is generally used to talk or ask about things already planned, whereas *will* is used at the decision-making stage itself.

Step 4
Students listen to the recorded text one more time, following it on the board. The teacher then rubs the text off the board and the students re-form in their original circle and improvise the conversation again from memory. They are encouraged to add more details if they wish.

Figure 10: Example taken from Thornbury (1999: 80f)

Using dictogloss: (cf. Thornbury, 1999: 82ff)
"A dictogloss is a form of dictation, but one in which the students hear and reconstruct the whole text rather than doing so line by line" (Thornbury, 1999: 82)

- teacher sets the theme
- after having elicited the pre-knowledge of the class, teacher presents a spoken text (as a whole)
- students take notes on what the teacher says (keywords)
- in groups learners reconstruct the full text à try to be as close to the original as possible (including the grammatical structures)
- by discussing their versions of the reconstructed texts negotiation of meaning takes place and supports implicit grammar acquisition (cf. chapter 9)

Using genre analysis: (cf. Thornbury, 1999: 85f)

- as language is context-sensitive it is essential that the learners also grasp the context of a text
- context also "determine[s] the kind of language that is used" (Thornbury, 1999: 85)
- genre analysis: "study of the ways in which social contexts impact upon language choices" (Thornbury, 1999: 85)
- by analysing a genre the learners also analyse "whose overall structure and whose grammatical and lexical features have been determined by the contexts in which it is used, and which over time have become institutionalised". (Thornbury, 1999: 85)

As we have seen, grammar is a vital part of any authentic communication act and can, thus, be brought into the foreign language classroom easily. However, teachers do have to know more about what is going on in the mind of the learners when acquiring a (foreign) language. Research in second language acquisition has provided a lot of insight into what is going on in the mind of the learners. Therefore, in the following part of this book we will take a closer look at the relationship between SLA research and grammar teaching.

Before we turn to theoretical and practical implications of psycholinguistic research in SLA, however, we provide a brief overview of the key issues captured in any of the language teaching approaches presented in chapter 3 and 4.

Further Reading

Larsen-Freeman, D. (2001). *Techniques and principles in language teaching*. Oxford: OUP.

Richards, Jack C. & Rodgers (2002). *Approaches and methods in language teaching*. Cambridge: CUP.

Thompson, G. (1996). "Some Misconceptions about Communicative Language Teaching." In: *ELT Journal Volume 50/1 January 1996*, pp. 9-15

Study Questions

1. Which is, in line with CLT, the main objective of language teaching?
2. Please describe the role of errors in CLT. Do you agree?
3. Please discuss the concept of Communicative Competence. Do you think that any sub-competence is more important than the others?

	Goal	Activity	Teacher	Student
Grammar Translation Method	• ability to translate • ability to read and write in the TL • mental discipline • intellectual development	• deductive teaching of grammar • detailed meta-analysis of grammar rules • translation • bilingual word lists • focus on grammatical accuracy: memorisation of, e.g. verb conjugations	• centre of the L2 classroom • acts as role model • presents material • provides solutions	• rather passive, apart from translating • not exploring • no authentic communicative interaction
Direct Method	• daily life communication	• inductive teaching of grammar • natural learning principles: extensive oral input and interaction in the TL • demonstrations • focus on everyday communication items • errors are a sign of learning	• provides extensive oral input • preferably NS	• active • exploring
ALM	• behaviourism: pattern drills and repetitions; errors are to be avoided at all costs • conversational proficiency • knowledge about the TL culture • short range: accurate pronunciation • long range: native-speaker proficiency • grammatical accuracy	• inductive teaching of grammar • contrastive analysis	• centre of the L2 classroom • acts as role model • presents material • provides solutions • active • immediate error correction	• passive, only repeating (practice makes perfect) • reactive
CLT	• communicative competence	• no grammar teaching • activities focusing on meaningful interaction, i.e. negotiation of meaning	• active • counsellor • develops tasks that suit the learners' needs	• learner-centred • learner is active

Interlanguage Grammars: Second Language Development | II

5 Grammar Teaching and SLA: A Role for Interlanguage

> Learning and teaching, then, are inextricably bound together – on the face of it, certainly not a particularly startling observation. If nothing else, the learning/teaching symbiosis would seem to indicate that for anything having to do with language, the 'teachability' of that phenomenon would depend crucially upon its 'learnability'. Yet we may have legitimate cause to wonder how much of what passes today for 'formal' language instruction is an actual realisation of this teaching/learning relationship.
>
> (William Rutherford 1987: 2)

teachability and learnability

By referring to the terms of 'teachability' (Pienemann 1984, 1989) and 'learnability' (Pinker 1984, Pienemann 1985) in the quotation above, Rutherford made it very clear that there is an important interface between SLA research and grammar teaching. It is an interesting – and in a way disappointing – fact that, despite having known about this interface for more than 25 years, most approaches to grammar teaching until today do not account for the findings of empirical SLA research. The approach to grammar teaching taken in this book integrates findings from SLA research to strengthen classroom-based grammar teaching. Figure 11 illustrates a simplified version of our approach:

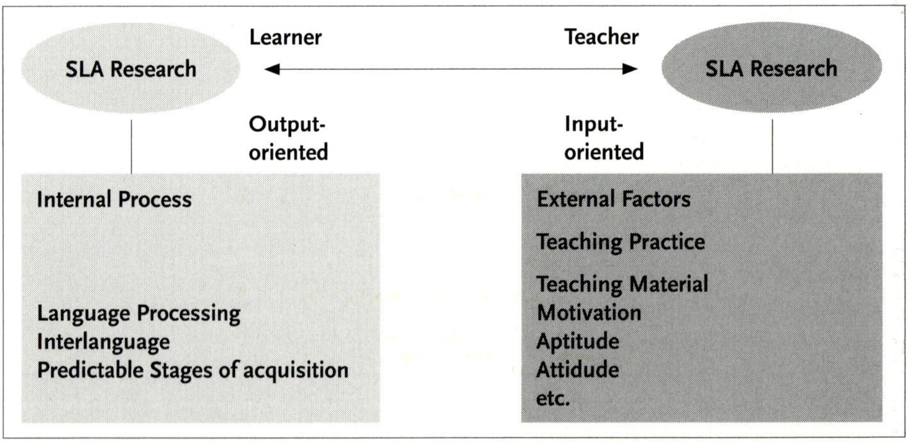

Figure 11: An integrated view of instructed foreign language acquisition (cf. Keßler 2006: 90)

grammar teaching and SLA

As can be seen in the illustration, SLA and teaching grammar are related. In instructed acquisition, both fields complement each other in that SLA research provides the empirical basis for understanding interlanguage development. Grammar teaching, in turn, applies SLA findings to the language classroom. The incorporation of research findings in to grammar teaching was discussed in the early days of SLA research, but without notable effect. In 1988, Sharwood Smith pleaded with educators to view grammatical knowledge in psychological terms because "we do not simply store lists of all possible words and combinations of units but rather programmes for enabling us to solve the myriads of problems involved in encoding and decoding utterances in a given language." (Sharwood Smith 1988: 207f)

In chapter 2, we briefly introduced the *Interlanguage Approach* as one way of teaching grammar. In this chapter we will now explain in more detail what, exactly, instructed SLA is and how it works. We will present a psycholinguistic approach to second language development with concepts that can be applied to the L2 classroom. Once some basic SLA concepts have been introduced, we will then relate those concepts to grammar teaching and its potential and limitations in the foreign language classroom (cf. chapters 7-10). Let us now take a closer look at what goes on in the mind of the learner.

This part of the book provides a non-technical summary of the basic components of psycholinguistic SLA research which are relevant to foreign language teaching. Until today, there have been competing views on instructed language learning, and the debate continues. Some SLA specialists claimed (e.g. Wode 1978, Felix 1982) that findings from SLA research should be applied in a one-to-one manner to the foreign language classroom. In direct opposition was the field of *Sprachlehrforschung* (e.g. Bausch & Königs 1983, Hüllen 1987). Its representatives claimed that instructed acquisition is totally different from natural acquisition. Therefore, they presumed that one cannot draw any conclusions for the foreign language classroom from SLA research. Luckily, this extreme position is no longer prevalent today, as most of the contentions have been found to be misconceptions between the representatives of the two fields. This is stressed by Börner & Vogel (2002) in the following:

> Nach langjährigen, von Extrempositionen gekennzeichneten Debatten wird die Grammatik von der Fremdsprachenforschung heute in ihrem Einsatz in der Lehre und in ihrer Rolle beim Lernen weder unreflektiert befürwortet noch grundsätzlich in Frage gestellt. Vielmehr bemühen sich Kognitionswissenschaften, Angewandte Linguistik, Sprachlehr- und -lernforschung sowie Zweitsprachenerwerbsforschung um ein differenziertes, theoretisch und empirisch abgesichertes Bild davon, unter welchen Bedingungen, in welchem Verhältnis und mit welchen Lernresultaten grammatisches Wissen den Fremdsprachenunterricht begleiten und unterstützen kann.
>
> Börner & Vogel (2002: blurb)

It would be beyond the scope of this book to re-analyse the tensions of the past. They have been discussed in detail by Keßler (2006: 169-183). We rather aim to provide a new approach to grammar teaching, namely the *Interlanguage Approach*. Figure 11 in the introductory part of this chapter illustrates how this approach accounts for a complementary view of second language acquisition and grammar teaching as advocated throughout this book.

all learners go through the same developmental Stages – but not all in the same way

There have been plenty of studies that have analysed natural and instructed second language acquisition (e.g. Ellis 1989, Pienemann 1989, Jansen 1991, Johnston 1997, Mansouri & Duffy 2005, Di Biase 2008). All of these studies came to the same conclusion: both environments of SLA follow the same path in the learners' minds. In chapter 2, we introduced the IL Approach to explain that learners develop their grammar along this very predictable path.

What still needs to be discussed is the question of whether all learners actually behave the same way when moving through the developmental Stages. As is commonly observed in L2 classroom practice, it is obvious that not all learners of a foreign language actually speak that language in the same way. Teachers will be well aware of the fact that there are quicker and slower learners and that some learners produce more errors than others. Would this not be evidence *against* any SLA theory that claims that all learners follow the same developmental path?

As a matter of fact, different learners produce different varieties of the target language. However, this is well in line with the theoretical basis of our approach (Processability Theory) as the theory accounts not only for Interlanguage development but also for Interlanguage variation. In the past, there have been competing approaches to Interlanguage variation (e.g. Ellis 1985 and 1994, Tarone 1988). For the *Interlanguage Approach* as we apply it here, we draw on the concept of Hypothesis Space as defined by Pienemann (1998 and 2007; cf. chapters 6 and 7 for details).

a case for grammar teaching

However, there are some major differences between natural and instructed acquisition that make a case for the teaching of grammar. Though learners can "produce and comprehend only those L2 linguistic forms which the current state of the language processor can handle" (Pienemann 2008: 9) the rate, route and success of development differ from individual to individual. It is here that instruction does make a difference, as the following two chapters will demonstrate.

A Role for Interlanguage

The view of grammar and its teaching put forward in this book is that the mental learner grammar develops gradually from an initial state towards the target language variety – ideally. Moreover, this gradual unfolding of the learner's interlanguage follows a universal developmental path every learner of any second language goes through. To be aware of this fact is of crucial importance in the L2 classroom, as factors such as attitude, aptitude or any other external factors in SLA are, at best, secondary. However, as classroom reality shows, even though every learner follows the same developmental path, many learners fall short of developing a target-like variety of the respective second language. Why? And what can be done about it?

To address these questions, one needs to know about the psycholinguistic dynamics underlying the second language acquisition process. To familiarise the reader with the basics of those developmental dynamics, we will offer an insight into a prominent psycholinguistic theory of SLA which has been empirically supported in numerous studies throughout the last years (cf. VanPatten and Williams 2007): *Processability Theory*. After we will have explained the theoretical background of the *Interlanguage Approach* in chapters 5 and 6, we show how the theory discussed here and classroom reality fit together. It will become clear that those teachers who know about fundamental concepts of second language acquisition research will only benefit from their efforts to familiarise themselves with the issues addressed here. They will be able to support their learners competently and effectively in the FL classroom. We expect neither our readers nor (future) teachers to be fully trained linguists. Still, they are language experts and, being experts, they will be interested in how to organise up-to-date grammar lessons that are based on a well-researched theory. This will be spelled out in detail in part III.

Let us now take a closer look at the key issues of Processability Theory (henceforth PT).

processability Theory

In 1998, Pienemann presented the SLA theory PT; it was further extended in 2005 (Pienemann, DiBiase & Kawaguchi). In his theory, Pienemann explores in detail what happens in the mind of an L2 learner during the acquisition process from the perspective of cognitive science. As stated at an earlier point, every L2 learner follows the same predictable developmental path, regardless of the L1 and the L2. Having revealed this very developmental path and defined its respective Stages of acquisition (see table 2), are the key findings of Pienemann, which he presented in his works: PT predicts exactly which linguistic forms of a foreign language are processable (and thus productive in the learner's IL) at which developmental Stage by the human language processor (see p. 86ff.). In other words, such structures as the English the English 3rd-SG-s,

> [...] will be produced by the language learner *only* if the necessary processing procedures are available. In this perspective the *language processor* is seen [...] as the computational mechanisms that operate on (but are separate from [!]) the native speaker's linguistic knowledge.
> *[PT] primarily deals with the nature of those computational mechanisms and the way in which they are acquired.*
>
> (cf. Pienemann 1998: 4f., emphasis added)

What is further important for language teaching is that the theory is typologically plausible; in other words, it can be applied to any language. In fact, PT was empirically validated for language-specific developmental features in the case of more than ten typologically different languages including English, German, Swedish, Italian, Spanish, Japanese, Chinese and Arabic (for detailed summaries see Keßler 2008 and Pienemann & Keßler in press).

focus and scope of PT

Pienemann approached SLA from a systematic point of view, addressing the following basic issues a theory of (second) language acquisition should account for[13]: 1) the logical and the 2) developmental problem:

1) *The logical problem*:

   Why are language learners able to accomplish the following even though respective linguistic constructions were not part of their input?

   1.1) recognise linguistic constructions which are possible and not possible in the target language

   1.2) produce an infinite number of sentences in the target language

2) *The developmental problem*:

Why does every L2 learner follow the same predictable developmental path?

The original version of PT, published in 1998, focused on the developmental problem, whereas in the extended version published in 2005 (Pienemann, DiBiase and Kawaguchi), the authors addressed the logical problem as well. The latter is briefly touched upon in chapter 6. However, in this book and, in particular, in this chapter we will lay the main emphasis on the developmental problem. In order to account for the developmental problem, PT is based on two principle concepts, which are supposed to motivate the second language acquisition process:

1) **Feature unification:** transfer of grammatical information within constituent structure (p. 88f.).

13 Cf. VanPatten & Williams 2007 for further information on what a theory of SLA ideally should account for.

2) **(Lexical) Mapping**: transfer of grammatical (and semantic) information between argument and functional structure and between constituent and functional structure (chapter 6).

In the following, the notions of 'learnability' and the 'linearisation problem' are introduced, as having defined working definitions of these concepts forms the basic prerequisite of an explanatory approach to (second) language acquisition. Afterwards, the provided insights are put into use when feature unification and mapping (chapter 6) are explained. In line with PT, we will refer to the psychology of language production (Levelt, 1989; 1999) and the formal linguistic framework Lexical Functional Grammar (Bresnan 2001). By doing so, it will become clear why the theory underlying the *Interlanguage Approach* is labelled *Processability* Theory.

learnability

To explore the cognitive mechanisms underlying SLA, Pienemann chose the concept of 'learnability'[14] as point of departure. He considered Weinberg's (1984) definition of learnability to fall short of processability, in that it excludes the human mind's procedural skills, which are psychologically constrained in language production (cf. Pienemann 1998: 1). These psychological constraints are:

- real-time speech *production* requires rapid on-line information processing, involving
  - word access: almost instantaneous word retrieval (a matter of milliseconds)
  - human memory: carrying out the message generation process without paying particular attention to any of the steps (see Levelt 1989).

Pienemann claims that "a learnability theory must [explain] how a learner develops from an initial state to the target grammar with the available input and the given learning device" (Pienemann 2005: 2). This way from the initial state towards the target grammar is what he aimed at capturing by defining the universal, predictable developmental path in second language acquisition. To recall, no matter which second language is acquired, and no matter what her/his first language is, any L2 learner goes through

[14] The mathematical theory of language learnability (also known as learnability theory, grammar induction, or grammatical inference) deals with idealised "learning procedures" for acquiring grammars on the basis of exposure to evidence about languages. (Pullum 2003)

the same Stages of acquisition. How, therefore, can it be that rates of learning and success of our students seem to be so heterogeneous, even though the developmental path is supposedly universal? This is due to the universal architecture of the human language processor (see page 88). In particular, PT claims that the shape of this universal developmental path is constrained by what is happening in our minds during language production. In other words, the unfolding of the interlanguage grammar in the mind of the L2 learner is dependent on the given make-up of cognitive mechanisms in language production. The basic premise of what underlies language production is that the output of the human language processor is restricted to be linear, since human beings can only produce one sound at a time. This restriction is called the 'linearisation problem' (Levelt 1989). In the following, it will be explained in detail how SLA and language production are related referring to the linearisation problem as the thread which will guide us through chapters 5 and 6.

The linearisation problem as just defined constitutes the main cognitive 'problem' to deal with when it comes to speech production, regardless whether in L1 or L2. The intended message in the individual's mind is initially 'chaotic', in the sense of of unstruc-

linearisation problem

Figure 12: Linearisation Problem

tured, non-linguistic pieces of information that then have to be given linguistic shape. As a result, the non-linguistic conceptual knowledge, or propositions (the information to be expressed), of what and how (e.g. statement, question, order) one wants to say has to be transformed into a *linear* linguistic form. In order for communication to be possible, the final utterance has to be clearly organised using the linguistic conventions of the chosen language.

several dimensions of the linearisation problem

One has to keep in mind that linguistic systems are rather complex in that they offer different ways of expressing one proposition (e.g. declarative sentence or question, active or passive voice). This, in turn, results in the linearisation problem being variable in complexity, as the present chapter and chapter 6 will reveal.

What makes the linearisation problem so relevant for second language research and classroom reality is that it occurs at several points in language production and SLA. Three of those dimensions will be presented in more detail, referring to English (as a second language): 1) The temporal dimension as manifest on the lexical and syntactic level, 2) the morphological, phrasal, inter-phrasal dimension and their impact on the syntactic level 3) and selected aspects of the dimension of grammaticalised discourse functions (Bresnan 2001: 98) and their impact on the syntactic level. The focus lies on 2) in this chapter and on 3) in chapter 6, whereas the explanation of 1), which follows in the next paragraph, serves primarily to give a general idea of the linearisation problem.

To begin with, there is linearity and non-linearity as to the linearisation of linguistic elements. At first glance, this sounds rather confusing which is why the following sketch of the temporal dimension of the linearisation problem also serves to illustrate the basics behind linearity and non-linearity.

The temporal dimension on the lexical, i.e. word, and syntactic level as one option of how the linearisation problem becomes evident in language production refers to the fact that the word order of the spoken sentence can, but does not necessarily have to mirror the real sequence of events (cf. Pienemann 1998: 56). Any sequence of events, both linear and non-linear, can be made explicit by using a temporal adverb in English (see page 81).

As can be seen in the above example of linearisation, non-linearity requires additional cognitive effort from the speaker,

linearity		**non-linearity**	
The man mounted his horse, then, he rode off.		*Before the man rode off, he mounted his horse.*	
event 1	event 2	event 2	event 1

(adapted from Pienemann 1998: 56)

because s/he has to "store one proposition in memory." (Pienemann 1998: 56) The speaker has to buffer, i.e. hold in his/her memory, the 'event' that "he mounted his horse", as the natural sequence is reversed in the statement. Accordingly, the speaker needs to alternately encode propositions and then buffer these pieces of information ("...,he mounted his horse") while the second event ("Before the man rode off") is audibly uttered first. To accomplish this, we need memory (see Chapter 9). In the particular case of second language production, this poses a further challenge for the learner: s/he is not only required to store a proposition in mind, but also has to encode it with the help of linguistic features s/he may not even have acquired yet. This means that a learner has to accomplish a more complex task than a monolingual speaker: in the particular case of a learner who may not have the simple past at her/his disposal, s/he would have to find a linguistic solution with the structures present at that point in time in her/his mental grammar (this example also touches upon 'interlanguage variation', which will be discussed in chapter 8).

Having explained the key aspects of the linearisation problem we will now turn to that area of the human mind where language production, second language acquisition and, in line with this, the constant linearising of conceptual material take place: the human language processor.

production constrains SLA

As mentioned before, the cognitive tasks (e.g. the linearisation problem) underlying language production which are accomplished in memory constrain the acquisition process (Pienemann 1998 and elsewhere). In order to gain a better understanding of the relationship between language production and SLA, it is vital to have an idea as to what actually constitutes the architecture of human language processing. This is depicted in figure 13 and explained in the following paragraph.

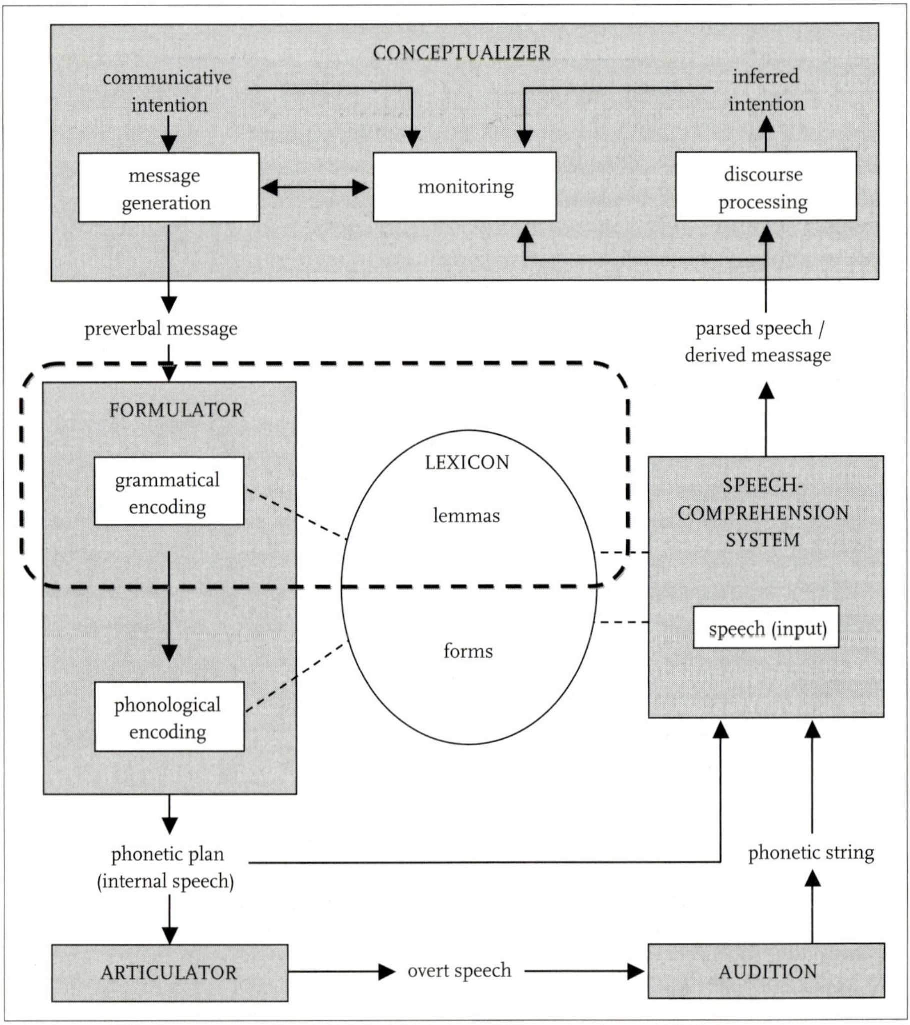

Figure 13: Psycholinguistic model of language production. Taken from Levelt 1999.

In 1989 and 1999, Levelt presented a model of speech production covering the range of processes involved in the conceptualisation of a message until its final articulation. Levelt's model is based on the view of the (adult) individual as a complex information processor who can transform thoughts, intentions and emotions into linguistic form. In terms of his speech production model this means that humans convert conceptual knowledge, i.e. what is intended to be said and how, into an articulatory plan. This transformation process happens incrementally, drawing upon and passing through three autonomous modules. These modules are defined as Conceptualiser, Formulator and Articulator. The central entity, the mental lexicon, plays a special role in speech production and SLA.

Keeping in mind the above basic technical terms, we will now turn to a sketch of the language generation process as proposed by Levelt and adopted by Pienemann (1998). Subsequently, we will turn to the relationship between language production and language acquisition, referring back to our connecting thread: the linearisation problem.

To begin with, the language production process is carried out with the help of algorithms which ensure the communication between the modules and the mental lexicon. Each module can only work with a particular kind of input and only produce a particular kind of output. This inflexible, highly specific nature of the modules accounts for the speed of producing a message.[15] First of all, in the Conceptualiser the 'preverbal message' is constructed. As the denomination suggests, the preverbal message does not have any linguistic shape at this point of the production process. It rather consists of pieces information which are taken from the discourse record such as situation knowledge and helps the speaker to keep the following in mind: who is the interlocutor? Which is the topic we are talking about? Am I going to produce a statement, an order, or a question? The preverbal message, thus, contains propositional information. Secondly, the preverbal message is passed on to the Formulator, which constitutes the interface between non-linguistic and linguistic material. As such, this module plays a very decisive role in the message generation process. Based on the conceptual material of the preverbal mes-

[15] By referring to the highly task specific nature of the modules, speech errors such as slips of the tongue can be explained. For reasons of relevance and space, however, we will not elaborate on this. For further information see Levelt 1989 and elsewhere.

sage, the Formulator retrieves the corresponding lexical entries from the mental lexicon. Here, the grammatical encoding of the message – which is the focus of Processability Theory – takes place. Basically, the grammatical encoder consists of procedures which guide, firstly, the retrieval of lemmas and, secondly, procedures which guide the ordering of the retrieved lemmas, i.e. the word order of the final sentence. In addition, these procedures enable the human language processor to construct noun phrases out of nouns, or verb phrases out of verbs (see p. 85) and, finally, full sentences. Apart from learning vocabulary or related issues, it is these procedures which learners of a second language have to acquire, in the first place. The above sketch of grammatical encoding, thus, affects the 'heart' of second language acquisition. To recall, in line with PT feature unification and (lexical) mapping are the driving momentums in second language acquisition. How is this related to language production? In fact, feature unification and (lexical) mapping *are* these very procedures which underlie grammatical encoding. We will come back to this at a later point in this chapter and also in chapter 6.

Finally, the surface structure built by grammatical encoding procedures has to be phonologically encoded, followed by the final articulation of the phonetic plan. All of this has to be carried out in a very limited amount of time in order to account for speech produced at a 'normal' rate, as it occurs in conversations.

production constrains acquisition

How, as maintained in PT, is language production as sketched above actually related to second language acquisition, i.e. the gradual development of the learner's interlanguage system? The particular mechanisms underlying message generation that Pienemann argues to constrain SLA take place predominantly in the Formulator. (However, as will be explained in chapter 6, PT also focuses on selected processes that characterise the relationship and 'communication' between the three modules and the corresponding levels of representation as defined in LFG, which is also discussed later). In line with Levelt (1989), Pienemann assumes that the message generation process is implicationally ordered and follows the sequence of processing procedures outlined below (cf. from Pienemann 2007: 14)

universal hierarchy of processing procedures

1 no procedure
2 category procedure
3 noun phrase procedure

4 verb phrase procedure
5 sentence procedure
6 subordinate clause procedure

The English noun phrase "the boy", for example, is formed in a speaker's mind as follows:

(1) The lemma BOY is retrieved from the mental lexicon.
(2) Since the lemma contains categorial information (BOY = N(oun)) the category procedure N (noun) is triggered.
(3) The particular NP can be built in that "possible complements and specifiers [as well as] diacritic features" (Pienemann 1998: 67) are identified in order to be linked, as a last step, to the NP. In this case, the specifier "the" would be selected and linked to "boy".

It should be pointed out here that the above sequence of six processing procedures is a universal hierarchy of processing procedures; that is to say it applies to any language. What Pienemann puts forward in terms of SLA is that every learner *must* acquire the processing procedures outlined above in order to be able to produce target-language specific structures, such as the 3rd-SG-s for English. This is why the theory of SLA discussed here is called '*Processability* Theory': SLA is constrained by the hierarchy in which the processing procedures unfold in the learner's mind. In PT, this gradual unfolding and development is defined through 'Stages of acquisition' (see table 3 at p. 86). These Stages, in turn, define the developmental path every learner has to go through in SLA, irrespective of the peculiarities of her/his first language and the target language.

ESL: developmental Stages

On the basis of this hierarchy of tasks that have to be accomplished by any individual during message generation and SLA, Pienemann (1998 and Pienemann, DiBiase & Kawaguchi 2005) developed language-specific hierarchies of morphosyntactic structures in order to describe the SLA process of different languages in detail.[16] These morphosyntactic structures, e.g. the English 3rd-SG-s, can only be produced in a target-like way if the respective processing procedures are available. In other words, this implicational hierarchy of the processing procedures, which

[16] For research on the emergence of discourse-pragmatic phenomena (e.g. active and passive voice, object topicalisation) see Pienemann, DiBiase & Kawaguchi 2005, Keßler & Keatinge 2008, Lenzing & Plesser (forthcoming).

every individual requires to build phrases and sentences, is the essence of what constitutes the learner's interlanguage.

In a nutshell, Pienemann suggests a universal, language-independent hierarchy of processing procedures as the basic matrix, plus the respective language-specific developmental hierarchy that results from it (see table 3).

developmental problem

By proposing that L2 learners' IL development follows a specific, unchangeable path, Pienemann accounts for the developmental problem introduced at the beginning of this chapter. As the developmental path is implicational in nature, no Stage can be skipped; this means that Stage 2 is the prerequisite for Stage 3 and so on. The learner has to be developmentally ready to acquire a particular Stage and, accordingly, produce a particular grammatical structure. This fact is of vital importance in terms of foreign language teaching. The learner *does not* learn the TL structures in the sequence in which they are presented by a teacher, but rather in the sequence in which the human language processor can handle them. These Stages of acquisition have been the subject of extensive research in the past and have been empirically validated (Pienemann 1984, 1985, 1987, 1989, 1998; Pienemann, DiBiase & Kawaguchi 2005; and others).

vital news for (future) teachers

The table below shows the relationship between the universal hierarchy of processing procedures and the respective morpho-syntactic structures of English:

processing procedure	**universal L2 process**	**English morphology**	**English syntax**
6 subordinate clause procedure	main and subordinate clause		**neg/auxiliary-2nd-?** *Why **doesn't** he go home?* **cancel inversion:** *I wonder why he sold the car.*
5 sentence procedure	inter-phrasal information exchange	**interphrasal morphemes, e.g. subject-verb-agr.:** ***He** gets up at six o'clock.*	**Passive construction:** *The ball was kicked by Peter.* **Wh-auxiliary-2nd** *Why **did** he sell that car* **Wh-copula inversion:** *Where **has** he gone?*

processing procedure	universal L2 process	English morphology	English syntax
4 verb phrase procedure	inter-phrasal information exchange		**yes/no inversion:** ***Has he** seen you?* **Wh-copula:** ***Where is** John?* **copula inversion:** ***Is** John at home?*
3 phrasal procedure	phrasal information exchange	**Phrasal morphemes, e.g. noun phrase agreement:** ***Two** boys* **neg + verb** *Me **no** come home.*	**adverb first** **In the morning, he drink coffee.* **Do-fronting** ***Do** you like it?* **Do he go home?* **Wh-SVO-?** ***Why** he go home?* **Aux-SVO-?** ***Can** he go home?*
2 category procedure	lexical morphemes	**plural:** *boy**s*** **past-ed** *walk**ed***	**canonical order (SVO)-Question:** **He go home?* **canonical order (SVO):** **He go home.*
1 word/ lemma	'words'/ formulae	**various lexical items, e.g. finite verbs; short sentences which are stored as one unit in the learner's mind. no creative use of those items!** *Hi. / How are you?/ What's your name? / ...*	

Table 3: Processability hierarchy for English. Adapted and modified from Pienemann (2005).

Up to this point, we have learned that IL development is defined as the gradual and accumulative unfolding of processing procedures in the mind of the L2 learner. As outlined by Pienemann, SLA is the acquisition of procedural skills and "the sequence in which they become available to the learner" (1998: 3). This takes place in the L2 learner's implicit memory, as will be explained in chapter 9. Pienemann's charting and validation of the invariant developmental path in SLA has shown that the latter is predict-

unchangeable developmental path

able. The fact that we can say which linguistic structures occur in which sequence in the learner's interlanguage is once again of crucial importance for (future) language teachers: to know what the learner will acquire next facilitates the design of learner-centred lessons, covering those aspects of the target language that the current developmental state of the learners requires (see PART III).

A further valuable aspect of PT for the foreign language classroom is that errors, or rather the types of those errors (see chapter 7, make up an integral part of the developmental process: as table 3 shows, in acquiring Stage 3 the English do-fronting becomes productive in the learner's IL. However, at this point of the production process such utterances as **Do he go home* occur. As the learner is at Stage 3, there is no point in correcting her/him; the 3rd-SG-s does and will not emergeuntil s/he has acquired Stage 5.

In PT, a distinction is made between morphological and syntactic target-language structures. 'Do-fronting' is a syntactic structure, as opposed to the morpheme 3rd-SG-s. As can be seen in the example sentence **Do he go home* , the learner has not yet acquired the 3-SG-s. As the do-fronting is a sign of development, despite the lack of interphrasal agreement, the non-target sentence in the example is still evidence for progress, and thus valuable information for the teacher. Not correcting such an inaccuracy in ESL may be irritating for (future) language teachers, but errors should be treated in a particular way in line with PT (see chapter 7). With respect to this concern, Pienemann highlights a distinction which is central in the discussion of mistakes in the L2 classroom: there is a difference between emergence and accuracy (see discussion on Interlanguage variation). Accuracy as a valid indicator for interlanguage development is not supported by empirical research. In 1981, Meisel et al. found out that there is no connection between learner variation, interlanguage development and accuracy (see Pienemann 1998: 143).

feature unification

As was mentioned at the beginning of this chapter, a major focus of PT is the exchange of grammatical information within phrases and sentences (see table 3) on the level of constituent structure. In short, this means that the learner progresses along a hierarchy of, for example, ESL morphemes which s/he can process (see also table 3):

Stage 2: lexical morpheme (e.g. the plural –s as in "boy**s**")
Stage 3: phrasal morpheme (e.g. **two** boy**s**)
Stage 5: inter-phrasal morpheme (e.g. he walk**s**)

As one can see, the inter-phrasal morpheme 3rd SG-s is acquired rather late. Why does it not emerge until Stage 5? At first glance, the 3rd-SG-s seems to be a little feature which 'simply' has to be attached to verbs in 3rd person. However, the processes required for this attachment are complex, compared to matching person and number as in the noun phrase "two boys". Subject-verb agreement happens across phrase boundaries and is, thus, a more complex task for the human mind than to achieve agreement within one and the same phrase.

How is this exchange of information across phrasal and inter-phrasal boundaries achieved? As can be seen in table 3, grammatical information exchange, expressed through the unification of diacritic features, has to be accomplished across phrasal boundaries (i.e. interphrasally) from Stage 4 onwards. This increasing complexity of feature matching within phrases and sentences leads us back to the linearisation problem. The linearisation problem applies not only to event sequences, but also to the encoding and buffering of syntactic or morphological information. With morphosyntax, the speaker has to match and buffer diacritic features, namely number, person, tense and aspect. This matching occurs either within a phrase (intraphrasally – Stages 2-3) or within a sentence, i.e. interphrasally (Stage 4 onwards). The described matching process is referred to as 'feature unification'. In short, through feature unification, it is "[ensured] that the different parts that constitute a sentence do actually fit together." (Pienemann 2000: 109) Feature unification takes place in the Formulator during language production (see page 82, figure 13). Two detailed examples of feature unification are given below:

- **Phrasal information exchange: *two boys***
  Feature: NUM = value: plural

- **Inter-phrasal information exchange: *the boy goes home.***
  Feature: NUM = value: singular
  Feature: PERSON = value: 3

Feature: TENSE = value: present
Feature: ASPECT = value: non-continuous
(examples adapted from Pienemann 2008: 19)

The example of interphrasal feature unification in the above declarative sentence demonstrates that speakers, and thus learners, first have to match the values of person and number in the noun and the verb. In technical terms, the NP and the VP procedures have to be acquired in order for the learner to be able to establish SV-agreement. In our example, the individual has to buffer the verb with the 3rd-SG-s attached, because in line with the canonical (=basic) word order of English, i.e. subject-verb-object (SVO), the subject is uttered first.

The word order of our example sentence is what leads us to the next chapter. In this section, we have discussed how feature unification accounts for various aspects of the linearisation problem. In the next chapter, we will turn to how so-called mapping processes account for a further dimension of linguistic linearisaton, namely that of grammaticalised discourse functions (Bresnan 2001: 98) along with their impact on the syntactic level (=word order).

Further Reading:

Pienemann, M. (2008). "A Brief Introduction to Processability Theory." In Keßler, J.-U. (ed). *Processability Approaches to Second Language Development and Second Language Learning.* Newcastle upon Tyne: Cambridge Scholars Publishing, pp. 9-29.

Pienemann, M. (1998). *Language Processing and Second Language Development: Processability Theory.* Amsterdam: John Benjamins.

Study Questions:

1. What does the term 'implicational sequence' mean?
2. Please find one synonym for each of the following: *(to) constrain, constraint.*
3. Please describe the process of message generation as defined by Levelt, 1989.

6 Interlanguage Grammars – Extending the Concept

Due to language, humans have various linguistic possibilities to express a single idea: declarative sentence, question, order, passivisation, etc.. However, each of the mentioned possibilities it is only declarative sentences which are organised rather simply, namely in canonical word order. To recall, the linearisation problem is concerned with linear and non-linear phenomena in language of different dimensions, which was introduced by referring to time courses of events. The dichotomy of linearity and on-linearity also applies to word order. Again, to establish linearity is less complex than to establish non-linearity. In this chapter, the reader will learn what happens in a speaker's/learner's mind each time s/he is about to produce structures which deviate from the basic word order of English, SVO, such as questions and passive voice. The following examples of English will guide the reader through this chapter whilst the third dimension of linearity – that of grammaticalised discourse functions (Bresnan 2001: 98) along with their impact on word order – is discussed.

- SVO: **Peter kick the ball.* (Stage 2)
- SVO-Question: **Peter kick the ball?* (Stage 2)
- Do-fronting: **Do Peter kick the ball?* (Stage 3)
- Wh-Aux-2nd-question: *What does Peter kick?* (Stage 5)
- Passive voice: *The ball was kicked by Peter.* (Stage 5)

meaning conveyance through word order

Why should teachers be aware of the processes underlying language production and SLA which have repercussions on word order? At this point, the structural differences between languages come into play: in this case, the fact that there are non-configurational languages and configurational languages. Languages of the first category encode much of their meaning through morphemes, i.e. affixes. Two such languages (also called agglutinative languages) are Turkish and Finnish. As opposed to non-configurational languages, configurational languages such as the Germanic languages (English, German etc.) convey a great deal of meaning through word order. That is to say, that English syntax is of greater importance for meaning than morphological structures such as the 3rd–SG-s discussed in chapter 5. A case in point is question formation. In Finnish, for example, questions are predominantly marked by morphological structures and in English by word order. As can be seen in the below example, the word order of English declarative sentences is different from that of questions. The most prominent difference is that the initial constituent is the subject of the declarative sentence, but the object of the question.

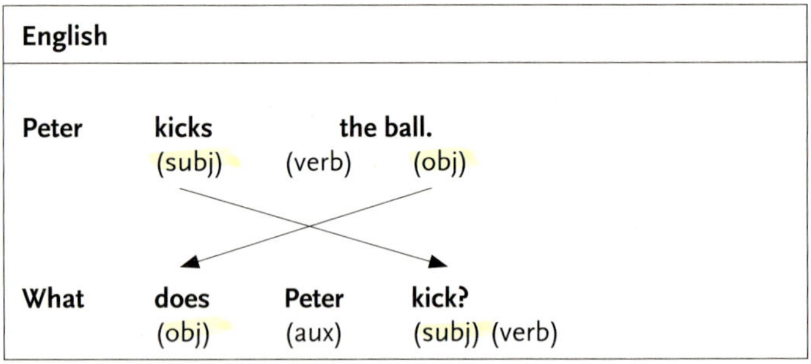

Figure 14: Mapping

This 'swapping' of constituent positions and their grammatical functions is a complex cognitive task which is acquired rather late, namely at Stage 5 of the PT hierarchy. The difficulty for a learner of English as a L2 is not merely the adding of an auxiliary (which cannot be accomplished before Stage 5; up to Stage 4, only WH-SVO or WH-copula questions are possible as Table 4
mapping shows), but the swapping of constituents. The phenomenon of swapping linguistic elements to encode the proposition <*kick*> with different meanings as in figure 14 is accomplished in a speaker's mind by carrying out different 'mapping processes'.

The term 'mapping' denotes how the so-called arguments of a verb (e.g. agent, patient) can be 1) assigned their corresponding grammatical functions (e.g. agent – subj; patient – obj), 2) and, in turn, their "slot" in the final sentence structure (1st , 2nd constituent: e.g. noun phrase, verb phrase) in order to create a meaningful message. In grammatical terms, it is of secondary importance in the above example (see figure 14) that the object is 'what' in the question and 'the ball' in the declarative sentence. Both fulfil exactly the same grammatical function, namely that of the object. What is of importance, however, is that the first construction conveys a different meaning than the second one – which is achieved through a change in word order. This alternation of word order, in turn, results from an alternation of the sequence in which the grammatical functions are realised. This sequence is a phenomenon based on the linearisation problem, which becomes manifest here in terms of linearising sentence constituents according to the intended form of the message, e.g. a statement or a question.

In order for the reader to understand the processes behind the above example, and in particular those behind the structures which guide the reader through this chapter, some useful terms will be introduced here. These linguistic terms are used in various theories of grammar, due to the general nature of their underlying phenomena, as the linearisation problem is, too. After having clarified some linguistic basics the reader may already know, we will turn to the different kinds of mapping processes as spelled out in Lexical Functional Grammar – the theory of grammar which the *Interlanguage Approach* is based on. Subsequently, we explore the relationship between mapping and speech production. Recalling that the reader learned that speech production constrains second language acquisition, and, thus, has consequences on the teaching of grammar, we will show towards the end of this chapter how mapping processes, speech production and SLA fit together.

To begin with, we aim at familiarising the reader with the three major levels of linguistic representation in each language user's mind:

1) **Argument structure:**
- The verb and the argument(s) it takes are represented in a-structure.
  *Please note: each verb takes its individually corresponding arguments!
- → for example: <*kick*> *agent, patient;* <*place*> *agent, patient/ theme, location*

2) **Functional structure:**
- The grammatical functions are represented in f-structure, which relates c-and a-structure.
  → for example: *subject, object*

3) Constituent structure:

- The final linear organisation of the sentence constituents is represented in c-structure.
  → for example: *noun phrase, verb phrase*

To know these three structures is so important for our Approach, as the 'mapping processes' discussed take place exactly between these levels of linguistic representation. There are two different mapping processes which happening in a speaker's mind during the production of any sentence:

- **Mapping between a- and f-structure: in the Mental lexicon**
  – This type of mapping is referred to as 'lexical mapping' and is based on 'Lexical Mapping Theory'.
  – What takes place: the arranging of who does what to whom. Mapping, or in other words, assigning grammatical functions (e.g. subject, object) to the arguments which the retrieved lexical entry takes.
  – Structures of English for which this has consequences, as explained in this chapter: *passive voice*

- **Mapping between c- and f-structure: in the Formulator**
  – in particular 'grammatical encoding' and 'surface structure':
  – This type of mapping is also simply referred to as 'lexical mapping.'
  – What takes place: the arranging of grammatical functions. Mapping, or in other words, assigning the grammatical functions to their slots in the final linear organisation of the sentence (e.g. noun before verb, etc.)
  – Structures of English for which this has consequences, as explained in this chapter: *SVO sentences, Do-fronting, Wh-Aux-2nd-question*

These two types of mapping processes can be further divided into linear and non-linear mapping processes. Whereas linear mapping (see figures 15 and 16) does not require much cognitive effort, non-linear mapping requires processing procedures which (in SLA terms) are acquired from Stage 4 onwards. We can say that the mapping processes are characterised by their increasing complexity, from linear to non-linear mapping. The common way to visualise mapping processes is to use arrows which depict whether the process is linear (see figures 15 and 16) or non-linear (see figure 17 and 18). In the examples below, we refer again to the structures this chapter is based on:

Level	**Example**
a-structure	*kick* <Agent Patient/Theme>
	↓ ↓
f-structure	Subject Object
	↑ ↑
c-structure	**Peter kick the ball.*

Figure 15: Example of linear mapping: SVO.

Level	**Example**
a-structure	*kick* <Agent Patient/Theme>
	↓ ↓
f-structure	Subject Object
	↑ ↑
c-structure	**Do Peter kick the ball?*

Figure 16: Example of linear mapping: Do-fronting.

Level	**Example**
a-structure	*kick* <Agent Patient/Theme>
	↓ ↓
f-structure	Subject Object
	↖ ↗ (crossing)
c-structure	*What does Peter kick?*

Figure 17: Example of non-linear mapping between c- structure and f-structure.

Level	Example			
a-structure	*kick*	<Agent	Patient/Theme>	
f-structure		Subject	Optional	Adjunct
c-structure		*The ball*	*is kicked*	*by Peter.*

Figure 18: Example of non-linear mapping between a- structure and f-structure.

mapping – language production

As the reader will recall, it was Levelt's model (1989) of speech production which was referred to several times before in order to explain how messages are created and how this process of message generation constrains second language acquisition. In the below figure, the three levels of linguistic representation, namely a-, f- and c-structure, along with their corresponding mapping processes are incorporated into Levelt's model of speech production (1989) (see figure 13).

The modules of Levelt's speech production model as well as the mental lexicon include the three levels of linguistic representation (see page 93f.) and their corresponding mapping processes as defined in LFG (Bresnan 2001). In his model, Levelt (1989) draws upon LFG in order to formalise the linguistic correspondences of the psychological processes underlying language production. What makes LFG particularly useful for Levelt (1989) (and PT) is that *Lexical* Functional Grammar assumes grammar to be lexically driven; this means that lexical entries stored in the mental lexicon contain the all of the required grammatical information in order to encode the message. As the reader already learned, the mental lexicon is the central element in both speech production and second language acquisition, as defined in PT. In PT and LFG, the mental lexicon is not merely seen as a simple lexical store, but rather as a lexical 'factory' (cf. Van Valin 2001) in which the mapping processes discussed above take place in order to ensure the generation of a meaningful message. This linking of speech production and mapping accounts for both monolingual and bilingual speakers. A pecu-

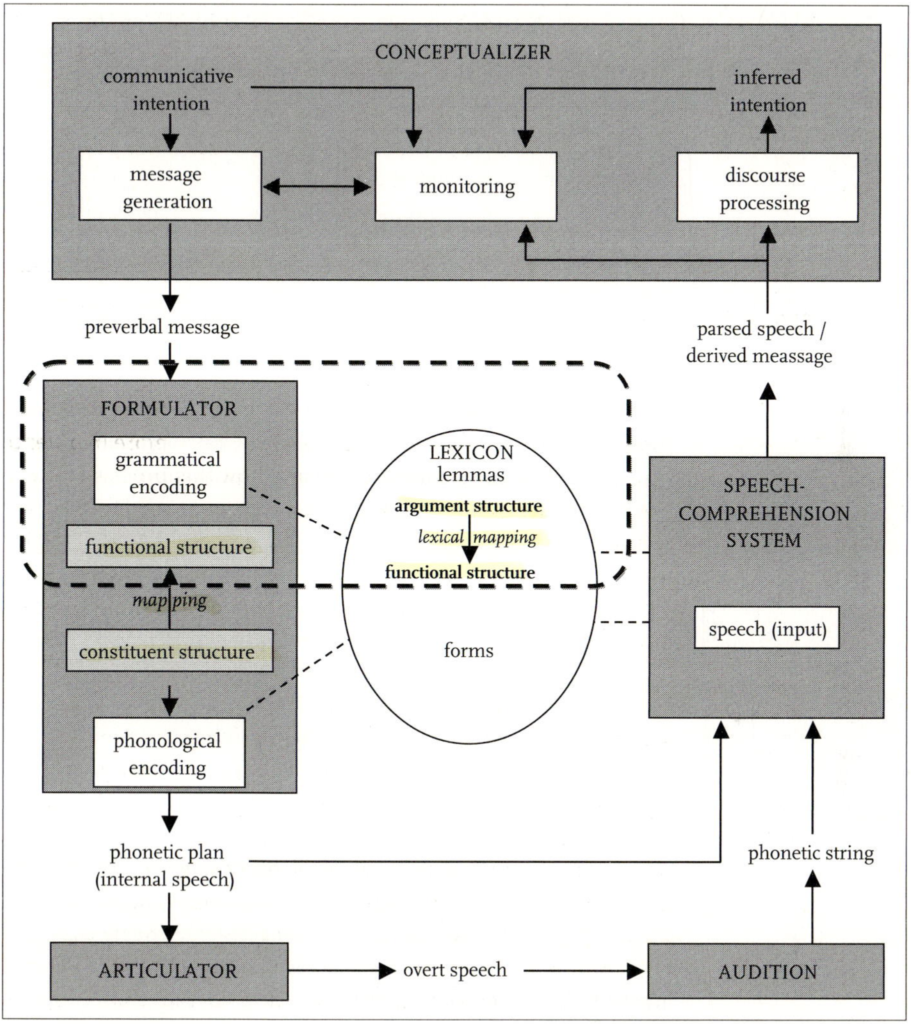

Figure 19: Psycholinguistic model of language production showing at which point in the message generation process the different mapping processes take place (Plesser in progress. Adapted from Levelt (1999) and Bresnan (2001)).

liarity concerning the bilingual speaker is, however, that s/he is required to have the mapping processes at her/his mental disposal in her/his Interlanguage. In fact, they need to acquire the processing procedures underlying linear and non-linear a- to f- and c- to f-mapping in addition to those processing procedures of the PT hierarchy which we introduced in chapter 5 (see table 3 on page 87). The reader may notice at this point once again how complex of a task second language acquisition and, in line with this, the teaching of grammar is. Keeping with our *Interlanguage Approach* and the underlying SLA theory, we will explain now what exactly happens in a learner's mind as regards mapping processes.

mapping – speech production – SLA

Originally linked by Levelt (1989), Pienemann (1998) and Pienemann, DiBiase & Kawaguchi (2005) elaborated on the complementary relationship of psychology (speech production) and formal linguistics (LFG). As was stated at an earlier point in this chapter, PT nowadays not only focuses on the processes which take place in the Formulator, but also on the relationship, or rather the 'communication', i.e. mapping, between the Formulator and the mental lexicon. As a brief summary, we can say that L2 learners' interlanguage systems consist of the following three components which gradually unfold in the form of processing procedures in the learners' minds: the L2 mental lexicon, the L2 Formulator, and the means of communication between these entities, i.e. mapping processes. Therefore, during the SLA process, a learner's lexical entries are being progressively annotated for various features, such as their syntactic distribution, i.e. in which slot of the sentence a word can occur, or diacritics, such as number, case, gender, tense etc.. Furthermore, learners have to acquire the system for how to form questions or passive constructions, which requires them to develop the necessary processing procedures for mapping. Let us now turn to the direct implications for the foreign language classroom of the relationship between speech production, mapping and SLA.

To recapitulate, argument structure refers to the basic ideas conveyed in a sentence (propositions). "[A-structure] is based on a universal hierarchy of argument roles including roles such as 'agent' or 'patient'. At this point, the central role of the lexicon in LFG shows again why LFG is used as the linguistic framework referred to in PT: the core argument roles for each verb are listed in the lexical entry of the verb. For instance, the argument roles of the English verb 'see' are 'experiencer' and 'theme'" (cf. Pienemann 2008: 22). In f-structure, universal aspects of grammar are encoded; it contains grammatical functions, such as subject or object. (cf. Lenzing: in progress) Thus, the extended version of PT also includes the relationship between what is intended to be said and the way this is expressed using grammatical forms. (cf. Pienemann 2008: 15)

An important question concerning the three structures which is relevant for language teaching is whether they are universal or language-specific. C-structure is language-specific; word order, for example, clearly differs across languages. Functional structure "consists of universal units (such as SUBJECT or OBJECT) [and is] related to [c-] structure in a language-specific way. [F-]structure serves [further] to connect argument structure and constituent structure." (Pienemann 2008: 22). This 'connection' is achieved by mapping, as the reader learned before.

How does this affect the foreign language classroom? At this point, the 'linearisation problem' once again comes into play, as this structural option of expressing events in variable ways requires the learner to buffer particular elements in memory. We learned that the IL system, predominantly consisting of the L2 mental lexicon and the L2 Formulator, unfolds from words/formulae in the direction of more complex morphosyntactic structures plus mapping processes (see page 87, table 3). In which sequence do the mapping procedures develop in the learner's mind? In line with the increasing complexity of the processing procedures underlying morphosyntactic structures (see table 3), the mapping principles also unfold in the learner's mental grammar 'from simple to complex'. In other words, the different relationships between the three structures develop stepwise in the L2 learner, in that their unfolding follows a developmental sequence (cf. Pienemann 2008: 23). In terms of LFG and PT, linear (or direct) mapping is the mapping process which is the least complex. Linear/direct mapping, which is also called Unmarked Alignment, results in canonical word order in c-structure such as SVO in English (see figures 14-18). In the case of our diagrams, this is the mapping with straight lines from top to bottom (or bottom to top). In line with the PT hierarchy, the SVO order is maintained until Stage 3. In other words, in early second language acquisition, the agent is directly mapped onto the subject and the patient onto the object function (see figure 20). The arrows depict again the direction of mapping processes. A 'straight' mapping relation is much easier to accomplish for L2 learners than carrying out a non-linear mapping relation – something that also holds true for native speakers.

Level	**Example**
a-structure	*kick* <Agent Patient/Theme>
	↓ ↓
f-structure	Subject Object
	↑ ↑
c-structure	**Peter kick the ball.*

Figure 20: Unmarked alignment – the initial state the learner starts off with in SLA.

Every teacher may have noticed that learners are indeed, at first, only able to produce SVO sentences such as **Peter kick the ball* – it makes no difference if, e.g. question forms were dealt with in class. The first type of questions in ESL to emerge in learner grammars are those which start with an auxiliary like *(to) do* (see figure 21) or a Wh-question word followed by an SVO construction. The reason for this is that, after Stage 2, the learner is able to front such features as questions words or adverbs as in *Every morning, I get up at 7 o'clock.* However, the basic word order is still SVO at this point in the acquisition process.

Level	**Example**
a-structure	*kick* <Agent Patient/Theme>
	↓ ↓
f-structure	Subject Object
	↑ ↑
c-structure	**Do Peter kick the ball?*

Figure 21: Linear mapping including do-fronting.

How do we know that the learner who produced the sentence in figure 21 is still at Stage 3, even though Table 3 shows that questions actually emerge at Stage 4? In fact, it is the erroneous agreement between the auxiliary 'do' and the subject 'Peter'. We learned that interphrasal information exchange is acquired at Stage 4 and 'do' belongs to another phrase than 'Peter'. Therefore, in the above example the auxiliary 'do' is simply fronted before the SVO structure, as depicted by the straight vertical line. Fronting is acquired at Stage 3 (see Table 3), but it still does not result in a deviation from Unmarked Alignment. Let us now focus on figure 19. In PT, it is hypothesised that learners do not acquire the processing procedures for non-linear mapping until Stage 4 (see also the discussion on stabilisation). With regard to ESL, this means such complex structures such as Wh-Aux-2nd or passive voice emerge late in the learner's IL (see Table 3 and Keßler & Keatinge 2008, Lenzing & Plesser, in prep.). This has, in fact, fundamental implications for the foreign language classroom: to be aware of the fact that all L2 learners start with canonical word order (English SVO) due to the way in which (lexical) mapping processes emerge in the learner's mental grammar helps teachers to understand and appropriately deal with such non-targetlike utterances as given in figure 21.

logical problem

Moreover, in charting a developmental sequence for the acquisition of different word order possibilities, PT accounts for the logical problem: Pienemann proposes Unmarked Alignment (UA) to be the initial state, i.e. the point of departure in SLA. For (future) language teachers this is momentous news, because UA rules out such factors as the learners' first languages as determining factors of the initial state. In other words, we can conclude that the different native languages of foreign language students have no impact on the development of their mental grammar: each learner starts off with the same prerequisites. In addition to the same cognitive starting point, the learners all follow the same developmental path in SLA, as we learned before. Of course, despite the fact that the initial state in SLA is the same for every learner language assessment and classroom practice reveal heterogeneous learner groups. There are two decisive factors which cause this well-known heterogenity, namely the rate and the route of the individual interlanguage development. Until now, we have only briefly touched upon the value of instruction in terms of

first language not relevant

teaching grammar. In PART III, however, we take a closer look at the question of whether instruction does make a difference in SLA. Before we turn to the practical implications of the theoretical foundations laid in this chapter, however, we will delve into the dynamics of one of the most prominent aspects of SLA, namely 'stabilisation'.

Further Reading:

Bresnan, J. (2001). *Lexical Functional Syntax*. Malden, Mass.: Blackwell.

Pienemann, M. (Ed.) (2005). *Cross-linguistic Aspects of Processability Theory*. Amsterdam: John Benjamins.

Study Questions

1. Please explain the linearisation problem in language production.
2. Please find two examples for linear mapping and two examples for non-linear mapping.

7 Interlanguage and the Language Classroom

As was pointed out at an earlier point in this book, there has been extensive research in the past on the question whether the developmental path in natural and classroom SLA is different. In terms of teaching grammar this means if instruction can alter the sequence of acquisition (see Pavesi 1984; 1986, Felix 1981 and Felix and Hahn 1985). Each of the studies, however, revealed that L2 learners follow the same developmental path, regardless of the learning environment. Does this render grammar teaching redundant?

The Teachability Hypothesis

Based on the results of the research mentioned, Pienemann (1984, 1985, 1987, 1989, 1998) proposed the 'Teachability Hypothesis' (henceforth TH), in which he assumes psychological constraints on the teachability of languages – based on the processing constraints on the learnability of second languages that were discussed earlier. The TH predicts that

- **Stages of acquisition can neither be skipped, or altered by instruction**

Why is it impossible to skip Stages? According to Pienemann,

> [e]ach Stage requires processing procedures which are developed at the previous Stage. 'Skipping Stages' in formal instruction would imply that there would be a gap in the processing procedures needed for the learner's language. Since *all* processing procedures underlying a structure [such as the interphrasal morpheme 3-rd-SG-s in English] are required for the processing of the structure, the learner would simply be unable to produce the structure.

- **instruction will be beneficial if it focuses on structures from 'the next' Stage.**

(Pienemann 1998: 250)

In line with PT, instruction is ineffective if it does not suit the developmental state of the learner. Teaching grammar that does not suit the current state of the learner can even be harm-

developmental readiness

ful, e.g. when an early learner is taught a complex morphological structure such as the 3rd –SG-s, s/he is not developmentally ready for.

At first glance, it may appear demotivating for (future) teachers that instruction does not make any difference as to the developmental sequence as such. However, the good news is that instruction *can* be beneficial – as long as it suits the developmental state of the learner. Instruction can influence variational features as these "appear to be free of the kinds of constraints which affect the teachability of developmental features: once a variational feature [such as the 'copula'] can be produced at all it can be said to be teachable" (Pienemann 1989: 61). In line with this, instruction can be beneficial to acquisition as regards

a) the rate of acquisition
b) the frequency of rule application
c) the different linguistic contexts in which the rule has to be applied

(Pienemann 1989: 63)

implications for language teaching

When it comes to implications for language teaching of the above predictions, (future) teachers should be aware of the fact that "teaching can only promote acquisition by presenting what is learnable at a given point in time. [...] Items in a syllabus need to be taught in the order in which they are learnable." (Pienemann 1989: 63). As Lenzing (2004) puts it, the fact "that not everything that is taught is necessarily also learnable [...], the [TH] has the potential to make a vital contribution to the question of 'what to teach' in the foreign language classroom."

In other words, the teacher can provide input and exercises that focus on structures that

1) a learner **is close to acquiring** the respective processing procedures for and that
2) a learner **has just recently acquired** the respective processing procedures required for.

Examples for ESL are given below. For a detailed study and presentation of classroom activities based on the PT framework, see section X of this book.

	Morphology	Syntax
Stage / structure	Stage 5: 3rd -SG-s	Stage 5: Aux-2nd-?
Example	*He gets up at ten o'clock every morning.*	*Why does he get up at ten o'clock every morning?*
Classroom activity	• Habitual action task This task provides the learner with a picture sequence showing the daily life of a person. S/he is asked to describe in one sentence each what s/he can see.	

Figure 22: Habitual action task

teachability in the classroom

The Teachability Hypothesis was also subject to criticism. For reasons of scope and space of this book, we can only focus on one aspect some critics have raised.[17] In 1985 and 1998 Lightbown claimed that one must not overestimate the impact of the Teachability Hypothesis for the foreign language classroom. Lightbown (1998: 179) warns that this hypothesis only deals with a "tiny fraction" of the elements important in any language classroom. Ad-

17 For a full discussion of critical approaches against the Teachability Hypothesis see Keßler, Liebner and Mansouri (in press).

ditionally, she fears that teachers who stick to closely to this hypothesis will start using "wrong" structures in their input. This criticism has also been refuted empirically by studies (e.g. Mansouri & Duffy 2005, Keßler 2006, Di Biase 2008, Pienemann & Keßler 2007) which show that the basic ideas of teachablity are indeed tailored to much of instructed foreign language learning. However, the Teachabilty Hypothesis was never claimed to be applicable to teacher input on a one-to-one level. On the contrary: when teaching in a foreign language classroom the teacher has to ensure the provision of L2 input in as rich a context as possible. How instruction can beneficially be applied in foreign language learning will be exemplified in detail in part III of this book.

When addressing learner output, however, a teacher who is familiar with the concept of teachability will be in a position to distinguish between different kinds of learner errors. This distinction can help the teacher to address different learner errors in a pedagogically appropriate manner. As errors are the result of which variant of the L2 a learner 'chooses' in SLA, the following section provides an overview of Interlanguage variation as one of the most prominent features in SLA. Afterwards, the role of errors is examined in detail.

Interlanguage Variation

As was mentioned several times throughout this chapter, every (future) teacher is aware of the fact that learners make mistakes. We have clarified so far that a certain type of errors is part of the acquisition process and that there is no case in pushing the learner towards a target-like production of , e.g. **Do he live here?* when s/he is at Stage 3. However, even though a learner seems to have acquired a particular TL structure, Pienemann points to the fact that "[t]here is overwhelming evidence that the shape of an interlanguage varies within one learner on one and the same day depending on which linguistic task the learner performs in which context (...)" (cf. Pienemann 1998: 273). However, when do we know that a particular TL structure is acquired? Pienemann applies the so-called Emergence Criterion (henceforth referred to as EC). That means that he does not focus on accuracy, but emergence.[18] In line with this, Pienemann defines a syntactic structure,

Emergence Criterion

[18] It has not yet been finally clarified as to when a structure can be considered automatised.

such as Aux-2nd (Stage 5 of the ESL hierarchy), to be acquired when it was produced systematically once when the target grammar required its use. As to morphological structures, such as the 3rd-SG-s (Stage 5 of the ESL hierarchy), he suggests three occurrences in obligatory contexts. In line with this, it is important to draw upon a testing framework which enables (future) language teachers to identify the shape of IL variation in order for instruction to be learner-oriented.

It is, in fact, of central importance to consider IL variation, since to ignore or misinterpret this common phenomenon of L2 performance may lead to a misjudging of what the learner is actually able to do in the target language (cf. Pienemann: 274). To be aware if this potential misjudging is particularly important in the context of L2 instruction. In SLA research, the study of IL variation has been the focus of numerous studies from different perspectives (Tarone 1988, Ellis 1985, 1994), as it is certainly an intriguing phenomenon a theory of SLA should account for (cp. VanPatten & Williams 2007). However, what exactly is 'IL variation'? As the following paragraphs will show, Pienemann found out that IL variation is, in fact, systematic and predictable. Therefore, it can be dealt with adequately in the foreign language classroom.

Steadiness Hypothesis

Pienemann (1998; 2005 and elsewhere) addresses the phenomenon IL variation with a well-structured line of reasoning: his argumentation is based on the concepts of the Emergence Criterion, the Steadiness Hypothesis, and Hypothesis Space. What the Steadiness Hypothesis predicts is "that despite considerable differences in performance the basic rule system underlying variable IL performance *does not change* within one learner between tasks" (Pienemann 1998: 278, emphasis added), it hence remains stable. In other words, Pienemann states that L2 learners cannot be influenced by external factors to such extent that they apply linguistic knowledge in a particular setting but not in another one. This hypothesis was tested and confirmed in numerous studies (e.g. Pienemann 1998).

Mode Steadiness Hypothesis

In the past, major research within the framework of PT was based on spontaneous oral speech production data; written data was not focus to interlanguage analyses until recently. The only PT-based studies on L2 writing are those by Håkansson and Norrby 2007 and Håkansson and Rahkonen 2008 and Plesser 2008.

In 2008, Plesser proposed the Mode Steadiness Hypothesis (MSH), which forms an extension of the Steadiness Hypothesis. The MSH predicts that (1) L2 production of individual learners is steady across the two modes of production, oral and written. She further claims that (2) mode steadiness is independent of processing time, because learners are constrained to using only those processing procedures which are available in their IL system. There is no reason to believe that processing procedures are different for the two modes. Nevertheless, the MSH allows for variation, but only within the range predicted in 'Hypothesis Space'.

In Plesser's respective pilot study on German ESL learners (2008), she analysed written and oral data for each individual informant focusing on the ESL PT-Stages defined by Pienemann 1998 (cf. figure 20). It turned out that for all informants the level of acquisition was identical in the written and the oral mode, irrespective of processing time, and performance varied only within Hypothesis Space (see page 109). That is to say, learners who did not apply the 3rd-SG-s in spoken production did not apply it in written production either. The same observation goes for, e.g. question formation. The students could not form such questions as "When do you go home?" in one, but not the other production mode. They could either produce a target-like variant of a question in none or both modes.

However, up to this point the MSH had only been tested for English morphosyntax. In 2010, Lenzing and Plesser conducted a study on learners of Spanish as a L2 – testing morphosyntactic as well as discourse-pragmatic phenomena, i.e. passive voice and object topicalisation. Preliminary results show that the MSH also holds for discourse-pragmatic structures. What is striking, though, is that the strategies to circumnavigate the target-like form (if the learner is not developmentally ready to produce it) are not exactly the same in oral and written production. That is to say, the number of structural hypotheses on the variational level becomes higher correlating with the increasing complexity of TL structures.

Before we turn to the implications for foreign language teaching of this crucial insight in IL variation as integral part of the acquisition process, it is explained how IL variation is defined in detail in the PT framework. Examples will be given in order to demonstrate how IL variation becomes evident in English as L2.

Hypothesis Space

In order to demonstrate that IL variation is indeed systematic and not, as commonly assumed, random in nature, it is argued in PT that learners operate within a constrained scope of possible strategies on each Stage of acquisition to solve linguistic problems, i.e. tasks. The range of these "structural hypotheses" (Pienemann 1998: 231) is what he refers to as *Hypothesis Space*. "The key assumption underlying the concept of Hypothesis Space is that variation and development can be captured by *one* dynamic linguistic system." (Pienemann 1998: 279, emphasis added). The figure below illustrates the conception of Hypothesis Space.

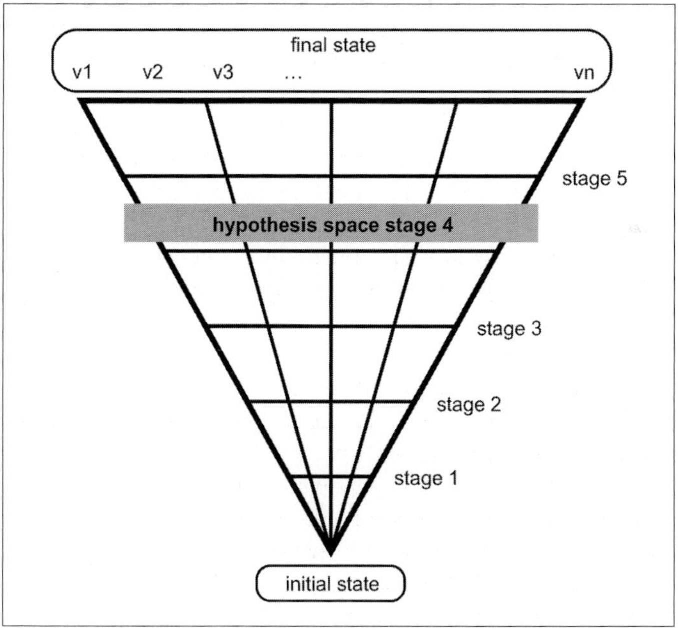

Figure 23: Hypothesis Space (adapted from Pienemann 1998: 232).

The horizontal level represents the developmental Stages (see page 87 table 3 for details) whereas the vertical dimension illustrates the scope of IL variation within each Stage. Within Hypothesis Space, every Stage is characterised by a continuum of poten-

tial linguistic options an L2 learner can produce – ranging from simplified to target-like variants, as demonstrated by the example given above. As can be seen, the range of possibilities to circumnavigate a target-like variant grows in proportion to the Stage acquisition: the higher the Stage acquired, the higher the linguistic options. To make a case in point apart from the example in figure 21, the teacher may observe the following solutions of "When did she come home?" in the classroom:
*"When she come home?"
*"She (did) come home when?"
...
In a nutshell, the errors teachers observe in the L2 classroom can be captured by hypothesis space. The fact that errors are not random, but systematic has direct repercussions for the treatment of errors in the L2 classroom.

This will be laid out in the following paragraph. It will become clear that not all errors are 'bad' errors. Knowing about different types of errors will help teachers to find the most efficient way of providing beneficial feedback to their learners.

The role of errors

> But we feel that just as a mother or father does not force a child to speak adult English from the start, for the *obvious reason that the child is unable to do it anyway*, so second language learners, adults included, should be given the same opportunity to practice and improve to the extend that they are able. It is useless and unnecessarily painful to attempt too much at once.
>
> Burt & Kiparsky: 1975: 7, stress added

In this section we will discuss a vital element of classroom-based foreign language learning, namely the role of errors.

Task

Before we introduce the role of errors in the *Interlanguage Approach*, take a few minutes and take some notes about the role you assign to errors in grammar teaching.

As Burt & Kiparsky (1975) pointed out more than 35 years ago, teachers often tend to measure language learners in the classroom against the standard of (adult) native speakers of the target language. An approach to errors like this, however, neglects the obvious fact that any native speaker of his/her first language is granted up to five years to gradually develop accuracy, fluency and proficiency. In view of this, why do teachers often tend to expect their learners to master the foreign language from scratch? We have seen that any second or foreign language learning also develops along a predictable path. In the previous sections of this chapter we have also discussed that this does by no means imply that all learners do exactly the same in their acquisition process but that we can distinguish between different Interlanguage variants that may be more simplified or more standard oriented. The following paragraphs are adapted from Keßler, Liebner and Mansouri (in press).

Interlanguage Approach to error correction

In the *Interlanguage Approach* as explained and discussed throughout this book, we have to distinguish between developmental and variational errors made by the learner. Though error correction may be considered as part of input (the teacher provides some kind of feedback as input to the learners), both PT as well as the *Interlanguage Approach* to error correction are closely related to learner output. Depending on the kind of output provided by the learner, corrective feedback should vary in quantity as well as quality. Before we discuss the details of the *Interlanguage Approach* to error correction in instructed L2 acquisition, let us briefly look at various possible learner errors. Note that the errors mentioned can be captured by the concept of Hypothesis Space introduced on page 109.

As mentioned above, an analysis of learner errors from a PT perspective first of all needs to distinguish between developmental and variational errors. Developmental errors are errors which occur because the learner wants to express something that s/he cannot yet process according to her/his current state of IL development. In chapter 5 and 7, we introduced the concepts of development and variation from a PT perspective. Applying these concepts to the field of error correction, we conclude that not all learner errors should be treated in the same way. In contrast to early approaches to the so-called communicative foreign language classroom, which invited teachers to neglect any errors as long as the message that the learner wanted to convey was understandable, a PT approach to error correction would not follow the idea 'anything goes'. Depending on the kind of error, the slogan 'message before accuracy' can be harmful for further L2 development. Let us look at the following examples, each provided by a Stage 3 learner of EFL:

(1) Peter go home.

(2) He Tarzan.

developmental errors

Sentence (1) provides an example of a developmental error: the morphological structure required in a target language version of this sentence would be "3-sg-s". This structure is not acquired until Stage 5 on the PT hierarchy for EFL. A learner who is still at Stage 3 is not yet developmentally ready to acquire this structure; thus, it can neither be taught nor learned by this learner at this point in time. Correcting the learner would not lead to any success in the acquisition process, as the learner may be able to repeat the target-like form of this structure after having been corrected by the teacher, but would make the same error again as soon as another context for 3-SG-s occurs. However, providing corrective feedback by the teacher might be beneficial for other learners in the same classroom who may already have acquired Stage 5 and can comprehend and process the corrective feedback provided by the teacher.

variational errors – need for correction

Sentence (2), on the other hand, is an example of a variational error. The underlying syntactic structure to be processed by the learner is SVO. This structure is acquired at Stage 2. As mentioned above, the learner in our example has reached Stage 3 already, so s/he is able to process the SVO structures. In Chapter IV.2, we discussed the concept of variation from a PT perspective and introduced the notion of hypothesis space. Looking at sentence (2) more closely shows that the learner makes an error by choosing an omission strategy for his interlanguage production. Instead of producing a complete SVO structure including the verb, the learner in our example produces an incomplete SVO structure, leaving out the verb. From a 'message before accuracy' point of view this sentence could be considered acceptable. In fact, many teachers tend to accept such an utterance without any correction, as they are satisfied that their learners are able to produce foreign language utterances at all. From a PT perspective, however, not correcting this error would be rather problematic. As will be discussed in detail in Chapter 8, the omission strategy will lead to a simplified interlanguage. We will demonstrate that simplified choices may accumulate and result in simplified interlanguage variation. If a learner only acquires the function but not the form of a structure, this can restrict and limit her/his future interlanguage development. In our example, the acquisition of the copula is vital for the learner's further development in EFL. Without having acquired the copula at a rather early point of the acquisition process, the learner will not be able to invert the copula as required at Stage 4. Thus, not correcting this error will lead to stabilisation in interlanguage development. This is why it is crucial to correct this error and to provide exercises (with rich linguistic context) for learners to develop a more standard-oriented variety of the target language.

The discussion of different types of errors has revealed that teachers should distinguish between – necessary – developmental errors that need not necessarily be corrected. Providing rich input in the target language in combination with vast opportunities for the learners to produce output through interaction and negotiation of meaning (cf. Long 1996) supports that learners will notice their errors eventually. Thus, these errors will be overcome once the learner is developmentally ready. Variational errors, on the other hand, are indeed a case for correction. As those errors reflect a simplified account of the target language at a developmental Stage the learners have already acquired, these errors need to be addressed by the teacher in order to support his/her learners in developing an Interlanguage variation as standard-oriented as possible.

A differentiated perspective on error correction as proclaimed in this section reveals that some common beliefs about grammar and its teaching (cf. Chapter 2; see also Pienemann 1995, Larsen-Freeman 1997) need to be reconsidered from an interlanguage perspective. This will be done in chapter 10.

Before we turn to applications of PT in the language classroom in part III we will introduce a further crucial characteristic of SLA, namely that hardly any learner ever achieves native-like competence in the L2.

Further Reading:

Mansouri, F. and L. Duffy (2005). "The Pedagogic Effectiveness of Developmental Readiness in ESL Grammer Instruction." *Australian Review of Applied Linguistics, 28*(1), pp. 81-99.

Pienemann, M. (1998). *Language Processing and Second Language Development: Processability Theory.* Amsterdam: John Benjamins.

Study Questions

1. What does the Teachability Hypothesis state?
2. How is the Teachability Hypothesis related to the concept of developmental readiness?
3. Please discuss the difference between variational and developmental errors. What does this mean for the foreign language classroom?

8 Interlanguage and Stabilisation

> "*Fossilization,* a mechanism [...] underlies surface linguistic material which speakers will tend to keep in their IL productive performance, no matter what the age of the learner or the amount of instruction is he receives in the TL.
>
> (Selinker 1972:229)

One of the most important questions in SLA is whether L2 learners can achieve native-like mastery of the target language. As is commonly agreed on among linguists and applied linguists, L2 learners do hardly ever reach native-like competence in TL (Towell & Hawkins, 1994). In 1972, Selinker suggested the technical term 'fossilisation' to capture this, maybe most prominent, feature of SLA. In 1996, he stated a more precise definition of fossilisation, referring to it as

> "the process whereby the learner creates a cessation of [IL] learning, thus stopping the [IL] from developing, it is hypothesized, in a permanent way [...] The argument is that no adult can hope to ever speak a second language in such a way that s/he is indistinguishable from native speakers of that language."
>
> (Selinker 1996)

In order to incorporate fossilisation into a theory of SLA, the concept should be operationalised precisely. In this concern, two major problems are frequently raised in literature:
1) How can fossilisation be defined accurately?
2) How can fossilisation, then, be empirically described?
As any research design is based on a clear-cut working definition of a particular concept, the two problems are closely related with each other. As Long (2003) highlights, regardless of how fossilisation has been described throughout the last three decades, each of the definitions fell short of measurability. As to Selinker's work(s), Long criticised that "[his] view is essentially ambiguous in that it suggests fossilisation to be both *explanandum* (i.e., the thing to be explained) and as *explanans* (i.e. an explanation)." (Han 2004: 21) That is to say, is fossilisation a phenomenon that should be explained, or is it an observation that explains something? Leaving this problem rather unresolved as it has to be

addressed within each theoretical framework individually, one further problem concerning an operationalisable definition of fossilisation has to be accounted for: how long does an L2 learner have to show a cessation in IL development before one can denote her/him 'fossilised'? One way to overcome this difficulty in theory construction is to concentrate on the term 'stabilisation' which, in contrast to fossilisation, is claimed to not be of permanent character (Bley-Vroman 1989), at least not in a measurable sense. Stabilisation, as an abruption of the learner's IL development, "[...] has become widely accepted as a psychologically real phenomenon of considerable theoretical and practical importance. (Long 2003: 496) Still, it is almost equally difficult to prove a learner to be temporarily stabilised as permanently fossilised since the time span appears to be defined somewhat arbitrarily within respective research designs. In this concern, Long concludes that "[...] while it is often said that stabilisation is pervasive [...], the evidence to date has been largely impressionistic." (*ibid.*)

fossilisation or stabilisation?

Selinker and Lakshmanan (1992) agreed on stabilisation as indicator for (putative) fossilisation. Han proposed a clearer delineation of the interrelation between stabilisation and fossilisation in that she defined fossilisation as follows: "invariant appearance of IL forms over *time*, backsliding over *time*, and stabilized variations over *time*." (Han 1998: 87, emphasis added) However, what the extensive academic discourse about stabilisation/fossilisation narrows down to is the notion of 'time'. This in turn, entails repercussions for empirical research on these phenomena as this view requires longitudinal studies conducted over a particular (arbitrary) period of time. Until today, researchers generally agree on longitudinal data as the only way to capture and empirically describe the phenomenon at all (Long 2003, Han and Odlin 2004 and others). If such data were collected, then, what exactly should be subject to measurement – the IL 'in general', or only particular features of it? In SLA research, this question is referred to as the distinction between global and local stabilisation: the first term suggests stabilisation to cover the entire IL, and the second one that stabilisation is limited to either

1) particular linguistic levels of the IL such as
   a. phonology

   b. morphology
   c. syntax
   d. semantics
   e. pragmatics
2) or only particular features of one or more the above.

In the past, stabilisation has been the focus of various research projects based on different theoretical approaches (cf. Selinker 1972; 1989, Long 2003, Han & Odlin 2004, Birdsong 2004). What is striking reviewing their works is that SLA researchers concentrated on other factors of SLA than the processing dynamics themselves, such as age of onset, L1, lack of intrinsic motivation to acculturate with the TL community (internal factors) and premature communicative pressure, e.g. inadequate instruction (see 'Teachability Hypothesis'), few occasions to use the TL, lack of instrumental motivation, e.g. the need to speak the TL at work, with friends/relatives/fellow students or not, or a simplified mental grammar that satisfies her/his communicative needs (external factors).

A further problem with research on stabilisation is that research results could not be implemented into an SLA theory in a way that the latter could predict stabilisation to occur under particular conditions, or not. In this concern, Long concludes that an explanation of stabilisation/fossilisation an SLA theory may include has to be of *predictive* power and not only a framework for description of the latter *after* the learner stabilised (cf. Long 2003: 514). An explanation on stabilisation that aims at differing from preliminary works exactly in predictability and, along with this, research design is presented in the following.

In their approach to tackle stabilisation in SLA, Pienemann (1998, 2005) and Plesser (in progress) focus on explaining stabilisation with the concept of *Generative Entrenchment* (GE) (Wimsatt 1988, 2005), which has its origin in philosophy and natural science (see figure 24). "The basic mechanism behind generative entrenchment is the principle that developmentally early decisions bias the further development of the interlanguage system." (Pienemann 2008: 21)

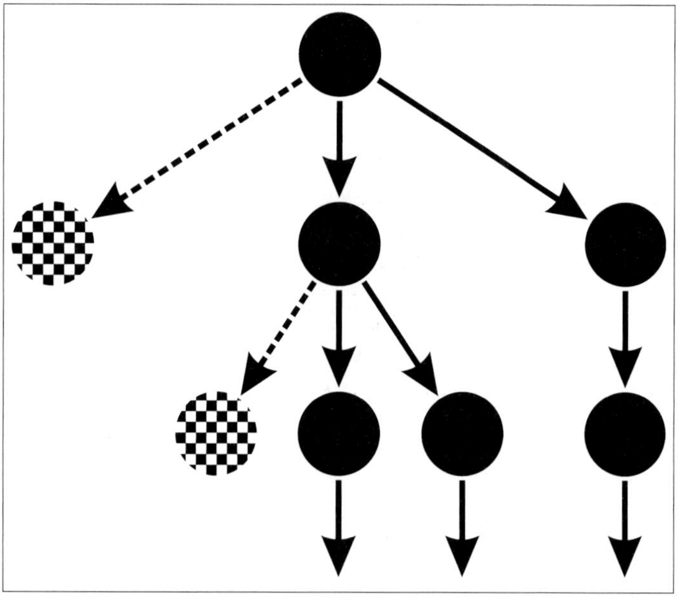

Figure 24: Simplified depiction of the dynamics of Generative Entrenchment. The chefuered balls represent a structurally wrong decision and the back ones a correct one leading to further development.

Pienemann first incorporated this concept into PT in the late 1990s to account for processing constraints inherent in the predictable developmental dynamics themselves. His account for stabilisation concentrates on the morphosyntactic development of the L2 learner. Along with our *Interlanguage Approach* to SLA this means that learners who (subconsciously) choose the simplified variety of the TL at an early point in SLA (see figure 25), will reach a point in their acquisition process from which they cannot progress any further. This can be exemplified with a house that is being built. When the foundations are laid on weak and not sufficiently robust materials, they will not be structurally capable of taking the weight of, e.g. more than three floors. Unfortunately, laying the foundations is hardly reversible, and if it was, only at a very high cost. This applies to the SLA process, too. Once a learner enters the simple route of SLA (see figure 25 and chapter 7) and is not being instructed in a developmentally adequate way (see DiBiase 2008 and chapter 11, s/he is likely to stabilise at some point in morphosyntactical development.

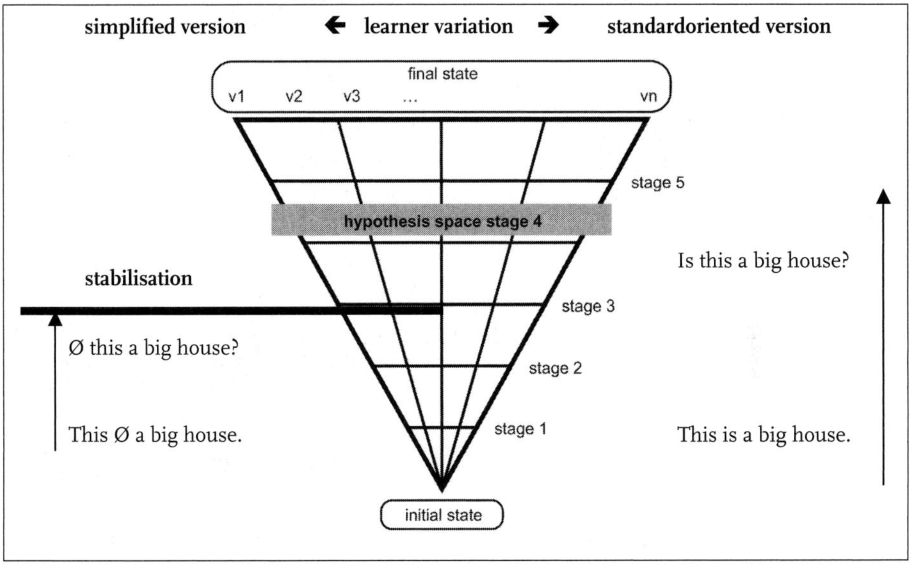

Figure 25: Stabilisation exemplified with the copula.

In looking at the cumulative nature of the cognitive processing dynamics underlying SLA, Pienemann achieved that research on stabilisation is not dependent on such factors as mentioned above, e.g. age of onset socio-pragmatic language behaviour. Using PT and GE as points of departure for an empirical study on stabilisation, we can collect spontaneous oral speech production data (see chapter 15) which allows us to make inferences on her/his current Stage of development and route of acquisition (simplified? target-like?). As the reader will recall from chapter 5, the unfolding of the learner's mental grammar as explained in PT follows a universal, *predictable* sequence. That is to say, Stage 1 precedes 2, which in turn is necessary for the acquisition of Stage 3 and so on. The Stages themselves, comprising the universal processing procedures together with their respective TL specific linguistic structures such as the English 3rd-SG-s are clearly defined. This idea of the SLA process to be *implicationally* organised enables us to draw conclusions as to stabilisation on the basis cross-sectional data?

of cross-sectional speech production data. By means of this, the vagueness and arbitrariness in the notion of 'time' as inherent in the design of longitudinal studies can be overcome.

So, what actually happens when, e.g. a learner of ESL stabilises? Plesser puts forward two core hypotheses. With reference to the Unmarked Alignment Hypothesis (see chapter 6), she claims that structures located at Stages 1-3 merely require default mapping processes, whereas structures located at higher Stages require the acquisition of functional categories, such as I°, C°, D°. Therefore, she hypothesises that (1) L2 learners who produce strongly simplified output cannot progress further than Stage 3, as they fall short of acquiring functional categories. She further hypothesises that (2) learners who progress beyond Stage 3 do not produce simplified varieties of such phenomena as 'copula inversion' (see figure 25), as they have acquired functional categories. To support her hypotheses empirically, Plesser collected cross-sectional as well as longitudinal data from both ESL and SSL learners. By looking at stabilisation cross-sectionally and longitudinally she aimed at demonstrating that cross-sectional data collected and analysed within the implicational framework provided by PT are sufficient to reveal a subject's IL as stabilised.

a case in point – a stabilised Russian learner of ESL?

Preliminary results of Plesser's study show a a Russian learner of ESL who apparently stabilised. Instead of the target-like version "She is in the house" which the task required he produced *"She Ø in the house" and a corresponding simplified, i.e. omitted inverted copula. However, the core question for (future) teachers when dealing with stabilisation is if this Russian learner, and accordingly all L2 learners found to be stabilised, can be *de*stabilised. In line with the argumentation presented above, i.e. stabilisation resulting from an early turning in a simplified SLA route, this seems hardly possible. This would suggest that a learner would have to 'go back' and 'choose' a more target-like variant of the L2. What may be possible as a language teacher, however, is to pedagogically intervene at an early point of the acquisition process. That is to say, at that point where the teacher realises, or rather diagnoses that a learner produces strongly simplified output, s/he can provide adequate instructional material and feedback to *prevent* the learner from potential stabilisation.

Further Reading:

Long, M.H. (2003). "Stabilisation and Fossilization in Interlanguage Development." In: Doughty, C. & M. Long (eds.); pp. 487-535.

Pienemann, M. (1998). *Language Processing and Second Language Development: Processability Theory*. Amsterdam: John Benjamins.

Plesser, A. (in progress). *Stabilisation in Second Language Development. A Case of Generative Entrenchment? Exploring English and Spanish as an L2*. Doctoral Thesis, Paderborn University, Germany.

Study questions

1. Please discuss the difference between 'stabilisation' and 'fossilisation'.
2. Please explain the concept 'Generative Entrenchment'.
3. Please as to how language teachers can prevent their learners from stabilising.

9 Implicit vs. Explicit Grammar Learning

> "One of the most frequently asked questions in language teaching circles is whether grammar should be taught explicitly, and one of the central issues in the psycholinguistics of second language acquisition is whether adults can learn a language fully through the same implicit learning mechanisms used by the child in learning a first language."
>
> (DeKeyser 2003: 313)

The present chapter focuses on major differences between implicit and explicit grammar learning. Even though the terminology may sound rather technical at first glance, this topic is closely related to language teaching in that teaching, basically, only affects explicit grammar learning. However, the mental grammar of language learners primarily results from implicit learning. What can be done in the language classroom, then, in order to support the students to progress? In fact, teaching grammar does have the power to influence the rate, route and success of the SLA process, which is laid out in the following.

To communicate authentically and virtually fluent in a foreign language, the human mind must be capable of rapid online processing, i.e. listening and speaking without conscious effort. For rapid online processing to happen, the learners must develop an IL system of automatised routines her/his language processor can draw upon (see chapter 5). That sounds indeed appealing, but *how* do these 'routines' develop? Do L2 learners simply pick up the TL as was put forward in CLT, i.e. deduce regularities and language specific features of the L2 implicitly as in first language acquisition? Or do L2 learners need explicit knowledge about the TL that can be converted into implicit knowledge, i.e. pre-structured presentation of regularities and language specific features as in Grammar Translation?

In order to provide both adequate input and classroom activities, it is crucial to be aware of and understand the difference between implicit and explicit learning mechanisms and their role in SLA. These learning mechanisms are both parts of the neuropsychological capability which physicians and psychologists refer to as 'memory' (see Levelt 1989). It is here where all kinds of learning and, thus, language learning takes place. The terminology of implicit and explicit grammar learning is often presented either in a rather technical way or remains vague and confusing. The present chapter provides an overview of the relevant facts concerning implicit and explicit language learning for the foreign language teacher. First, the key concepts of memory are presented. Subsequently, memory is related to language acquisition with reference to the *Interlanguage Approach* put forward in this book based on the psycholinguistic SLA theory PT (see chapters 6 and 7). We will then turn to the implications of these human cognitive prerequisites for language teaching.

Memory

Memory plays a decisive role in both SLA and L2 production. In fact it is the psychological constraints of human memory which principally shapes the SLA process. Be as it may, what *is* memory? From a psychological point of view, memory refers to an individual's ability process information. With the help of memory, one can notice, encode, decode, build routines, store and retrieve different types of information.

Recalling the explanations on Levelt's model on language generation, it was shown that the individual draws upon three components that are part of implicit memory and work automatically, and two knowledge stores located in explicit memory. Apart from implicit and explicit memory, each individual has got a short-term memory, too, which plays an important role in cognition. In the following, short-term and long-term memory are presented with particular emphasis on SLA and L2 use. First, definitions of short-term memory and long-term memory are given, followed by a more detailed discussion of the scope of functions memory fulfils in both language use and acquisition.

INFOBOX: 'Short-Term Memory' (i.e. 'Working Memory')

Short-term memory (SHORT-TERM MEMORY) is located in the prefrontal cortex of the brain. Common knowledge suggests memory to be related merely to the aspect of time span, which means that events can only be remembered for a 'short' time. Accordingly, short-term memory is assumed to store those events that were experienced recently, which is assumed to apply conversely to long-term memory. However, these assumptions are rather inaccurate. In fact, short-term memory rather serves to buffer verbally encoded information, which has to be currently held 'in mind', e.g. during a conversation (see chapter 6, Levelt 1989). This buffering is a kind of loop, the information is not evaluated or used in any way, it is simply held here until it is used. With regard to language use and acquisition, the term itself is often used synonymously to phonological short-term memory or working memory. The concept of working memory, though, is different from short-term memory in that working memory can store information as well as 'work' with it. short-term memory rather implies passive retention of material.

As regards capacity *of short-term memory researchers assume that about 7 +/-2 items can be buffered at a time, varying in time course only from seconds to minutes (cf. Gazzaniga 2002: 307). Once this volume is used to full capacity, the intake of new items entails the erasure of the oldest ones (Schmidt, Lang and Thews 2005: 228), i.e. are 'overwritten'. Accordingly, short-term memory is of very limited capacity.*

INFOBOX: 'Long-term Memory'

Contrary to short-term memory, data stored in long-term memory (LONG-TERM MEMORY) can last from seconds to decades; in fact, long-term memory is assumed to be of unlimited capacity. This results from the neuronal plasticity of the brain, which refers to the ability of neurons to shape new synaptic structures or deform existing ones. Researchers assume this to be the neuroanatomical analogy of learning. The feature of plasticity is age-dependent in that it decreases with the being growing older.

According to the multiple memory systems approach by Nyberg and Tulving (1996), long-term memory consists of several components, to store and/or process different types of information. The two major categories which the different components can be assigned to are memory stores being con-

[19] Please note the Critical Period Hypothesis (CPH) in this regard. The CPH as proposed by Lenneberg (1967a, 1967b) suggests the concept of a time period during which humans can acquire every language as a native speaker when exposure begins in infancy. This period of time closes around the age of puberty, since lateralisation has then reached a relatively steady state and the assignment of tasks to structures of the brain is less adaptive.

sciously accessible or not. In view of this, the following terms refer to either the first or the second group:

(1) Consciously accessible	***(2) Not consciously accessible***
Declarative memory/explicit memory	*Non-declarative memory/implicit memory*
Episodic memory	*Procedural memory*
Semantic memory	

These different types of memory comprise further subsystems which are interrelated, as is illustrated by the following chart:

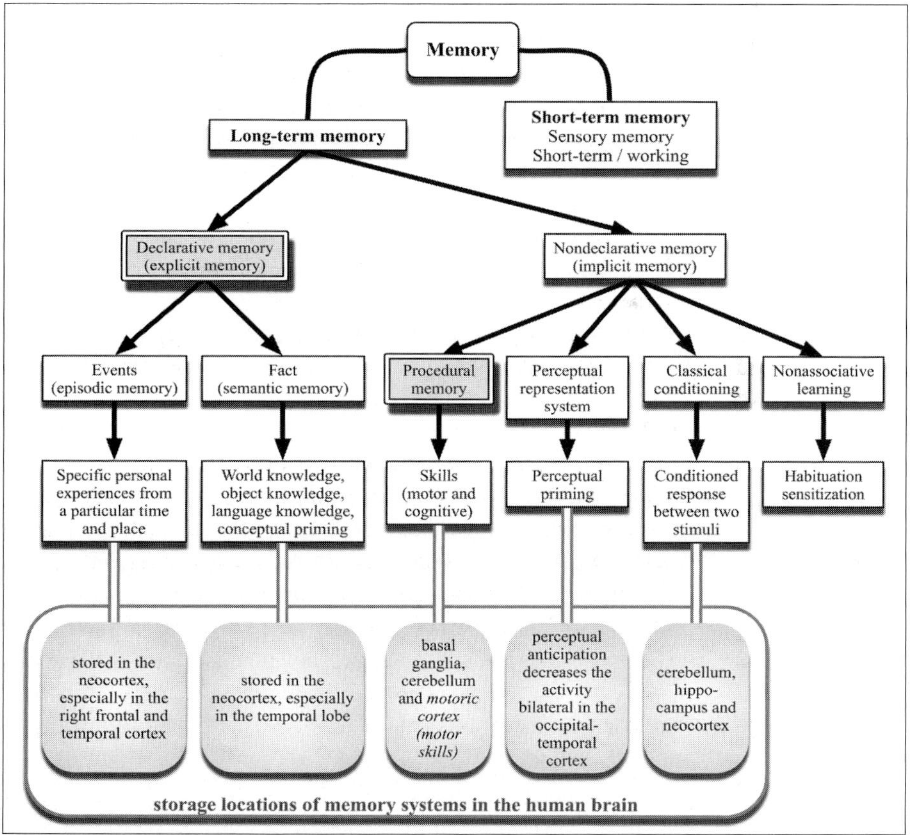

Figure 26: Sketch of the different memory systems complemented by their location of storage in the brain (combined and adapted from Gazzaniga 2002: 314 and Schmidt, Lang and Thews 2005: 226).

The subsystems serve *to process different types of information. In explicit memory, such kind of information as vocabulary, or events an individual experienced are stored (and not in short-term memory). In contrast, implicit memory is not a mere place of storage, but an area close to the brain stem where routines are acquired and carried out, such as how to walk and speak. That is to say, with the help of implicit memory, we can carry out everyday actions we have acquired without conscious effort. To be more specific, in procedural memory, a subsystem of implicit memory, motor and cognitive skills are located. As speaking requires motor and cognitive skills, it is, thus, procedural memory where SLA takes place. Procedural memory works highly task specific, which why it is so efficient. That is to say, each particular part of procedural memory is in charge of one respective specific task. In terms of language learning this means, that once an L2 learner has acquired the processing routines underlying specific TL structures (e.g. the 3rd-SG-s in ESL), these structures can be used without extensive cognitive effort (Pienemann 1998 and elsewhere).*

Functions of Memory in Language Use and SLA

Once introduced the terms and scope of tasks of short-term memory and long-term memory, we will take a closer look at the functions memory fulfils in SLA and language use.

short-term memory

Short-term memory plays a decisive role in language perception and production. As regards auditory language perception, phonological memory as part of short-term memory refers to the ability to buffer audio-input, sounds and their order of occurrence to support message decoding. The productive use of language requires the ability to encode and buffer lexical, grammatical and phonological information which is retrieved from implicit memory. This capability affects a speaker's fluency and, what is more, can predict the success rate of further SLA processes. Baddeley even claimed phonological memory to be a "language learning device" (cf. Baddeley *et al.* 1998: 159).

Contrary to long-term memory, short-term memory does not have adaptive, i.e. learning capacity. Its functioning is characterized by rotary neuronal potentials (a 'loop' as the reader will recall) and is not dependent on plasticity.

Long-Term Memory: Implicit or Explicit Learning?

> *Implicit learning* dos not require an intention to learn; that is, it occurs incidentally while performing some other task. Nor does it require conscious hypothesis testing, or comparisons between consciously recalled events. Such processes fall under the province of *explicit learning*.
>
> (Williams 2004: 203, emphasis added)

As far as *implicit memory* is concerned, the building and automatisation of new routines requires a larger amount of time, but is of *enduring effect*. Furthermore, information is retrieved subconsciously from implicit memory and its processing is, thus, less effortful. In contrast, the storage in and retrieval from information stored in *explicit memory* does not require much time (e.g. learning of new words), but is more *susceptible to be forgotten* Paradis points at a basic difference in the conception of declarative and procedural memory: "while declarative memory is very flexible in that it integrates information from various modalities, procedural memory is available only for very specific tasks; it is inflexible (each motor or cognitive skill is subserved by its specific procedural memory." (Paradis 1994: 395) He further claims that metalinguistic explicit knowledge, which is formally learned, does not become part of the learner's IL. Accordingly, rules of thumb such as the German "He/She/It '-s' muss mit" which is frequently presented in German ESL classrooms are, therefore, of limited or no effect as to L2 development. Accordingly, metalinguistic knowledge is thus not available to the automatic processes underlying language production (see chapter 6) and acquisition.

rules of thumb in the language classroom

These conclusions are of central importance for SLA and L2 use. In the 1990s, Weber-Fox and Neville found out that learning of new vocabulary is not necessarily age-dependent, in contrast to the acquisition of foreign morphosyntactic structures. This finding leads to the assumption of a lexicon/morphosyntax dissociation in the human brain (cf. Paradis 1994) and, accordingly, supports the idea underlying Levelt's 'Blueprint for the Speaker' and PT that lexical entries are stored in declarative memory, whereas the respective annotations (the diacritic features) are part of implicit memory (Pienemann 1998 and elsewhere). This is also

As was pointed out at an earlier point in this chapter, information that is stored in implicit memory is harder to memorise, but more securely stored on the long run. The fact that plasticity decreases with age has, in view of the above mentioned dissociative organisation of language knowledge, **two major implications for SLA**:
(1) new words can be learned at any age and
(2) the procedural skills which shape the matrix onto which those words are mapped during language generation are unlikely to be fully acquired (see, e.g. Birdsong 1992).

Thus, the older the learner, the more improbable becomes native-like competence as far as the TL grammar[20] is concerned. What results from this for the adult learner of a L2 is the question as to what extent declarative and procedural memory can interact with each other to circumvent poor L2 performance, mere pattern learning of chunks or even stabilisation. In short, can metalinguistic, i.e. explicit knowledge, convert into implicit knowledge? Does explicit grammar learning help, then? In SLA research, there are, generally spoken, three basic views to be found: the so-called (1) non-interface position, the (2) interface position, and the (3) weak interface position.

(1) Supporters of the non-interface position (e.g. Krashen 1985) argue that explicit learning, i.e. teaching grammar, does not have any influence on the acquisition process whatsoever. They do not only maintain that explicit knowledge could convert into implicit knowledge, but also negate any kind of cognitive relationship between the two.

(2) Researchers maintaining the interface position (e.g. DeKeyser 2003, N. Ellis 1993, 1994 and Robinson 1997) claim that explicit knowledge can convert into implicit knowledge. Their view is based on 'information processing theory' and, in line with this, practice and attention as principle impetus of acquisition. According to the interface position, SLA is driven by the will to understand the interlocutor and to get oneself understood. However, even though this position was supported by some studies (Norris & Ortega 2001), it is not adopted here as it would require

[20] And target-like pronunciation, of course.

too much cognitive effort for L2 learners to constantly consciously decode and encode messages. Moreover, studies could not prove long-term effects of explicit knowledge that did not suit the developmental state of the learner.

(3) Here, the weak interface position is adopted as it is largely in line with the *Interlanguage Approach* promoted in this book. According to the weak interface view, SLA is an implicit process. Based on studies Pienemann (1985, 1987, 1989, 1998), Long (1991) and others carried out on the effectiveness of formal instruction one can summarise that L2 learners will not incorporate an L2 structure into their implicit IL system they are taught, unless they are developmentally ready for the very structure. With reference to Pienemann, Ellis summarises that

> even if learners' [sic] have their consciousness raised about specific linguistic properties (i.e. are equipped with explicit knowledge) and then are subsequently given opportunities to practise [...] they do not acquire them to the point where they become evident in their communicative language use.[... However], formal instruction appears to work with some features that are not developmentally constrained (e.g. copula-be).
>
> (Ellis 1994: 88)

However, as the reader will recall, the question we are addressing here is as to whether explicit knowledge can be converted into implicit knowledge. To be precise on this, we do not claim this to virtually happen, but rather that explicit knowledge can facilitate and accelerate SLA in that may support the automatisation of emerged structures. Besides, teaching grammar, i.e. providing explicit knowledge, can above, all help the learner to develop a target-like variety of the TL. Therefore, we claim explicit knowledge to be rather complementary to implicit knowledge – given the developmental readiness of the L2 learner[21].

implications for L2 use and SLA – monitoring

As we have learned up to this point,

> [s]peech requires automatized processing routines [which are stored in procedural memory], or else, with the limited capacities of Working Memory, it would become impossible to find, within

21 However, what one has to keep in mind in the discussion of implicit and explicit L2 learning is that competing SLA theories define the underlying acquisition processes involved in SLA in different ways. This is why it is of crucial importance to be aware of the SLA framework one refers to.

> fractions of a second, the words and morpho-syntactic structures that can translate concepts [i.e. the preverbal message] into linguistic forms appropriate to them [which are processed in the Formulator].
>
> (Multhaup 2002: 186)

However, the interaction between short-term memory and long-term memory is also important in L2 performance. These two kinds of memory do interact in language production in that information buffered in working memory is monitored, i.e. checked against the information processed during conceptualisation. Sometimes, once an utterance is recognised as unacceptable the speaker can repair what has been said or s/he is about to say. Otherwise, s/he produces a Freudian or a slip-of-the-tongue. In the case of successful monitoring it becomes apparent that information currently held in short-term memory is able to transmit the information of an item being unacceptable to long-term memory, at least if a repaired utterance is to be generated. From the perspective of brain research monitoring

monitoring

> is the process of relating information currently held in mind back to the task requirements. [...] [The right dorsolateral prefrontal cortex] may be important both for monitoring the content of internally held information, such as monitoring the content of episodic or working memory [which is included in declarative memory].
>
> (cf. Ward 2006: 282)

What is mainly unclear in this concern is if speech in an L2 is checked against both declarative and procedural knowledge[22]. Universally spoken, L2 learners are able to draw on both implicit and explicit knowledge. Whereas monitoring on the basis of implicit knowledge requires the learner to merely notice "that you just don't say it that way" (cf. Paradis 1994: 401), self-repairs on the basis of explicit knowledge derive from the learner knowing that "the preceding direct object is feminine" (cf. *ibid.*). Hence, the second type of monitoring requires the L2 learner to

[22] As Ellis (1994: 85) states, monitoring is a frequently occurring phenomenon in the early Stages of adult SLA. Therefore, declarative knowledge may be monitored at the beginning of the acquisition process to be later complemented by monitoring procedural knowledge as well.

be taught the language and its properties formally for the reason that L2 learners whose learning environment is the classroom "are likely to form declarative memories for the grammatical and phonological rules of the target language" (Lee 2004: 67). In this regard, Levelt (1989) and Krashen and Terrell (1983) proposed the monitor to be involved in the language generation process. Krashen and Terrell propose that declarative knowledge cannot become procedural[23] and that, therefore, learned language knowledge[24] can only be accessed in the form of the monitor by the learner. From the neurophysiologic point of view, once the monitor detects incorrect SV-agreement (**He go home*), which respective rule ("He, She, it – s muss mit!") is stored in explicit memory a signal is sent that the generated utterance is incorrect. By means of this, the human brain may be prevented from shaping a wrong memory trace (cp. Lee 2004: 67). This procedure applies conversely to monitoring a correct sentence, as target-like structures are memorised correctly and, by means of this, the corresponding neuronal trace becomes stronger (cp. *ibid.*). At this point, Lee's ideas are not adopted, since the logical consequence of his claim would be that learners acquiring language by formal instruction above all perform correctly as a result of monitoring. Here, it is claimed in line with *Processability Theory* that the monitor of L2 learners can only draw upon such knowledge s/he has acquired at that point in time. If the student is taught a structure s/he cannot process, the provided explicit knowledge is not integrated into the learner's L2 system. In fact, it is memorised as a metalinguistic piece of knowledge the learner can talk *about,* but not apply in real communication. L2 learners can only make use of one IL system (cf. Pienemann 1998), as is also supported by the Mode Steadiness Hypothesis (see chapter 7). Even though L2 learners may have sufficient time in written L2 production, they are not able to correct mistakes they would not have corrected in spoken language. Their IL system can only process those structures s/he has acquired by then.

23 See Krashen and Terrell's non-interface position (Krashen: 1985).

24 Krashen and Terrell refer to grammar as learned knowledge.

Figure 27: Explicit grammar teaching

This can be exemplified by English SV-agreement as follows: a learner who has not acquired the respective processing procedure to process the 3rd–SG–s is not able to monitor this TL structure correctly, even though this particular phenomenon was explicitly taught before and s/he can cite the rule ("He, She, it – s muss mit!"). In this concern, Ellis (2000) supports the findings within the PT framework and suggests the following options concerning the potential interaction of declarative and procedural knowledge in SLA:

Once the L2 learner has reached the Stage of acquisition the corresponding TL structures of which are currently taught in the classroom, s/he is able to integrate explicit knowledge in implicit knowledge.

Since L2 learners are likely to notice (see chapter 11 of this book) a recently acquired structure in the input, explicit knowledge may thus support the consolidation of the neuronal trace to automatise a procedural routine. In other words, explicit formal instruction that suits the learner's developmental Stage supports automatisation of processing routines as was explored above in terms of a potential interface between implicit and explicit memory. In a nutshell,

> [w]hile practise is absolutely necessary to achieve a certain level of skill in the use of a language, it does not necessarily guarantee that the skill will be acquired. The learner might be practising

> things he or she is not ready to learn [cp. developmental readiness] at that particular point in time.
>
> Pienemann (1995: 7)

Basically, foreign language teaching supports the L2 learner in that it provides input as well as feedback. Both are particularly important when the L2 learners' contact with the TL is limited to the classroom environment. Nevertheless, the process of SLA follows a predictable path which is hardly sensitive to formal instruction as we learned at an earlier point (see chapter 6). This might sound demotivating for (future) teachers at first glance, as teachers aim at smoothing the learning process as much as possible. However, as will be shown in the following section, teaching that is based on the empirical findings explained here, will be beneficial for the learners and enhance the acquisition process.

Further reading:

DeKeyser, R. (2003). ?Implicit and Explicit Learning.? In Doughty, C. J. and M. H. Long (eds). *The Handbook of Second Language Acquisition*. Malden, MA: Blackwell, pp. 313-348. Gazzaniga, M. S. (2002). *Cognitive Neuroscience*. New York: Norton.

Study Questions

1. What type of information is stored in a) explicit memory and b) implicit memory?
2. Please state a) the non-interface, b) the weak interface, and c) the interface position.
3. Why do language teachers need to know about selected aspects of human memory presented in this chapter?

10 Teaching vs. Learning Grammar

Why don't learners learn what teachers teach? (Allwright 1984)

Does instruction make a difference? (Long 1983)

Is language teachable? (Pienemann 1989)

Throughout this chapter we have discussed the interface between SLA research and grammar teaching. We have seen that any kind of SLA – both natural and instructed – follows the same predictable path of IL development. At first glance one might get the impression that teaching grammar does not make sense at all. Looking at the quotations above, we can see that in the early days of SLA research scientists raised questions that supported the view that teaching grammar might be a vain endeavour. However, that would be far too pointed and was not intended by the persons who asked those questions. Obviously, it would be wrong to believe that a good teacher can teach any structure at any time (as representatives of Sprachlehrforschung have claimed; cf. Bausch & Königs 1983). Long (2005) summarises the insights from SLA for grammar teaching as follows:

> [...] language learning both inside and outside classrooms is a gradual, cumulative, often non-linear process. It involves zig-zag developmental paths, U-shaped behaviour, passage through fixed developmental sequences in such areas as negation, interrogatives and relative clauses, plateaus, reconstructing, lengthy periods when non-target forms and constructions are the norm, fluctuations in error rate, only gradually improving accuracy.
>
> Long (2005: 3)

instruction does make a difference

Yet, despite the fact that the developmental sequences found in L2 acquisition are equal in natural and instructed settings, teaching grammar does make a difference (Doughty 1991). In the following sections of this chapter we will take a closer look at why and in what way instruction does make a difference in the foreign language classroom. First of all, we summarize what every teacher should know about SLA.

Summarising: What every teacher should know about SLA

Traditionally, many teachers (and actually researchers, too) have the impression that in the foreign language classroom a target language is *taught* in the first place. However, this approach towards language (and grammar) teaching is not a very learner-centred one as it does not take into account that whatever is taught in the language classroom has to be processed in the mind of the learner. In other words: teaching and learning seem to be quite distinct subject matters.

In the introduction of this chapter we have quoted Rutherford (1987) on this teaching/learning relationship. SLA research can help language teachers to understand what is going on in the minds of learners when they are acquiring a language after having acquired their mother tongue. In section 4 of this chapter we will come back to this in more detail.

In the traditional approaches to grammar teaching (cf. chapter 3) the teacher plays the active role in the classroom. The teacher has to choose the material as well as the structures to be learned by the learners. Additionally, the teaching method is also exclusively chosen by the teacher. According to Littlewood (1984: 1), the learners can then only "react to stimuli and instructions provided by the main actor in the classroom, the teacher." In approaches to the foreign language classroom from an SLA perspective the active role in the learning process is shifted to the side of the learner. By analysing empirical data of how learners actually speak a foreign language SLA research contributes to explaining both the linguistic and the communicative competence of the learner (cf. Lakshmanan & Selinker 2001, Keßler 2006).

analysing learner language

This analysis of Interlanguage data provides a sound basis for the teacher of how learners actually develop their second language grammar gradually in a predictable way. In other words: when knowing about acquisition processes as explained by SLA, research teachers are equipped with a yardstick of reference of what a learner can and cannot process in the target language at a given point in time (cf. Pienemann 1995).

grammar develops gradually

One branch of SLA research is the field of psycholinguistics. Teachers need to know essential basics from this discipline in

psycholinguistics

order to support their learners in the best possible way in their instructed foreign language learning. Psycholinguists provide insight into what happens in the mind of a learner when the latter is learning a language different from his/her first language. According to Sharwood Smith (1994: 143f), the psycholinguistics of language processing studies "how language users access and integrate structures in order to produce and understand utterances. Looking at how linguistic structures arise and change over time should as part of the learner's mental repertoire be called 'developmental psycholinguistics.'" The following figure illustrates how language and mind are interrelated.

Figure 28: Language Processing

When familiar with basic findings and concepts from SLA research, teachers can understand in what way foreign language learners develop their Interlanguage and why they do it in just this way. This understanding allows them to evaluate learner errors in a different light. In chapter 9 we discussed that in many EFL classrooms the learners are able to state the rule of when and why to apply the 3- SG -s to a verb. However, many of those students are not able to apply this rule in spontaneous speech production. SLA research can explain in detail why the application of 3-SG-s is so complicated. Knowing about this problem helps the teacher to understand foreign language learners and find adequate treatment for language errors. We will specify the role of errors and their treatment in section 4 of this chapter.

Critical voices may claim that instructed acquisition differs immensely from natural acquisition and that therefore findings from SLA research cannot be transferred to the foreign language classroom. Of course, the settings of natural and instructed acquisition do indeed differ a lot. However, the underlying processes in mind of learners are very similar. Pienemann (1995: 14) has illustrated the differences and similarities of natural and instructed acquisition by comparing language development with the development of a plant. He points out that "a rose will still be a rose inside a greenhouse or outside in the garden".

Figure 29: A rose in a greenhouse and a rose outside in the garden (drawing by Verena Wendel)

Taking up the image of the rose and applying it to the language classroom, we can say that the role of the teacher is comparable to that of the gardener. Knowing about nutrition, water, light and other factors and caring about the plant makes it grow more beautifully than wild roses. Knowing about SLA helps teachers to support their learners in grammar learning und thus enhance foreign language acquisition, especially in terms of a more standard-oriented Interlanguage variation. Summing up, we ought to bear in mind the following reasons why teachers should know about SLA:

Summary

- Knowing about acquisition processes provides language teachers with reference points that tell them what their learners are ready to acquire/learn at a given point in time. This knowledge can then serve as a guideline as to what to teach and what rather not (yet) to teach to these learners.
- Teachers who understand SLA basics of Interlanguage development can also alter their approach towards learner errors. By evaluating the actual kind of error and its cause from an SLA perspective teachers can develop effective treatment of those errors.
- Knowing about the developmental hierarchy of Interlanguage structures we can adapt syllabi and even textbooks according to learner needs. Grading textbooks according to the 'learnability' of the structures can be one way to accelerate grammar learning in the foreign language classroom.
- Finally, but not least important, knowing about SLA basics makes the teacher able to challenge some of the common beliefs about grammar and replace them by more learner-centred principles.

However, we must not forget that SLA research is not a discipline that is concerned with language teaching methodology. Theories in SLA provide the description and explanation of phenomena (the acquisition processes) that occur and can be observed when someone acquires a foreign language. SLA research does not claim to provide any teaching methodology on its own. Nevertheless, approaches to grammar teaching can draw profitably on SLA findings. In the next step these approaches would have to develop their own way of successfully teaching language structures in the classroom.

In the following sections of this chapter we will provide a more detailed account of some of the basics of SLA. The application of SLA theories to actual foreign language teaching will then be discussed in part III.

Reviewing: Grammar Myths

After you have studied this book up to this point, your views of grammar and its teaching may have been confirmed, changed or proven to be unidimensionally focused on the structure of language itself, leaving the L2 learner's cognitive prerequisites as to language learning mostly unconsidered. Before we turn to the re-evaluation of the common beliefs about teaching grammar discussed in chapter 2, please take some minutes and answer the below questions again.

- What is grammar?
- Is grammar teachable?
- If so, should grammar be taught explicitly?

In chapter 2, we identified six views of teaching grammar which are common among language teachers. In the following, these views will be subject to a second closer analysis. This analysis, however, will be complemented by observations as to grammar learning and teaching from a psycholinguistic SLA perspective (see VanPatten and Williams 2007; Pienemann 1998, 2005; Keßler 2008) and some of the 'myths' as to grammar teaching identified by Larsen-Freeman (1995).

do learners learn what teachers teach?

Based on a rather static view of grammar and traditional views of teaching grammatical structures, most teachers believe that learners learn what teachers teach. L2 instructors do, of course, notice that learners make mistakes and in most cases fall short of 'immediate' internalisation of a linguistic feature and its use they have been explained. Still, this is rather seen as a result of the 'myth', as Larsen-Freeman (1995: 3) calls it, that "[s]tudents have different learning styles. Not all students can learn grammar." This is a very radical view disrespecting the cognitive abilities of each learner. While it is, in fact, evident that different learners follow different routes and rates (see 7) in SLA, there is no empirical evidence whatsoever supporting the idea of particular learners being generally unable to acquire the grammatical structures of the L2. As was shown in this book, learners' output follows paths with predictable Stages in the acquisition of a given structure (Pienemann 1998, 2005; VanPatten & Williams 2007). This, in turn, results in limits on the effects of instruction in SLA (*ibid.*) as the developmental path itself cannot be altered (cf. figure 30).

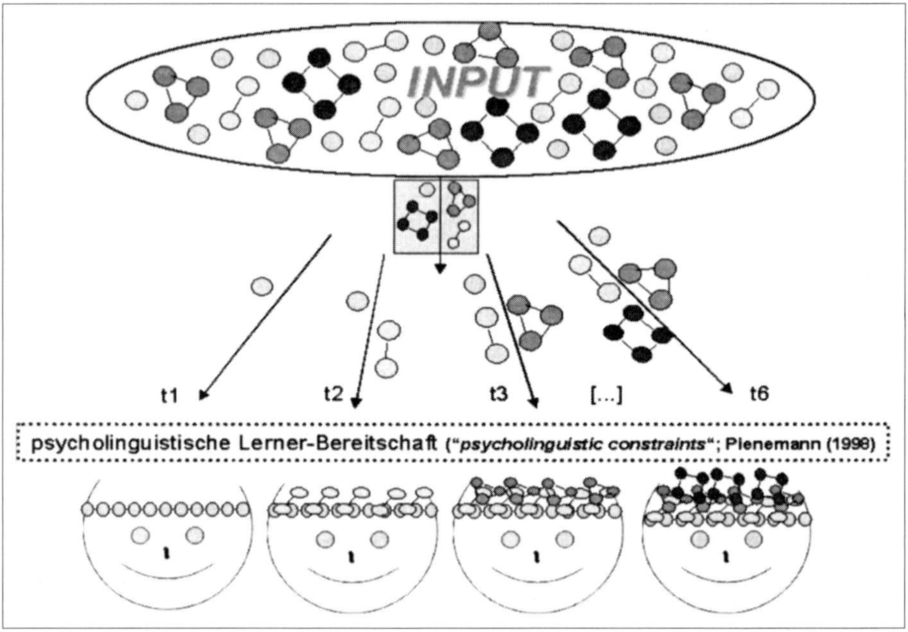

Figure 30: Taken from Keßler 2006: 96

We have learned, however, that variational features are sensitive to instruction and it has further been demonstrated that instruction is supportive and conducive to both route and rate of SLA. How these findings can be effectively used and implemented in the L2 classroom is shown in the following chapters of this book. As learners do not necessarily learn what teachers teach, second language learning is variable in its outcome (VanPatten & Williams 2007). This is mainly due to the developmental and variational dynamics of learner grammars.

The fact that SLA follows predictable developmental sequences as discussed in the above section sometimes misleads readers from outside the field of SLA to think that that would imply that all L2 learners would acquire this language in exactly the same way. However, a look at any second language learning environment very quickly shows that this is clearly not the case. There are plenty of differences amongst language learners: although they all follow the same developmental sequences learners differ e.g.

> in pace and in the amount of standard-orientation or simplification of the target language.
>
> (Keßler 2008: 75)

languages and its grammars: a fixed set of rules?

The last issue introduced by Keßler as to standard-orientation or not leads to a further common belief we identified, namely that languages and its grammars are assumed to be a fixed set of rules. In chapter 2 we demonstrated that Standard English actually is a minority variety of the English language. Therefore, *the* grammar (future) teachers could reliably refer to in the ESL classroom does not exist. The tridialectical future of the use of English(es) predicted by Crystal (see page 19) is a strong case in point. We further presented different kinds of grammar, acknowledging that prescriptive grammars can serve as point of reference for teachers and learners. We aimed at highlighting, however, that these grammars ignore the dynamicity of language, and the social and historical value of linguistic varieties which should be part of what learners learn *about* the TL. In this regard, we made a case for descriptive grammars, which do not include any kind of evaluation of the grammatical system described. Pedagogical grammars, as we concluded, ideally comprise relevant features of pre- and descriptive grammars filtered for the needs and potentials of foreign language learners. The last 'kind' of grammar we introduced was the IL grammar, i.e. the state of a mental representation of the L2 that has not yet been fully developed by an L2 learner. This grammar is different from the other grammars in that it does not refer to any 'external' system of reference but to an internal reconstruction of the respective TL grammar. This results from the learner not yet having (fully) acquired the L2 but only approximated to it. IL contains features from the target language but also 'innovations' by the learner, which are neither target-like nor totally in line with the learner's first language. It was shown in 5 to what extent these innovations are systematic and predictable, making a clear case for instruction as a facilitator of SLA.

Practice makes perfect. Doesn't it?

Advocating instruction as beneficial for the SLA process does not necessarily imply that practice makes perfect, as was also shown in 5. That is to say, there are limits on the effect of frequency on second language acquisition (VanPatten & Williams 2007). In PT terms and thus in line with the *Interlanguage Approach*, we can state that "frequency cannot override the constraints of the hierarchy." (Pienemann 2007: 152) An example which occurs repetitively throughout this book is the English 3-SG-s. The structure itself is highly frequent yet not acquired until Stage 5 of the processability hierarchy as a result of a complex processing procedure required for its emergence in the learner's IL (see chapter 5). Unless the learner is developmentally ready for it, the structure will not emerge – despite highly frequential occurrences in the input.

errors should be eradicated – no error correction at all

Given that the 3-SG-s is being omitted by many learners, can't we push them to 'simply' attach it to the verb in correcting her/him? Or would it be in line with the *Interlanguage Approach* to wait until s/he is developmentally ready for it, trusting that the structure emerges without any instructional support anyway? As to the particular case of the 3-SG-s, the rather bad news is that this is a developmental error, as specified in chapter 7. However, as was stated before, corrective feedback can be beneficial for other learners in the same classroom who may already have acquired Stage 5. They can comprehend and process the corrective feedback concerning the use of the 3-SG-s. It is important, in this regard, to not create an atmosphere of stupidity or anything like it when an error occurs. This may have a harmful effect on the ongoing SLA process as premature and inadequately accuracy-based instruction can make learners feel unease and result in unauthentic or even compulsory communication. In a nutshell, developmental errors should be treated under the premise of 'message before accuracy'.

As opposed to developmental errors, variational errors are sensitive to instruction. Referring to the example "*This ø your new colleague John" given in chapter 8, 'message before accuracy' could hinder the learner to develop a target-like mental representation of the L2 grammar. To not correct a variational error such as the omission of the copula at an early point of the SLA process could, hence, result in a simplified variety of the L2.

teachers have to know everything about the L2 grammar

The ability to differentiate between developmental and variational errors, Standard English(es) and pedagogical grammars deriving from the latter does not imply that teachers have to know everything about the L2 grammar. The most important skill, as it were, in the L2 classroom is that a teacher is aware of the fact that those different kinds of grammar exist, with particular emphasis on the fact that learners follow their 'own' grammar they make up in their minds. The teacher should further consider that variations from the standard are a productive and creative part of the restructuring process learners undergo in SLA.

To make a long story short, language instructors should aim at balancing the below elements of classroom SLA in a learner-centred way based on the research findings so far presented in this book from psycholinguistic SLA research and Applied Linguistics.

Further reading:

Keßler, J.-U. (2006). *Englischerwerb im Anfangsunterricht diagnostizieren. Linguistische Profilanalysen am Übergang von der Primarstufe in die Sekundarstufe I*. Tübingen: Narr.

Larsen-Freeman, D. (1995). On the teaching and learning of grammar: Challenging the myths. In F. Eckman et al. (Eds.), *Second language acquisition theory and pedagogy*. Mahwah, NJ: Lawrence Erlbaum.

Study Questions:

1. Go back to questions at the beginning of this chapter and answer them again.
2. Compare and discuss prospective changes in your answers.

Grammar Teaching in the EFL Classroom | III

> The only contribution that classroom instruction can make is to provide comprehensible input that might not otherwise be available outside the classroom.
>
> Krashen (1985: 33f)

In the previous chapters we discussed the role of second language acquisition research in grammar teaching. We showed that it is beneficial for language teachers to have a basic understanding of SLA research. However, following the *Interlanguage Approach* as we do in this book, one might argue that most grammar learning happens rather incidentally. In chapter 7 we made the point that no teacher – however well-trained and inspired s/he is – is able to teach any grammatical structure at any given time in the acquisition process. Rather, the learner has to be developmentally ready to acquire the structure that is taught.

Would this then imply that grammar teaching is a useless exercise? Unfortunately, there is not a simple answer to this question. Doughty (2004: 181) points out that even amongst SLA theorists there is no common agreement "concerning the potential value of instructional intervention in SLA." From a theoretical perspective we can distinguish at least two contradicting strands of research within this field: some researchers assume that instruction has no effect on second language acquisition. This group of researchers promotes the so-called non-interventionist approach. The second group of SLA experts promotes the idea that the right kind of instruction provided at the right time is beneficial for classroom-based acquisition of languages.

instruction does make a difference

In this book we have chosen an *Interlanguage Approach* to grammar, its teaching and its learning. We strongly believe (and we are backed by many empirical studies, e.g. Pienemann 1984 and 1989, Ellis 1989, Mansouri & Duffy 2005) that there is a case for grammar teaching. In other words: there are more contributions that classroom instruction can make to grammar teaching than the quotation by Krashen (1985: 33f) mentioned above might assume. However, any grammar teaching that is meant to be beneficial for individual learners ought to follow the developmental path. Knowing about the developmental path of language acquisition supports the teachers in selecting those structures for the language classroom that their learners are psycholinguistically ready to learn next.

Focus on Meaning vs. Focus on Form

There seem to be two competing approaches to the foreign language classroom. According to the communicative approach language teaching has to be meaning-focused: language is then not supposed to be treated as the object of instruction but rather "experienced meaningfully, as a tool for communication – perhaps with target grammar structures physically highlighted or embedded within communicative activities." (Fotos 2001: 268). At the other end of the scale we find an approach that merely focuses on forms and offers fairly explicit ways of grammar teaching. Neither approach, however, addresses all learner needs in the modern foreign language classroom. In accordance with Fotos (2001) who points out the "considerable research support" for this position, we suggest the following mix: focus on Meaning whenever the goal is on communication and on the processing of meaning and Focus on Form to practice language patterns needed for discourse (cf. Fotos 2001: 268).

In this part of the book we will now take a closer look at three selected approaches to grammar teaching, namely:

- Focus on Form (chp. 11)
- Task-based Language Teaching (chp. 12)
- Immersion Programmes (chp. 13)

All these approaches can easily be integrated into language classrooms that follow the *Interlanguage Approach* as discussed throughout this book. The emphasis on (explicit) grammar teaching, however, varies within these approaches. Whereas grammar instruction does play an important role in the Focus on Form concept, there is no explicit grammar teaching at all to be found in Immersion Programmes. Nevertheless, learners on Immersion programmes can acquire the target grammar and teachers can integrate some implicit grammar teaching/learing even into more traditional foreign language classrooms.

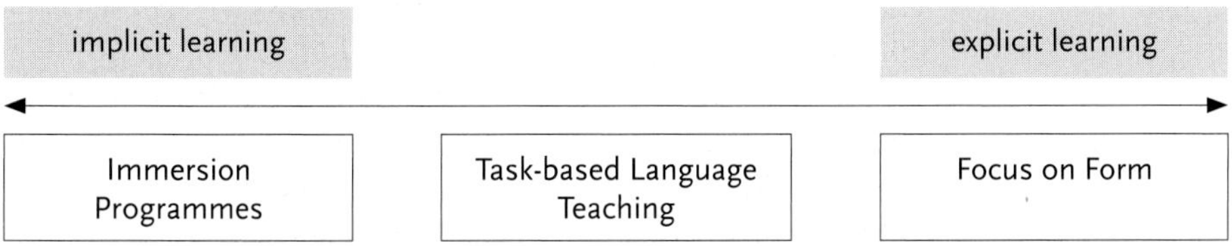

Figure 31: Three selected approaches on a continuum from implicit to explicit learning

As can be seen from figure 31, on a continuum Focus on Form would be the most explicit approach to grammar teaching discussed in this book and Immersion Programmes would be the most implicit approach to grammar teaching. Task-based language teaching can be found somewhere in between these two extremes. However, one must bear in mind that all these three approaches are in line with the *Interlanguage Approach* and that there are other approaches to grammar teaching that are by far more explicit.

11 Focus on Form

> Focus on Form refers to how attentional resources are allocated, and involves briefly drawing students' attention to linguistic elements (words, collocations, grammatical structures, pragmatic patterns, and so on), in context, as they arise incidentally in lessons whose *overriding focus is on meaning, or communication,* the temporary shifts in focal attention being triggered by students' comprehension or production problems.
>
> (Long 1997: 1, emphasis added)

Focus on Form (FonF) was proposed by Long (1988; 1991; 1997), Long and Crookes (1992) and Long and Robinson (1998) and was further developed by Doughty and Williams (1998) and others. Their approach met with enthusiastic approval among applied linguists and teachers who sought to overcome the limitations of the two extreme perspectives on language teaching, i.e. a sole focus on meaning or focus on formS in the L2 classroom. Long suggests a combination of both in that FonF sticks to the principles of authentic communication and learner-centeredness promoted in CLT and, at the same time, the explicit teaching of grammar when appropriate. What is central in this concern is that in the original version of FonF (Long 1991), attention is only then drawn to form when the students have comprehension or production problems in a meaning-based activity. That is to say, grammar teaching occurs on an unplanned, irregular basis resulting from the learners' current needs. However, Doughty and Williams (1998) proposed a distinction between (1) *proactive* and (2) *reactive* FonF. That is to say, attention to form can be drawn by (1) instructional materials prepared in advance which promote the elicitation of a particular TL structure (e.g. the past –ed) or (2) by the need arising occasionally in class, as suggested by Long (1991). The table below illustrates the sequence in which the form in focus occurs in proactive and reactive FonF. The example structure is the English past –ed.

proactive vs. reactive FonF

Proactive FonF	Reactive FonF
1) Input enhancement activity[25] • Teacher provides enriched material: – e.g. the learners listen to a dialogue between two individuals talking about their last holiday	**Main task** • Picture description task: the learners are given a picture sequence which shows an individual carrying out different activities. The title says that these pictures refer to a past event. The learners are asked to describe the pictures.
2) Production activity • Pair work: the teacher asks the learners to talk to each other about their last holiday	**Input enhancement activity** • Teacher provides enriched material: – e.g. the learners listen to a dialogue between two individuals talking about their last holiday
3) Main Task • Picture description task: the learners are given a picture sequence which shows an individual carrying out different activities. The title says that these pictures refer to a past event. The learners are asked to describe the pictures.	**Production activity** • Pair work: the teacher asks the learners to talk to each other about their last holiday • Main task completed

Table 4: Suggested sequence of focusing on the English past –ed in proactive and reactive FonF.

Figure 32: A sample picture sequence showing how Lisa spent yesterday morning.

25 See page 152 of this book.

Whichever kind of FonF an L2 teacher may apply, s/he should always keep in mind that "the fundamental assumption of [FonF] instruction is that meaning and use must already be evident to the learner at the time that attention is drawn to the linguistic apparatus needed to get the meaning across." (cf. Doughty and Williams 1998: 4) That is to say, teachers using FonF do not begin a lesson with an explicit, i.e. metalinguistic introduction of a particular grammatical structure with the idea of making learners apply it rather in respective grammar exercises.

Interaction Hypothesis

As to the theoretical motivation, FonF is based on the 'Interaction Hypothesis' (Long 1981, 1983, 1996), which claims, that SLA is a process that is explicable by neither a purely linguistic nativist nor a purely environmentalist theory (cf. Long and Robinson 1998: 22). This hypothesis holds that IL development is promoted by negotiation of meaning in authentic interaction between L2 learners, and most prominently, between L2 learners and advanced or even native speakers of the TL. In order to prevent learners producing somewhat simplified output in meaning-based classrooms to achieve their communicative goal (as was criticized with the early versions of CLT), FonF includes the explanation of form-function relationships when the need arises in class. Negotiation work does not necessarily result in simplification, but in fact, "also elicits negative feedback [...] including corrective reformulations of [...] utterances that preserve the learner's pretended meaning." (Long and Robinson 1998: 23)

effectiveness of FonF

How effective is FonF when it comes to help the learners to reach target-like L2 proficiency? Which are the cognitive processes underlying the potential effectiveness of FonF? The primary means to enhance the acquisition process aimed at in FonF classrooms is to aim for *noticing* to occur. Noticing means that a learner registers a particular linguistic form, e.g. the plural –s in ESL, in the output of a speaker or in the instructional material. Schmidt first proposed the *Noticing Hypothesis* in 1990 when the roles of attention and awareness became more and more important in cognitive psychology and related SLA research. He initially defined noticing as nothing but the "*registration* of the occurrence of a stimulus event in conscious awareness and subsequent storage in long term memory, not the detection of form/meaning relationships or inductive formation of hypotheses or other processes that may lead to the organisation of stored knowledge in a linguistic system

noticing

(Slobin 1985; Chaudron 1985)." (Schmidt 1994: 179, emphasis added). Thus Schmidt claims that the individual simply recognizes a particular TL structure without further cognitive generalization of potential underlying patterns or rules of the latter. In a more recent work Schmidt refined his claim in that he pointed to a clear distinction between noticing and metalinguistic awareness (cf. Schmidt 2001: 5). To make a case in point, the fact that s/he notices the plural –s does not imply her/his understanding or rather analysis of the structure and its regularities.

How does a feature noticed from the input become implicit knowledge? There are three basic steps according to which implicit knowledge is acquired that describe how noticing fits into the SLA process:

1) **Noticing**
2) **Comparing: noticing the gap**
   - The learner compares the linguistic feature, e.g. the past –ed noticed in the input with his or her own mental grammar, registering to what extent there is a 'gap' between the input and her/his IL
3) **Integrating**
   - The learner integrates a representation of the new linguistic feature into his or her IL

(adapted from Richards & Renandya 2002: 171)

Consciousness Raising

According to Long and Robinson (1998), noticing can be achieved by 'Consciousness Raising' (CR). CR as originally defined by Rutherford and Sharwood Smith (1985) refers to a "deliberate attempt to draw the learner's attention specifically to the formal properties of the target language" (p. 274), i.e. to make particular TL features more salient to perception. In the meantime, CR has been replaced by the term 'Input Enhancement' (IE). This change in terminology is based on the difference between what the learner is exposed to in the L2 classroom, i.e. input, and what s/he actually integrates into his or her IL, i.e. intake. In this sense, intake is that part of input the L2 learner was able to process, that is to say, intake is in a way constrained by processability[26]. Ac-

Input Enhancement

[26] In this concern, we have to distinguish between L2 perception and production: PT primarily makes predictions about the developmental sequence in which TL structures become productive in the L2 learners' IL.

cording to Sharwood Smith, the term CR is imprecise as it suggests "the learner's mental state is altered by the input; hence, all input is intake. Input enhancement implies only that we can manipulate aspects of the input but makes no further assumptions about the consequences." (Sharwood Smith 1993: 176) How can input be enhanced, as it were, in order to facilitate noticing? With reference to Gascoigne (2006) and Haley and Rentz (2002), we can identify the following implicit and explicit IE techniques:

	Feedback (Teacher)	**Material**
implicit	• recasts • clarification requests • oral equivalent of textual enhancement: stress, intonation, gestures	• visual textual enhancement via typographical alterations: italicising, boldface type, colour coding • input flooding[27] • Task-essential language
explicit	• discussion of the target forms • metalinguistic feedback • negative evidence through overt error correction *with* explicit reference to the learner's error • negative evidence through overt error correction *without* explicit reference to the learner's error	• processing instruction[28]

Table 5: Implicit and explicit techniques of Input Enhancement (IE)

As Gascoigne states, CR/IE are technically speaking the "forefathers of FonF" (2001: 70). In today's FonF classrooms, CR/IE, corrective feedback and noticing are related and implemented.

27 Input flooding: here, learners are bombarded by an artificially increased number of the target forms, while maintaining a communicative focus.

28 See VanPatten (2004) for a detailed elaboration on Processing Instruction.

Reviewing Long and Robinson (1998: 24f.), we can identify three ways within FonF, already mentioned in figures 28 and 29, of raising the L2 learners' consciousness in order to facilitate noticing and thus acquisition. They are explained in further detail in the following:

1) **Frequency**
2) **Explicit negative feedback**
3) **Implicit negative feedback**

1) When learners have problems with either the comprehension or production of, say the plural –s, the teacher can provide enriched instructional material containing this structure at a high frequency. This way, the instructional material serves to raise the learners' consciousness concerning the respective structure. More precisely, in terms of material, CR can be instrumentalised through italicising, colouring or underlining a TL structure in order to make it perceptually salient for the learners. These techniques are generally referred to as 'Input Enhancement' (Sharwood Smith 1991). Input enhancement serves to facilitate noticing. The learners who are to solve a communicative task based on this material, *may* allocate their attentional resources (*ibid.*) to the TL structure in question.

The following figure illustrates the relationship as assumed within the *Interlanguage Approach* based on PT between consciousness raising through enhanced input, noticing and the implicit mental grammar (IL) of the L2 learner:

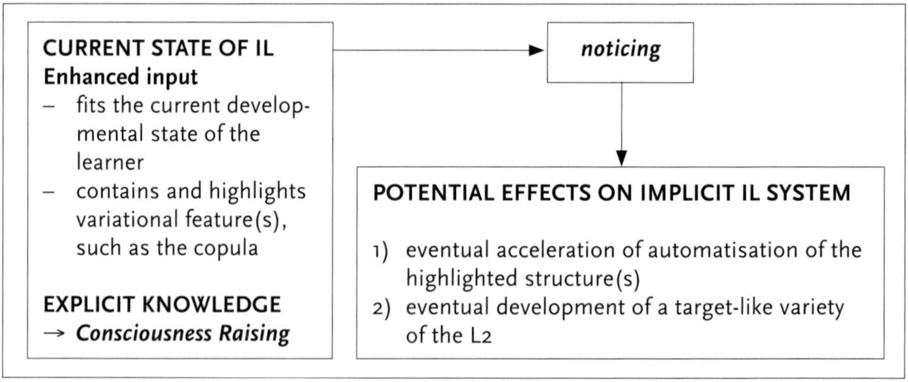

Figure 33: The relationship between Input Enhancement, noticing and the IL system of the L2 learner.

2) According to Long and Robinson (*ibid.*), occasional explicit negative feedback, i.e. metalinguistic explanation, is useful. When an error occurs frequently in class such as the omission of the plural –s, the teacher can intervene pedagogically and draw the learners' attention explicitly to that particular issue. When a teacher gives explicit feedback, s/he usually not only presents the target-like form, but also refers to the non-target-like form produced by the learner.

However, explicit negative feedback only results in an advantage for short-term learning (DeKeyser 1995; Robinson 1996). We have learned (see Chapter 7) that language teaching is constrained by learnability and, moreover, that language learning means the accumulative acquisition of processing procedures which are part of implicit memory. It is, therefore, not surprising that explicit negative feedback does not have long-term effects on the learner's developing IL system when it does not fit the current developmental state of the learner. This is also supported by empirical findings of studies conducted within the PT framework (Pienemann 1984, 1985, 1987, 1989, 1998; DiBiase 2008). These findings are also in line with the explanations of the weak interface position (see chapter 9 of this book): teaching grammar can have positive effects on rate and development of a target-like variety of the L2, once the L2 learner is developmentally ready to acquire the structure.

3) As to implicit negative, or rather interactional feedback, Long and Robinson suggest corrective reformulations, known as recasts. Studies on L1A showed that recasts are frequently noticed by the children. Research in SLA supports the efficacy of recasts in adult L2A, too (Oliver 1995; Ortega & Long, 1997; Richardson 1995). As opposed to explicit negative feedback, when giving implicit negative feedback the teacher confines her/his corrections to saying the target-like form, without reference to the non-target-like form produced by the learner. As holds for explicit negative feedback, in line with the *Interlanguage Approach* implicit negative feedback is only expected to be effective when the learner is developmentally ready for the particular structure.

Even though further research has to be conducted on the effectiveness of corrective feedback, recent studies indicate that a learner's IL develops in a rather target-like way when there is an developmentally guided form-oriented instruction

adequate focus on form (see Norris and Ortega 2001). With reference to the PT framework highlighting developmental readiness of the learner as a crucial variable in instructed SLA, DiBiase proposes the refined definition of FonF, namely 'developmentally guided form-oriented instruction' (DiBiase 2008). An empirical study DiBiase conducted with L2 learners of Italian demonstrated

> that developmentally guided form-oriented instruction plus FonF feedback is **effective:** it promotes faster acquisition of learnable structures (e.g., beginning to differentiate marking with additional features). In this sense, the question of 'more accurate use' is also positive (development in marking both number and gender) while the issue of overall accuracy remains unresolved. It can also be said that it is **efficient** since no additional inputs in terms of program time and teacher allocations were necessary to achieve these results.
>
> DiBiase 2008: 215f.

How can FonF then be incorporated inro the FL classroom? As was stated several times throughout this book, explicit knowledge is seen as a means to facilitate attention to form and thus accelerate SLA, but the actual SLA process is the gradual development of implicit knowledge which is by nature not sensitive to conscious control of the individual. Teachers are, in the first place, required to diagnose the learners' current Stages of development (see Chapters 7 and 15) regularly. Secondly, it is necessary to identify the nature of errors made by the learners: do they affect developmental or variational features? On this basis, s/he can adapt his or her communicative instructional materials to encourage the learners to notice-the-gap, i.e. the mismatch between their IL variant and the TL variant. In a further step, the teacher has to decide whether the pedagogical intervention should be either 1) the proactive or 2) the reactive variant of FonF (Doughty and Williams 1998). Finally, the teacher should draw attention to form when appropriate according to FonF, but without giving up the communicative nature of the respective classroom activity. One instructional technique which has turned out to support the *Interlanguage Approach* very well in FL classrooms is *Task-based Language Teaching*(see chapter 12).

Further reading:

DiBiase (2008) Di Biase, B. (2008): "Focus on Form and Development in L2 learning." In: Keßler, J.-U. (ed.): *Processability Approaches to Second Language Development and Second Language Learning*. Newcastle upon Tyne: Cambridge Scholars Publishing; pp. 197-219.

Doughty, C. and Williams, J. (2003). *Focus on form in classroom second language acquisition.* Cambridge: CUP.

Long, M.H. and Robinson, P. (1998). "Focus on form: Theory, research, and practice." In C. Doughty and J. Williams (1998), pp. 15-41.

Study questions:

1. Explain the differences between proactive and reactive FonF. Conceive a proactive and a reactive lesson focusing on the English 3rd-SG-s.
2. Explain why the term Consciousness Raising has been replaced by Input Enhancement.
3. Explain the relationship between Input Enhancement, noticing and the implicit IL system of L2 learners.

12 Task-based Language Teaching (TBLT)

> TBLT addresses questions which are at the center of attention in second language acquisition research. These are concerns such as the relationship between target language perception, processing, production, and language learning. The central goal, then, was to establish a close relationship between a certain learning environment (the task), a communicative behaviour resulting from this learning environment (task-based L2 performance), and second language acquisition (task-based L2 learning).
>
> Eckerth (2008: 13f)

As can be seen from the quotation above from Eckerth (2008) tasks play an important role both in SLA research as well as in language teaching. In this chapter we will focus on how communicative tasks in classroom-based foreign language instruction are utilized in order to allow for interaction among learners. In chapter 15 we will then return to the notion of communicative tasks and show how they contribute to eliciting speech samples of spontaneous learner language in order to yield a linguistic profile of the internal state of the learners Interlanguage development.

The use of tasks on the pedagogical front has been researched quite widely (e.g. Long & Crookes 1987, Long 1996, Ellis 2003, Littlewood 2004, Van den Branden 2007, Willis & Willis 2007). In Germany, among others, Müller-Hartmann & Schocker-v. Ditfurth (2004, 2005 and 2011) and Keßler (2006 and 2008b) promote the TBLT approach to language and (implicit) grammar teaching.

Though there seems to be some consensus that TBLT provides an alternative approach to a rather teacher-centred and form-oriented classroom practice (Van den Branden 2006a) there is more controversy as to what extent "learners react to the linguistic data and the learning environment they are exposed to, and to what extent they act as reflective and intentional agents making use [...] of learning opportunities" (Eckerth 2008: 14). Nevertheless, a minimum consensus in terms of what a task is can be found in the literature (cf. Prabhu 1987, Skehan 1998, Ellis 2003). On the other hand, however, a definition of the term tasks has not yet been agreed on, although we can find competing lists of definitions by various authors (e.g. Johnson 2003, Ellis 2003, Littlewood 2004; for a summary see Keßler & Kohli 2006).

definition of 'task'

For the purpose of this book the concept of "task" may best be defined along with Nunan (1989: 10) as "a piece of classroom work which involves learners in comprehending, manipulating, producing, or interacting in the target language while their attention is principally focused on meaning rather than form. The task should also have a sense of completeness, being able to stand alone as a communicative act in its own right". Lee (2000) takes Nunan's definition as a point of departure for a slightly extended definition that also includes the idea of a task being a kind of a workplan. For a detailed summary of various definitions of "task" see Ellis (2003: 4f) and Van den Branden (2006: 6ff). Table 5 is taken from Van den Branden (2006: 7f) and provides an overview of various "definitions of 'tasks' as an educational activity":

Author	Definition
Long (1985)	A task is a meaningful and viable unit of analysis in all four of what I take to be the major issues in programme design: (i) identifying learners' needs (ii) defining syllabus content (iii) organizing language acquisition opportunities (iv) measuring student achievement [...] Tasks have the initial advantage over linguistic units of analysis in that they are meaningful for the participants. That is, tasks are the way non-linguists conceive what they do. People talk about the kind of day they have had that way, children play that way ('Let's go and get some ice-cream'), job descriptions are written that way.
Richards, Platt & Weber (1985)	An activity or action which is carried out as the result of processing or understanding language, i.e. as a response. For example, drawing a map while listening to a tape, and listening to an instruction and performing a command, may be referred to as tasks. Tasks may or may not involve the production of language. A task usually requires the teacher to specify what will be regarded as successful completion of the task. The use of a variety of different kinds of tasks in language teaching is said to make teaching more communicative ... since it provides a purpose for classroom activity which goes beyond practice of language for its own sake.
Crookes (1986)	A task is 'a piece of work or an activity, usually with a specified objective, undertaken as part of an educational course, at work, or used to elicit data for research'.

Author	Definition
Krahnke (1987)	The defining characteristic of task-based content is that it uses activities that the learners have to carry out for non-instructional purposes outside the classroom as opportunities for language learning. Tasks are distinct from other activities to the degree that they have non-instructional purposes.
Breen (1987)	Any structured language learning endeavour which has a particular objective, appropriate content, a specified working procedure, and a range of outcomes for those who undertake the task. 'Task' is therefore assumed to refer to a range of workplans which have the overall purpose of facilitating language learning from the simple an brief exercise type to more complex and lengthy activities such as group problem-solving or simulations and decision-making.
Prabhu (1987)	An activity which requires learners to arrive at an outcome from given information through some process of thought and which allowed teachers to control and regulate that process is regarded as a task.
Candlin (1987)	One of a set of differentiated, sequenceable, problem-posing activities involving learners' cognitive and communicative procedures and applied to existing and new knowledge in the collective exploration and pursuance of foreseen or emergent goals within a social milieu.
Breen (1989)	A task is 'a structured plan for the provision of opportunities for the refinement of knowledge and capabilities entailed in a new language and its use during communication'.
Nunan (1989)	A piece of classroom work which involves learners in comprehending, manipulating, producing or interacting in the target language while their attention is primarily focused on meaning rather than form.
Willis (1996)	Activities where the target language is used by the learner for a communicative purpose (goal) in order to achieve an outcome.
Skehan (1998)	An activity in which: • meaning is primary • there is some communication problem to solve • there is some sort of relationship to comparable real-world activities • task completion has some priority • the assessment of the task is in terms of outcome
Lee (2000)	(1) A classroom activity or exercise that has: (a) an objective obtainable only by interaction among participants, (b) a mechanism for structuring and sequencing interaction, and (c) a focus on meaning exchange; (2) a language learning endeavour that requires learners to comprehend, manipulate, and/or produce the target language as they perform some set of workplans.

Author	Definition
Bygate et al. (2001)	An activity, susceptible to brief or extended pedagogic intervention, which requires learners to use language, with emphasis on meaning, to attain an objective. An activity, influenced by learner choice, and susceptible to learner reinterpretation, which requires learners to use language, with emphasis on meaning, to attain an objective.
Cook (2001)	The archetypical communicative technique is an information gap activity. [...] Students look at one or the other set of photos and have to discover what the differences are, if any, by talking to each other without looking at the other set. [...] [This technique] might use visuals, tapes or models – in fact anything where the teacher could deliberately engineer two sets of slightly differing information so that the students had an information gap to bridge. [...] They have to use their own resources to achieve a communicative goal with other people, thus bringing communication directly into the classroom.
Ellis (2003)	A task is a workplan that requires learners to process language pragmatically in order to achieve an outcome that can be evaluated in terms of whether the correct or appropriate prepositional content has been conveyed. To this end, it requires them to give primary attention to meaning and to make use of their own linguistic resources, although the design of the task may predispose them to choose particular forms. A task is intended to result in language use that bears a resemblance, direct or indirect, to the way language is used in the real world. Like other language activities, a task can engage productive or receptive, and oral or written skills, and also various cognitive processes.
Van den Branden (2006)	Classroom tasks [...] should primarily be directed towards meaning exchange. Classroom tasks should facilitate meaningful interaction and offer the learner ample opportunity to process meaningful input and produce meaningful output in order to reach relevant and obtainable goals. In other words, tasks invite the learner to act primarily as a language user, and not as a language learner.
Eckerth (2008)	Task-based language pedagogy uses tasks as the basis unit in planning, structuring, carrying out and assessing foreign language teaching [...] In line with the communicative approach, TBLT favors activities which require and encourage meaning-oriented language use and target language communication, and both are understood as ways of using language in order to achieve a communicative goal rather than merely displaying the mastery of a certain L2 structure.

Table 6: Definitions of 'tasks' as an educational activity (compiled from Ellis 2003: 4f and Van den Branden 2006: 7f, extended by Keßler & Plesser)

focus on meaning

A look at Table 6 clearly demonstrates that tasks in TBLT focus on meaning rather than on form. This observation points to another important feature of the nature of tasks: tasks are always open in outcome. In other words, it is the learner and the interaction between learners or learner-teacher interaction that makes the difference in TBLT. Tasks as workplans support implicit language learning. However, it is the 'task-in-progress', i.e. the actual work of the learners on the task, that provides the learning opportunities. According to Seedhouse (2005), it is rather the task-in-progress that both teachers and researchers should focus on.

In contrast to more teacher-centred approaches to language teaching, tasks provide vast opportunities for language learners to experiment both with content as well as with language. Thus working with tasks in the foreign language classroom opens the grammar teaching focus to a more learning-centred scenario as learners can solve the task using their own ideas as well as L2 structures according to their individual state of Interlanguage development. As meaning is more important than form, learners need not fear being corrected immediately for using a non-target like structure but can complete the task. Then, a short form-focussed session (cf. chapter 11) might follow.

task continuum

TBLT enjoys great popularity amongst SLA researchers, as well as among language teachers. However, there are also some critical voices to be found. Foster (1999: 69) for example raises concern that too much focus on meaning might lead to neglecting formal aspects of the target language, especially in the fields of morphology and syntax "because language does not have to be well-formed in order to be meaningful". Obviously, Foster is right in her assumption that ill-formed language can also be meaningful. Nevertheless, in terms of active L2 learning following the *Interlanguage Approach* as sketched out throughout this book teachers ought to allow for rather standard-oriented Interlanguage variations to be produced by their learners (cf. Chapter 7 on the role of IL Variation and on how to distinguish 'developmental' from 'variational' errors). Littlewood (2004: 321f) addressed the concern raised by Foster and developed a task continuum that differentiates "between tasks which focus on language forms and tasks which focus on the meanings that are communicated. This is not a dichotomy, however, but a continuum along which the students may operate with differing degrees of focus on form and meaning". Figure 34 illustrates Littlewood's task continuum:

Focus on forms		←	→	**Focus on meaning**
Non-communicative learning	**Pre-communicative language practice**	**Communicative language practice**	**Structured communication**	**Authentic communication**
Focusing on the tructures of language, how they are formed and what they meand, e.g. substitution exercises,' discovery' and awareness-raising activities	Practising language withsome attention to meaning bit not communicating new messages to others, e.g. question-and-answer-practice	Practising pre-taught language in a context where it communicates new information, e.g. information-gap activities or 'personalized' questions	Using language to communicate in situations which elicit pre-learnt language, but with some unpredictability, e.g. structured role-play and simple problem-solving	Using language to communicate in situations where the meanings are unpredictable, e.g. creative role-play, more complex problem-solving and discussion
'Exercises'	←	*(Ellis)*	→	*'Tasks'*
'Enabling tasks'	←	*(Estaire and Zanon)*	→	*'Communicative tasks'*

Figure 34: Task continuum (taken from Littlewood 2004: 322).

As can be seen in figure 34 Ellis (2000: 195f.) distinguishes between 'exercises' which do not serve any communicative aim and 'tasks'. He reserves the notion of task exclusively for those activities that focus on meaning and interaction. Estaire & Zanon use the same basis for their distinction between 'enabling' and 'communicative' tasks.

TBLT as answer to P-P-P

So has TBLT become just a fashionable way also to teach grammar through meaningful – so-called real-world – activities? A point to emphasis here is that the TBLT approach to grammar instruction is far from being new. It was first introduced by Prahbu (1987) and then quickly adapted both by SLA researchers as well as language teaching specialists. Eckerth (2008) even raises the question as to whether TBLT is "old wine in new bottles". Is there more than a fashion that TBLT can offer to grammar teaching? According to Carless (2009) TBLT is an answer to the severe criticism of the P-P-P Approach[29] to language teaching. The P-P-P has been subject to severe criticism not only for a "lack of research basis" (Richards & Rodgers 2006: 249) but also for not being compatible with findings provided by SLA research on how languages are learned (e.g. the *Interlanguage Approach*, see Chapter 7). Skehan (1996) summarises this criticism as follows:

> The underlying theory for a P-P-P approach has now been discredited. The belief that a precise focus on a particular form leads to learning and automatization (that learners will learn what is taught in the order of which it is taught) no longer carries much credibility in linguistics or psychology.
>
> (Skehan 1996: 18)

Skehan's criticism reflects a major problem in many grammar teaching settings. Throughout this book we have demonstrated how Interlanguage develops gradually and how SLA research and language teaching have to go hand in hand. Pienemann (1998) laid out a theory that explains in detail why learners learn the foreign language in exactly the way they do it (cf. Chapter 7; developmental problem). With Carless (2009: 51) we can stress that "the basis of TBLT in SLA theory has been well-articulated (Ellis, 2003; Skehan, 1996)". Additionally, a more recent summary of how TBLT is embedded in SLA is provided by Eckerth (2008) and by Pienemann & Keßler (in press).

Müller-Hartmann & Schocker-v Ditfurth (2004: 40) point out that "TBLT has become an important approach which allows psycho-linguistic and sociocultural approaches to language learning to find common ground". According to these authors, the Common European Framework of Reference (see Chapter 15 of this book for more detail) "supports the combination of focus on meaning and form in TBLL: '[...] a changing balance needs to be established between attention to meaning and form, fluency and accuracy, in the overall selection and sequencing of tasks so that both task performance and language learning progress can be facilitated" (Müller-Hartmann & Schocker-v Ditfurth 2004: 40).

[29] "P-P-P" stands for the raher traditional model of "presentation – practice – production". This approach has been extremely popular in many teacher training settings throughout the world (cf. Richards & Rodgers 2006: 47).

This view is also supported by Carless (2009: 52) who acknowledges that "a major issue in TBLT is how form-focused work is managed".

If TBLT offers such a potential for theory-based grammar teaching by integrating the *Interlanguage Approach* into it, what then would TBLT-based grammar instruction consist of? Eckerth (2008: 31) offers the following points on how TBLT accounts for grammar learning in instructional settings:

- tasks provide the conditions for input, interaction, and output that are assumed to be conductive to second language acquisition (Long & Norris 2000);
- though not limited to group- and pair-work, the bulk of tasks involve oral learner-learner interaction. Such a participation pattern increases students' speaking time and provides a sheltered communicative space where students can develop their own voice (Nunan 2004);
- typically confronting the learners with a 'referential problem' (Yule 1997), tasks require the kind of authentic referential communication that links L2 classroom learning to L2 use outside the classroom;
- via a 'focus on form' (Long 1991, 2000), specific learning difficulties can be addressed and teaching can be adapted to particular pedagogical needs

taken from: Eckerth (2008: 31)

focused vs. unfocused tasks

In TBLT we have to distinguish between two "general types of tasks" (Ellis 2003: 16). These two types are:

- **focused and**
- **unfocused tasks**

Unfocused tasks support language learning in general and focus on communication and meaning. However, they do not focus on any particular language structure that the teacher might want his/her learners to use in particular. According to Ellis (2003: 16) these tasks "may predispose learners to choose from a range of forms but they are not designed with the use of a specific form in mind". On the other hand, teachers can administer focused tasks that allow the learner to "process, receptively or productively, some particular linguistic feature, for example a grammatical structure" (Ellis 2003: 16).

In the context of this book we will concentrate on the focused tasks as they contribute to teaching grammar in a far more exact way than any unfocused tasks would allow. The distinction between focused and unfocused tasks, however, must not be misunderstood in the way that focused would not need to fulfil the requirements of 'tasks' discussed above. In other words, focused tasks also have to provide meaningful activities connected to the real world. A communicative, non-linguistic outcome is the core even of focused tasks; otherwise they would be exercises (cf. figure 34 above).

Figure 35: Example of a focused task (picture dictation task); picture taken from Elsner (2007); task created by Keßler for this section

Focused tasks can be designed in two ways: first, a task can be designed to be a focused task by making sure that it can only be completed if the learners use a specific linguistic form. Figure 35 provides an example of a picture dictation task where Learner A has to describe where the items listed in the worksheet can be found in "his/her" room to Learner B. Only by listening and comprehending the prepositions used by Learner A is Learner B placed in a position to draw the lines according to the locations in Learner A's room. This is a focused task because the task can only be fulfilled if both learners focus on prepositions. The result may be different for different pairs of learners as each learner might arrange the room individually. In other words, this task is open in outcome. The task is communicative because it can only be solved by discussing and negotiating meaning between the two participants. As this list illustrates, this tasks meets all the major features of a task and provides a learning opportunity of a highly complex grammatical feature (prepositions) in a communicative way.

A second approach to designing a focused task is to put the language itself into the focus of the task. Ellis (2003: 18) provides an example of a focused task of this type. Activity 2 illustrates this task. In his example, Ellis focuses on prepositions of time. According to Ellis (2003: 17)

> Learners use the data supplied to complete a table by classifying the time phrases into those that use 'in', 'on', and 'at'. They then try to work out a rule to describe how these prepositions are used. This kind of activity, which I have called 'consciousness raising (CR) tasks' (Ellis 1991), is a task rather than an exercise because it requires the learners to talk about the data together. This talk, like talk about any other topic, involves the exchange of information and ideas, and is, therefore, meaning-centred.
>
> Ellis (2003: 17)

Activity 2
Prepositions of time

1 Underline the time expressions in this passage
I made an appointment to see Mr. Bean at 3 o'clock on Tuesday 11th February to discuss my application for a job. Unfortunately, he was involved in a car accident in the morning and rang to cancel the appointment. I made another appointment

to see him at 10 o'clock on Friday 21st February. However, when I got to his office, his secretary told me that his wife had died at 2 o'clock in the night and that he was not coming into the office that day. She suggested I reschedule for sometime in March. So I made a third appointment to see Mr. Bean at 1 o'clock on Monday 10th March. This time I actually got to see him. However, he informed me that they had now filled all the vacancies and suggested I contact him again in 1998. I assured him that he would not be seeing me either this or the next century.

2 Write the time phrases into the table.

AT	IN	ON
3 o'clock		

3 Make up a rule to explain when to use 'at', 'in' and 'on in time expressions.

taken from Ellis (2003: 18)

At first sight both focused tasks introduced in this section my look very similar. Both tasks deal with prepositions and thus are focused on a particular grammar feature. However, the main difference between the two tasks is that in the one featured in figure 35 the task reflects the real world and the learners have to come up with everyday language in their communication in order to solve the task. The task is open in outcome as there are hardly any limitations on where the learners may put the items in their own picture.

Activity 2 can also be considered a task as has been illustrated in the quotation by Ellis above. However, here the main task activity takes place when learners discuss their ideas on how to explain the use of different time expressions. In doing this, they negotiate meaning in the target language. This negotiation of meaning is beneficial for (instructed) second language acquisition (cf. Long 1996).

We have seen how focused tasks can be used to support implicit grammar learning and also contribute to consciousness-raising for more explicit approaches to grammar teaching. It would be beyond the scope of this introductory textbook to demonstrate in detail how tasks can be developed for primary and secondary school foreign language classrooms. Van Gorp & Bogaert (2006) provide a comprehensive overview of how to design tasks. Their paper puts special emphasis on how tasks can be manipulated to "enhance language learning" (Van Gorp & Bogaert 2006: 76).

task cycle

Of course, TBLT does not happen in isolation and teachers would not present a set of tasks – focused or unfocused – in a series without any introduction or follow-up work. There have been several suggestions of how tasks can be integrated into a teaching unit (e.g. Estaire & Zanón 1994, Willis 1996, Ellis 2003, Keßler 2008b). The most straightforward suggestion was put forward by Willis (1996) who considers a task cycle to consist of three main phases, namely:

1. pre-task
2. task
3. language focus

Ellis (2003: 33) points out that there are "opportunities for attention to form in all three phases". In the pre-task phase the focus can be on new vocabulary and useful phrases the learners might need for the actual task work. In the second phase the emphasis is on task completion with the main focus on meaning. However, as the examples provided above show, in this phase of working on a focused task, form comes into play in an implicit way, too. In the post-task phase the language focus can be on consciousness-raising towards specific linguistic forms needed to communicate and negotiate meaning. In this phase, TBLT can closely be linked to FonF as discussed in the previous section of this chapter. Obviously, the post-task phase can go far beyond a mere language focus. During this phase a discussion task can also be administered as a follow-up activity. The learners would then have to use information gained during their work on the task (Phase 2) and reinterpret it according to the question raised in the follow-up task (cf. Bygate et al.'s 2001 definition of 'task' listed in Table 5).

teacher's role in TBLT

So far we have discussed how TBLT supports grammar learning from the pupils' perspective. In this last part of our section on TBLT let us now briefly discuss the teacher's role in this approach to grammar teaching. According to Van Avermaet et al. (2006: 175) the teacher plays a crucial role in TBLT, even though this is a rather learner- and learning-centred approach to foreign language instruction. These authors stress the following two "core actions" that teachers carry out to activate their learners in order to offer the richest learning opportunities possible:

- motivating the learner to invest intensive mental energy in task completion;
- interactionally supporting task performance in such a way as to trigger processes such as negotiation of meaning and content, the comprehension of rich input, the production of output and focus on form, which are believed to be central to (second) language learning

These two core actions summarise the underlying (SLA) theory of TBLT in a nutshell. We have discussed the role of negotiation of meaning, input, output and focus on form in various sections throughout this book and explained how these factors contribute to successful instructed foreign language learning from the Interlanguage perspective. With Van Avermaet et al. we would like to recall Breen's (1987: 25) four basic questions teachers should ask themselves to investigate the learning potential of any language learning task. These questions are:

1. What is the objective of the task?
2. What is the content of the task?
3. How is the task to be carried out?
4. In what situation is the task to be carried out?

Like the three phases of task performance discussed above, the teacher's role in TBLT can be split into three Stages. Figure 36 illustrates these three Stages. The four questions listed above are part of the planning Stage. During this Stage the teacher will have to choose and/or develop the tasks to be administered in classroom work. This phase comprises all mental and physical activities by the teacher in order to choose the right tasks for his/her learners. As the selection of the right task depends very much both on the learning aims as well as the individual learning group we refrain from offering any "recipes" for teachers in this book. We rather provide some theoretical background combined with practical examples as we do not believe in "ready-to-cook" activities that could be copied by any teacher for any classroom. In contrast to Harrington & Ware (2007) we do not believe in "Recipes for Success in Foreign Language Teaching" or "Ready-Made Activities for the L2 Classroom". Certainly, we understand the desire of teachers to use templates of best practice for their own teaching. However, we are sure that any "ready-made" recipes do not cater for individual classroom situations and individual learners' needs.

planning Stage

performance Stage

post-task assessment

Figure 36: Three Stages of teacher activities in TBLT (cf. Van Avermaet 2006: 175ff)

The second phase of teacher activities in TBLT is the performance Stage. During this Stage the teacher observes his/her learners in task performance. S/he overlooks the mental processes that take place and perhaps records on how the learners perform in their interaction. These notes can be useful in the post-task assessment and may be used as a basis for a FonF (see chapter 11) session once the performance Stage has been completed. Additionally the teacher may use this phase to point out the task's potential for the learners and act as a facilitator of learning (cf. Weskamp 2001).

The third phase is the phase of post-task assessment. During this phase both teacher and learners evaluate how the learners participated in the interaction and how they solved the problem raised by the task. This phase can also be used to address some of the grammar features covered in the task more overtly and focus on certain trouble areas the learners encountered during their actual task work. This phase also provides the basis for the next planning Stage within TBLT.

In this chapter we discussed the main ideas of TBLT and showed how they relate to (implicit) grammar learning. We demonstrated that TBLT is focused on meaning and thus caters for the communicative language classroom. However, focused tasks as explained in this chapter are particularly useful in grammar teaching as they combine the merits of communicative language teaching with a widened perspective for meaning-based instruction by allowing for a rather implicit practice of linguistic features. This approach is not particularly new, as Eckerth 2008 pointed out. Yet, the integration of TBLT into the *Interlanguage Approach* to language teaching as fostered in this book also offers a learner- and learning-centred approach to (individual) grammar learning according to each learner's developmental readiness (cf. Chapter 7 of this book).

Further Reading

Eckerth, J. & S. Siekmann (eds.) (2008): Task-Based Language Learning and Teaching. Theoretical, Methodological, and Pedagogical Perspectives. Frankfurt and New York: Peter Lang.

Ellis, R. (2003): Task-based language learning and teaching. Oxford: Oxford University Press.

Keßler, J.-U. (2008b): "Communicative Tasks and Second Language Profiling: Linguistic and Pedagogical Implications." In: Eckerth, J. & S. Siepmann (eds) (2008): pp. 291-310.

Müller-Hartmann, A. & M. Schocker-v. Ditfurth (2011): Teaching English: Task-Supported Language Learning. Paderborn: Schöning/ UTB.

Van den Branden, K. (ed.) (2006): Task-based Language Teaching. From Theory to Practice. Cambridge: Cambridge University Press.

Study Questions:

1. Choose one of the definitions of "task" (Table 6) and explain why you consider this definition to be useful.
2. Explain the difference between a focused and an unfocused task.
3. Why are focused tasks especially beneficial for (implicit) grammar learning?

13 Immersion Programmes and Grammar Teaching

> "Comprehensible subject-matter teaching *is* language teaching. [...] [Immersion focuses] on "what is being said rather than how."
>
> Krashen (1984: 62f)

> "It is the teaching of content or information in the language being learned with little or no direct or explicit effort to teach the language itself separately from the content being taught."
>
> Krahnke (1987: 65; cited in Richards & Rodgers 2006: 204)

> "The teaching of language through content is not so much a method as a reorientation to what is meant by *content* in language teaching. The literature offers strong theoretical support for content-based approaches and abundant examples of successful programs in both the foreign and second language settings which effectively teach language through content."
>
> Snow (2001: 317)

In this chapter we will now turn to a teaching approach that might not at first glance reveal a close connection to the idea of teaching grammar. As stated in the quotations above, the focus of any immersion approach is not on explicit grammar teaching. The underlying principle of immersion approaches is rather that learners implicitly pick up the target language grammar by using the language in authentic situations when dealing with subject matter. Content is the key to language acquisition in these programmes. However, as we will demonstrate in this chapter, learners do acquire a lot of grammar of the target language.

Snow (2001: 303) points out that throughout history the notion of content has been interpreted rather differently. The following table (table 7) is adapted from Snow. It includes all the historical approaches to language teaching featured in chapter 3 of this book.

Teaching Approach	Definition of "content"
Grammar Translation	grammatical structures of the target language
Audio Lingual	grammatical structures, vocabulary, sound patterns
Natural Approach	language use for problem solving
Communicative Language Teaching	communicative purpose for which the learner uses the target language
Immersion/Content and Language Integrated Learning (CLIL)	subject matter of the (non-language) subject taught in the target language

Table 7: Definition of "content" in various teaching approaches (adapted from Snow 2001: 303)

As Immersion Programmes are meant to be an approximation to natural acquisition (Lightbown & Spada 2006, also see table 8) learners actually do go through quite a few Interlanguage structures during their acquisition process. If one compares some key characteristics of natural acquisition and traditional teaching approaches on the one hand and Immersion Programmes on the other hand, it becomes clear that Immersion Programmes offer an alternative to incorporating as much of natural acquisition as possible into an instructional setting of language learning. Table 8 is adapted from Lightbown & Spada (2006) and illustrates how Immersion Programmes draw from natural acquisition.

Characteristics	Natural Acquisition	Traditional Instruction	Immersion Programmes
error correction	–	+	–
learning on e thing at a time	–	+	–
high ratio of inter-action between users	++	–	+
genuine questions	++	–	+

Characteristics	Natural Acquisition	Traditional Instruction	Immersion Programmes
pressure to speak	++	–	+
negotiation of meaning	++	–	+

Table 8: Comparing natural acquisition and traditional instruction to Immersion Programmes (adapted from Lightbown & Spada 2006)

Immersion Programmes are far from being uniform. Many different implementations can be found throughout the literature and in teaching practice. "All share, however, a common point of departure – the integration of language teaching aims with subject matter instruction" (Snow 2001: 303). This observation has been confirmed by substantial empirical research over a number of years (e.g. Scott 1974, Wesche 1993; for details see Richards & Rodgers 2006: 209).

In the following part of this chapter we will firstly address some notational issues. One has to distinguish between a few key concepts of Immersion Programmes (Immersion, Content and Language Integrated Learning – henceforward CLIL – and Bilingual Modules). After a brief introduction to and discussion of these three concepts we will take a closer look at some research results that show the benefits of Immersion Programmes to the foreign language classroom. We will close the section on Immersion Programmes by looking at some key features of CLIL methodology.

Immersion

50% plus of all subjects taught in target language

Immersion is definitely the most intense instructional approach to the target language. According to Richards, Pall & Weber (1992) who provide the probably shortest definition of immersion, this form of bilingual education involves the subject-teaching of learners through the medium of the target language (i.e. a language that is not their native tongue). The term immersion is derived from the verb "to immerse"; the idea is that the language learner is immersed in a language bath by being surrounded by the target language in authentic situations. The target language is used as the means of instruction rather than the matter of instruction. There is no explicit grammar teaching in Immersion

Programmes. Classrooms that follow a full immersion approach (see below) do not offer any lessons dedicated to teaching the target language as such. Also, in Immersion Programmes language errors are not addressed unless they change the meaning of the content under discussion. Nevertheless, learners do acquire target language structures and rules implicitly as we will show in a later section of this chapter.

St. Lambert Project

The origin of (modern) immersion dates back to the year 1965 when in St. Lambert, Quebec in Canada parents of monolingually raised English-speaking children opted for an immersion education for their children in French. French is the majority language in Quebec and those parents assumed that there would be better job opportunities for their children if they were similarly literate in French as compared to their English mother tongue (cf. Swain & Lapkin 1982, Genesee 1987 and 1994). In this Canadian Model the first-graders were fully taught in their L2 (French). Even literacy skills were first taught in the foreign language. Only in the second grade was literacy also taught in their native language.

Though there are some reservations about the merits of immersion education (cf. Cummins' (1976) Threshold Hypothesis) and research has shown that learners in Immersion Programmes are far from developing the kind of balanced bilingualism (cf. Genesee 1987) that had been hoped for at the beginning of the St Lambert Project, Immersion has proven to be one of the most successful approaches to classroom-based foreign language learning – both in primary as well as in secondary schools (e.g. Wode 1988, Wesche 2002, Burmeister 2006, Pienemann, Keßler & Liebner 2006, Kersten 2009).

We speak of Immersion if the programme contains at least 50% of the tuition provided is in the target language. Depending on the number of subjects involved in the Immersion Programme as well as the starting point within the education curriculum we distinguish two basic types of immersion:

1. full versus partial immersion (→ are all subjects or a subset of the curriculum taught in the target language)
2. early versus late immersion (→ when do learners start to be taught in Immersion Programmes?)

Of course, in our schools we are often confronted with blended forms of the basic types of immersion. Some primary schools follow an early partial Immersion Programme, and many secondary school learners do not start their immersive education until the age of 10 or 12. Then we speak of late partial immersion. Within the German state school system one hardly finds any full immersion programmes – literacy is taught in the majority language German to the learners. However, within the private sector we can find international schools that follow the full immersion approach.

Content and Language Integrated Learning (CLIL)

up to 50% of subjects taught in target language

CLIL is used as an umbrella term for many approaches to bilingual teaching. Legutke et al. (2009: 105) translate CLIL as the "German equivalent [of] Bilingualer Sachfachunterricht" and adopt a definition of CLIL by Edelenbos et al. (2006: 93f), who claim that CLIL "is a keyword which is appearing increasingly and can be interpreted very broadly, from teaching a 15-minute sequence about apples as part of a lesson on fruits, to teaching some topics within a year in the foreign language, to teaching one or more subjects in the other language." We will refer to CLIL whenever at least one subject but less than 50 % of all the subjects are taught in the target language. Additionally, classroom routines are also addressed in the target language above the level that would be found in traditional foreign language classrooms. Anything below at least one subject being taught continuously in the target language will be referred to as bilingual modules at a later Stage of this chapter. When looking at instructed bilingual education throughout German state schools CLIL is the most widespread approach to be found. Predominantly, CLIL is applied in secondary schools and follows the principles of late partial immersion. A typical case of CLIL (German-English) to be found at secondary school level is the following programme:

Grade	Subject involved	Languages involved	Focus on...
from grade 5	English	English	• (authentic) communication • intercultural competence • role plays • fluency • (pronunciation) • implicit knowledge of selected grammar structures such as "passive voice
from grade 7	Geography	English	• subject matter • authentic communication • visual elements (photos, charts, diagrams, tables, maps, etc.)
from grade 8	History	English and German	• subject matter • authentic communication • historical sources • Language of choice depends on the topic and its connection to a certain language background
from grade 9	Politics	English and German	• subject matter • authentic communication

Table 9: An exemplary selection of subjects to be taught in a CLIL.

Needless to say, any other subject can also be taught in the target language in CLIL programmes. The choice of the subjects very much depends on the resources a school can draw from. Needless to say that appropriate teaching staff is needed. Ideally, teachers are fully trained foreign language teachers and also trained teachers in the subject taught in CLIL. A wide range of subjects are taught at various secondary schools all over Germany. For a recent overview of subjects taught in CLIL programmes see Hollm et al. (2010).

According to Werlen (2007) any approach to bilingual teaching (and its didactic foundation) has to meet certain challenges by addressing the following four learning/teaching aims:

- Sachlernen
- Kommunikationslernen
- Sprachlernen
- Strategielernen

As this hierarchical list reveals quite bluntly, language learning ranges only in third position – after content and communication. However, Werlen points out that "Kommunikationslernen" also comprises lexical items and grammar structures of the target language. By developing the meaning from words and phrases the learners – implicitly – also develop a greater understanding of the target grammar.

CLIL teaching practice

What does this mean for teaching practice? Larsen-Freeman (2000: 136ff) provides a CLIL sample lesson in geography. The lesson is about the Earth (see figure 37). When analysing the lesson Larsen-Freeman lists the following observations and their underlying principles. Figure 37 illustrates the content of the lesson which was provided originally by Christelli (1994):

Figure 37: A sample geography lesson on "The Earth" (taken from Larsen-Freeman 2000: 138)

In her example, Larsen-Freeman (2000: 139) points out that the design of this geography lesson addresses both the functional needs of the content matter by focusing on special vocabulary such as "degree, distance, equator, globe, hemisphere, latitude, model" as well as the linguistic needs by providing an authentic framework for the use of the passive voice. The teacher can introduce verb patterns such as "are located, are called, is used" etc. Larsen-Freeman (2000: 139) suggests that the teacher can explain "that the passive voice is used to defocus the agent or doer of an action." Looking at the four key aims suggested by Werlen (2007) and discussed above, the teacher addresses rather the "Kommunikationslernen" than the "Sprachlernen" aspects within this lesson as no explicit grammar rules are provided. As the next step in this sample lesson, the teacher can then provide various examples of how the geographical concepts of longitude and latitude "can be used to locate any place in the world [...] By stating 'This city is located at latitude 60° north and longitude 11° east,' the teacher integrates the present passive and the content focus at the same time" (Larsen-Freeman 2000: 139).

The following nine observations and principles can be derived from this sample lesson. The observations may be lesson-specific, but the underlying principles can be generalised and serve as a model for any other CLIL lesson as well:

Observation	**Principles**
The class is studying geography.	The subject matter content is used for language teaching purposes.
The teacher asks the students what they know about a globe.	Teaching should build on students' previous experience.
The students call out their answers enthusiastically as the teacher writes them on the blackboard.	When learners perceive the relevance of their language use, they are motivated to learn. They know that it is a means to an end, rather than an end in itself.
The teacher supplies the missing language when the students have troubles in explaining a concept in the target language.	The teacher 'scaffolds' the linguistic content, i.e. helps learners to say what it is they want to say by building together with the students a complete utterance.
The teacher reads the new vocabulary and then the students watch a video entitled "Understanding Globes".	Language is learned most effectively when it is used as a medium to convey informational content of interest to the students.
The students fill in the vocabulary words in the blanks in the modified cloze passages as they watch the video	Vocabulary is easier to acquire when there are contextual clues to help convey meaning.
The teacher provides a number of examples using the present passive with latitudes and longitudes co-ordinates.	When they work with authentic subject matter, students need language support. For instance, the teacher may provide a number of examples, build in some redundancy, use comprehension checks, etc.

Observation	Principles
The students are given the latitude and longitude co-ordinates, and they have to come to the front of the classroom to find the city on the globe.	Learners work with meaningful, cognitively demanding language and content within the context of authentic material and tasks.
For homework, the students are given a map, which they are to label based on a descriptive reading they have been given.	Communicative competence involves more than using language conversationally. It also includes the ability to read, discuss, and write about content from other fields.

Table 10: Observations and Principles of a CLIL Lesson (Larsen-Freeman 2000: 140f)

Table 10 illustrates how lesson-specific observations relate to general principles of the CLIL classroom. It becomes clear that though grammar structures are not formally taught there is a role of raising the learners' awareness for the use of certain structures in authentic contexts. The table also reveals that language teachers may even incorporate some rather traditional elements of teaching into their CLIL lessons like providing a set of examples and building in redundancy. This may take away some pressure from teachers who might otherwise fear that they have to change their teaching style completely to something they might not have been fully prepared for.

major principles of CLIL

On the other hand, table 10 also illustrates how learners work with meaningful, cognitively demanding language and content within the context of authentic material and tasks. In Chapter 12 we have discussed the TBLT approach to grammar teaching in detail. However, task-based language learning is also a major principle of CLIL. Müller-Hartmann & Schocker-v. Ditfurth (2004: 154f) list three major principles of CLIL:

- Task-based approach and authenticity
- Learner-centredness and learning-centredness
- Intercultural Communicative Competence

TBLT

These principles can also be found in other teaching approaches, but they form the core principles in CLIL. More precisely, TBLT contributes to focusing on meaning rather than language structures and language is used in an authentic way (cf. Prahbu 1987). As discussed in our section on TBLT (see chapter 12) learners negotiate for meaning also in CLIL. In terms of teaching grammar the TBLT approach supports Interlanguage development as the learners can take risks when they negotiate content matter in communicative situations. Risk-taking supports the acquisition of a more advanced Interlanguage (e.g. Keßler 2006 and 2008b).

learner- and learning-centredness

CLIL caters for a rich learning environment through the discussion of relevant topics and the provision of authentic texts and materials. In the process, learner-centredness and learning-centredness are addressed in a natural way as the learners can choose from a range of materials and learn about subject matter. Learners can pursue those questions within the range of the topic that are relevant for them content-wise. Additionally, they can adjust the material and their output to their individual linguistic needs. According to Müller-Hartmann & Schocker-v. Ditfurth (2004) learner- and learning-centredness is also achieved by the use of New Media in the EFL classroom, as these contribute to increasing the pool of material and also support the learners in finding and selecting as well as producing material.

Considering learner- and especially learning-centredness from the Interlanguage perspective as pursued throughout this book, CLIL like TBLT, is very much learning-centred, as one focus is on the output produced by the learners. This output may not only be evaluated according to its relevance of content but also according to learners' current state of Interlanguage development (cf. Chapter 6 of this book). This is essential not only for the approach to error correction but also in that it allows for an individual, and thus learner-centred, approach to implicit grammar teaching in communicative situations (cf. Candlin 1987, Larsen-Freeman 2000, Ellis 2003, Keßler 2006).

Intercultural Communicative Competence

Byram's model of ICC

Focusing on content matter opens the door in many subjects to experience of another culture (e.g. in geography or in history). Looking at authentic data from the target language background thus contributes to alternative interpretations of the same event (cf. Byram 1997). In his model of Intercultural Communication, Byram points out that skills need to be divided into two strands. The first is the "ability to interpret a document or event from another culture, to explain it and relate it to documents from one's own" (Byram 1997: 52). The second is the "ability to acquire new knowledge of a culture and cultural practices and the ability to operate knowledge, attitudes and skills under the constraints of real-time communication and interaction" (Byram 1997: 52). In CLIL we can add a third strand, namely the ability to actually verbalize the new knowledge by making use of the necessary linguistic features according to one's individual state of Interlanguage development. By comparing one's own culture to other cultures learners can learn not only to understand other cultures in a prejudice-free way but also reconsider and – if necessary – revise their own society's views (cf. Delanoy & Volkmann 2006, Keßler 2006b).

In addition to the major principles of CLIL as introduced by Müller-Hartmann & Schocker-v. Ditfurth (2004) and discussed in more detail here, Burmeister (2006: 204) completes the list of principles with the concepts of scaffolding and contextualisation. Scaffolds help the learners to gain the linguistic confidence needed for the discussion of the content matter dealt with during the CLIL lessons (see Burmeister 2006: 204-207 for details).

Bilingual Modules

bilingual modules

Bilingual Modules form a subcategory of CLIL. The main difference is the frequency and intensity. In contrast to CLIL, bilingual modules are taught in one or more subjects but rather in addition to traditional monolingual subject teaching. Individual teaching units are then taught in the target language following the same principles discussed in the CLIL section above. However, after the teaching unit is completed the language of instruction moves back to the majority language used at that school. Bilingual modules fit well into any kind of instructed language learning and are backed by curricula and are part of the "Bildungsplan" in Baden-Württemberg for EFL classrooms from primary school to grammar school. Bilingual modules can be well integrated into traditional teaching at German Hauptschule. In a recent study, Huber (2009) was able to show that bilingual modules applied at Hauptschule can contribute to new motivation in language learning and more equal learning opportunities in heterogeneous classrooms without compromising on content matter.

How do Immersion and CLIL Programmes contribute to Grammar Learning?

There is ample research on the positive effects of Immersion and CLIL Programmes (e.g. Swain & Laptkin 1982, Wode 1995, Burmeister & Daniel 2002, Wesche 2002, Burmeister 2006, DESI-Konsortium 2006, Piske 2006, Zydatiß 2000 and 2007, Kersten 2009). In this section we can only briefly look at one of the studies in more detail. To show how Immersion can be implemented from a very early Stage we chose an example from primary school (Piske 2006). A detailed study of the effects of Immersion on grammar learning in secondary school can be found in Burmeister & Daniel (2002). In this section we will restrain ourselves to the illustration of how grammar learning develops in Immersion and CLIL Programmes.

Piske (2006) provides three short transcripts of a learner from an Immersion Programme at a primary school near Kiel. The study was based on oral language production. Piske used the Frog Story (cf. figure 38; Mayer 1969) to elicit spontaneous speech samples. The learners had to describe the first three pictures of the story. Piske (2006) provides one example from his longitudinal study. The following transcripts are taken from Piske (2006) and show the Interlanguage development of one learner from the end of the first grade to the end of the third grade.

Figure 39 is an adaption from Piske (2006) and illustrates how learner B08 – a monolingual L1 German speaker – described the three pictures shown in figure 38. When analysing the transcripts one has to bear in mind that this learner has never enjoyed any traditional EFL lesson. Any grammar was acquired by the learner through the Immersion Programme at her school.

Figure 38: The first three pictures of the Frog Story (Mayer 1969)

Transcript 1: Child 08.1B (Grade 1)
There ***is*** a dog and a boy, and the d/ dog ***looking*** in a glass, and in the glass ***sitting*** a frog, and the moon ***shining***. And then the boy *are* ***sleeping***, and the dog *sleeping*. And then the boy ***looking*** in the glass, and the frog ***is***/ *is* not there.

Transcript 2: Child 08.2B (Grade 2)
There ***was*** a boy and he ***has*** a frog in a gr/ glass and he ***look*** at the frog, he ***love*** the frog and the dog ***look*** at the frog. And then the boy ***goes*** into bed and ***sleep*** and the frog ***goes*** out/ out of the glass and ***go*** in his home, and the dog ***sleep*** by the boy, and the f/ next morning the frog ***is*** away and the boy ***look*** at it/ at the glass, and the boy ***is*** awa/ and the frog ***is*** away. The dog ***look*** at the f/ ***look*** at the glass but the frog ***is*** not there.

Transcript 3: Child 08.3B (Grade 3)
Ehm one night a little boy ehm ***has catched*** a little frog and ***put*** him in a glass and ehm then he ***took*** the glass and ***bring*** it in his bedroom, and then he ***looks*** at the little frog, and the frog ***thinks***, when the little boy ***sleeps*** I ***go out*** in the forest to my family. And ehm the light ***is*** on, and the little dog ehm ***looks*** in the glass exactly on the frog. And when the frog ehm ***go out*** of the glass in the night, the little dog and the little boy ***are sleeping***, and ehm the moon ***is shining*** in the window, and ehm all ***is standing around*** and ***is*** dark. And when the day ***comes*** and the ehm sun ***shines*** on the glass and the little boy ehm ***wakes up*** and the dog a/ as well, ehm the glass *was* empty because the frog ehm in the night *go* ehm to his family again, in the forest.

adapted from Piske (2006)

Figure 39: Interlanguage development (Learner Grammar) at Primary School level from grade 1 to grade 4 (adapted from Piske 2006)

This learner, who has never been taught English grammar in a formal way, has developed her Interlanguage according to the developmental trajectory introduced in Chapter 7 of this book. It is particularly interesting to take a closer look at the development of verbs through the three transcripts. In Transcript 1 the learner uses a variety of verbs and attaches an "-ing" to most of them. Here, we cannot yet speak of the development of the progressive form. The learner overgeneralizes the "-ing" rather as a verb marker. This is a typical feature of early Interlanguage development and can also be found in other EFL contexts (cf. Keßler & Lenzing 2008: "The dog is *grab*ing").

Only one year later the learner has abandoned the "-ing" verb marker completely and replaced it by non-continuous verb forms. Now, the learner produces a past-tense form (was), additionally the "3-sg-s" starts to emerge (goes). As this form is not yet produced with any other lexical verb and "goes" does not occur in any morphological variation we cannot yet assume this structure to be acquired.

In Transcript 3 we can find a large range of different lexical verbs that are also used in morphological variation (e.g. shines, is shining). The learner now also produces a present perfect form, although, here the learner still overgeneralises the "past-ed" rule to an irregular verb. Lightbown & Spada (2006) report similar overgeneralisations in the acquisition of English as a first language.

Summary

In this section we have discussed in detail an approach to the foreign language classroom that does not at first glance reveal its connection to grammar teaching. However, we demonstrated that Immersion Programmes in fact contribute very well to a natural acquisition of (Interlanguage) grammar by providing relevant and authentic content input from which learners implicitly pick up fundamental grammar aspects as they go along. In line with Richards & Rodgers (2006: 220) we can conclude that "because CBI [content-based instruction, JK/AP] is based on a set of broad principles that can be applied in many different ways and is widely used as the basis for many different kinds of successful language programmes, we can expect to see CBI as one of the leading curricular approaches in language teaching."

Further Reading

Burmeister, P. & A. Daniel (2002): "How successful is late partial immersion? Some findings from a secondary school program in Germany." In: Burmeister, Petra; Piske, Thorsten; Rohde, Andreas (Eds.) (2002): An Integrated View of Language Development. Papers in Honor of Henning Wode. Trier: Wissenschaftlicher Verlag Trier; pp. 499-515.

Krashen, S. (1984): "Immersion: Why it works and what it has taught us." In: Language and Society 12: 61-64.
Larsen-Freeman, D. (2000): Techniques and Principles in Language Teaching. Oxford: Oxford University Press.
Snow, M.A. (2001): "Content-Based and Immersion Models for Second and Foreign Language Teaching." In: Celce-Murcia, M. (ed.); pp. 303-318.
Wesche, M.B. (2002): Early French Immersion: How has the original Canadian model stood the test of time? In: Burmeister, P./ Piske, T. / Rohde, Andreas (Hrsg.): An Integrated View of Language Development. Papers in Honor of Henning Wode. Trier: WVT, pp. 357-379.
Piske, T. (2006): „Zur Entwicklung der Englischkenntnisse bei deutschsprachigen Immersionsschülerinnen und –schülern im Grundschulalter"; in: Schlüter, N. [Hrsg.] (2006); S. 206-212.

Study Questions

1. Immersion and CLIL Approaches to foreign language learning differ from other approaches in their conceptualisation of grammar. Explain the major differences.
2. Explain the difference between full and partial immersion. Which of the two would you prefer at primary/secondary levels of education? Give reasons for your answer.
3. Name at least four major principles of CLIL. Can you see parallels to other approaches to grammar teaching? Explain.
4. Look at the transcripts in figure 37. Discuss the development of Interlanguage grammar by the learner from grade 1 to grade 3.

14 Course Books and Media

'Should we teach grammar, or shouldn't we?' Often presented with this apparent all-or nothing choice, even teachers asking the question may not have clear instructional goals for teaching grammar; they may simply think they *should* teach it. Sometimes they have other reasons, though, for thinking they ought to teach grammar: they find parents, the public, or even the politicians clamoring for grammar instruction in the hope that teaching traditional grammar from handbooks or CDs will somehow improve students' writing, or at least their ability to avoid 'errors'. Most often it doesn't.

Weaver et al. (2001: 17)

In the previous chapters we have looked at grammar teaching and learning from different angles. In chapters 5 and 6 we laid the theoretical foundation for grammar teaching from an Interlanguage perspective. This perspective has been substantiated by extensive empirical research in SLA. We have introduced and discussed three selected approaches to grammar teaching that we consider to be most relevant to teaching grammar in a less traditional way. With Weaver et al. (2001) we strongly believe that it is not a questions as to whether teach grammar or not. The question is rather how to teach grammar in such a way that individual learners in heterogeneous classrooms benefit most from its teaching.

Some 25 years ago, Allwright (1984) asked the question "Why don't learners learn what teachers teach?" Having discussed what is going on in the mind of the learners during the process of (instructed) second language development throughout this book we hope to have made it clear that it is neither the learners' nor the teachers' fault that grammar teaching has not always been as successful as intended. It is rather the traditional approaches to grammar and its teaching that neglect the development of Interlanguage as a successive process that happens to a large extent implicitly. However, especially the discussion of the selected approaches to grammar teaching in the previous chapter illustrated that grammar can be taught more successfully if inspired by basic findings from SLA research.

In this chapter we will now take a closer look at how grammar is still introduced and practised in textbooks. We will not dismiss the idea of textbooks as such, as they provide a vital pillar of any classroom-based foreign language teaching. However, we will point out some limitations of textbooks and show how teachers can easily adapt current textbooks to the needs of a foreign language classroom that follows the *Interlanguage Approach*.

This section will be followed by a practical application of the *Interlanguage Approach* to the EFL classroom. We will introduce and discuss our rationale of grammar teaching tasks and provide two samples of how those grammar teaching tasks can easily be integrated into the language classroom in order to foster grammar learning.

Course Books and Grammar – some limitations

> As it often is the case, crucial insights into how learners acquire a language have not been considered in the design of curricula and textbooks [...]. Therefore, the question arises whether the learning goals that are promoted in the textbooks are realistic ones.
>
> Lenzing (2008: 221)

Throughout the book we have been evaluating the *Interlanguage Approach* to grammar teaching. We have seen that not even the best teacher in the world can teach any grammatical structure at any time. It is rather the learners who have to be developmentally ready (e.g. Mansouri & Duffy 2005; cf. chapter 6 of this book) to acquire a given grammatical structure. In fact, this applies both to natural as well as instructed foreign language acquisition.

However, many textbooks for foreign language teaching give rise to the impression that grammar structures only need to be graded from simple to more complex in order to facilitate the learning of them. This might apply to lexical learning as there is no hierarchy in terms of which words can be acquired at an early or later Stage. In terms of grammar learning – as we have discussed in detail – the situation is a different one. In Chapters 5 and 6 we saw that the acquisition of grammatical items is constrained by what is processable for the learner at a given point in the acquisition process. In other words, the developmental hierarchy introduced in Chapter 5 holds for textbooks, too. Textbook authors claim to have sequenced the grammatical items in their books from simple to more complex. Unfortunately, they do not specify why they consider structure A to be less complex than structure B (cf. Keßler 2006, Lenzing 2008).

path of learnability

There have been several studies of whether the sequences in which grammatical features are presented in textbooks actually follow the "path of learnability predicted by Processability Theory" (Lenzing 2008: 221). For L2 English at primary level Lenzing (2006 and 2008) shows that the presented order of grammatical structures in two major textbooks used in Germany for English at primary schools indeed violates the developmental hierarchy of morpho-syntax as presented by SLA research. Using a similar approach for English at secondary school level in Germany Keßler (2006) found corresponding results for secondary school EFL textbooks.

There are, indeed, some major problems in the presentation of grammatical features as productive learning goals in textbooks. This does not mean that we are promoting a "learnable syllabus" in any such way as to implement Interlanguage structures in textbooks. What is meant is that textbooks ought to distinguish between productive use of grammatical structures that must follow the developmental hierarchy in order to be learnable and receptive use of grammatical structures that are needed in order to provide rich and authentic language input. The latter can not be learned by any learner at any time but only when s/he is ready to learn the structure. Nevertheless, these structures are important for the comprehension of the input and can well be produced by the learners at a formulaic level from the beginning of the acquisition process.

Seen in the light of the *Interlanguage Approach* it is more than questionable why learners at beginner level (both in primary as well as in secondary schools) are confronted with an active use of the *third-person-singular-s-structure* from a very early Stage of their acquisition process. This structure can only be acquired at Stage 5 (cf. Chapter 5, Table 3); most learners have not yet acquired this Stage when the structure is introduced in textbooks.

explicit rule presentation

Textbooks put a lot of emphasis in explaining the *third-person-singular-s-structure* in the first volume of their series. Figure 40 provides an example of how the grammar section of one of the major textbooks for L2 English in Germany at secondary school level explains this structure to learners.

1 Die einfache Form der Gegenwart
a Bejahte Aussagesätze

Mit dem *simple present* (der einfachen Form der Gegenwart) drückt man aus, dass etwas wiederholt (regelmäßig, immer, jeden Tag, oft, manchmal) oder nie geschieht.
Man benutzt diese Form auch, um allgemeine Aussagen zu machen:

- *I speak German.*
- *Cats eat mice.*

Wenn jemand etwas öfter macht, ist simple present angebracht.

Die einfache Form lässt sich wirklich einfach bilden: Sie entspricht dem Infinitiv – außer in der dritten Person Singular. In der dritten Person Singular wird ein -*s* an den Infinitiv angefügt.

He, she, it – das „s" muss mit!

The simple present
Positive statements

I **start**
You **start**
He/She/It **starts** at 8.45 every day.
We **start**
You **start**
They **start**

→ P 1, 2, 3, 4, 5 (p. 76/77)

Figure 40: Explanation of the third-person-singular-s-structure in a German textbook for grade 5 learners (Schwarz 1997: 145; emphasis taken from Keßler 2009: 95)

Of course, learners can very quickly state the rule explicitly. However, this by no means implies that they have acquired the rule for an active production in their Interlanguage (cf. Chapter 9 for the distinction between implicit and explicit grammar learning).

Whereas this grammatical structure, in terms of acquisition highly complex one, is introduced as a learning goal at a very early state in textbooks, another structure that is far simpler to acquire (at Stage 2 as compared to Stage 5) is not introduced until the second year of instruction at secondary school level. The structure in question is the simple past structure (*past-ed*). Learners are confronted with the *past-ed-structure* from a very early point in their instruction: in primary schools, the story telling approach is pursued for good reasons even in the first year of instructed foreign language instruction. Most of the stories told to the learners are fairytales that are familiar to the learners in their L1. Obviously, most fairytales are set in the past – thus requiring a lot of past tense structures. However, those structures are not part of the learning goals, either at primary school level or in the first year of secondary school education in Germany. Learners have to "wait" for one year in secondary school until textbooks actually present the *past-ed-structure* as a learning goal at the beginning of the second volume of their textbooks. Only after the summer holidays, is this simple structure introduced and practised.

textbooks and authenticity

Even if one does not wish to follow the *Interlanguage Approach* to grammar teaching there are some major limitations to textbooks and their presentation of grammar. Among others, Kieweg (1996) points out that textbooks feature an unnatural density of grammatical structures they want to introduce. Even in communication-oriented textbooks most of the texts presented to the learner have been constructed in order to introduce selected grammatical features. Content is less important and those texts very often compromise on authenticity. Figure 41 features a sample page taken from a recent text book for L2 English for secondary schools at beginners' level (year 5). It should be borne in mind that it is not our intention to censure a particular textbook or publisher. Our aim is rather to illustrate some general limitations of textbooks when dealing with grammar.

As can be seen from this sample page this textbook presents new grammar items in a "language section". In this example the learners are confronted with the present progressive. In terms of learnability and the *Interlanguage Approach* this is unproblematic as the *ing-structure* is acquired at Stage 2 of the developmental hierarchy. The problem with this introduction of the present progressive is the rather unnatural text that is full of samples of the targeted structure. In natural conversations and settings this is hardly to be found.

grammar structures presented in isolation

Additionally, the exercises below the text again focus on an isolated grammatical item which is neither in any relation to the real world of the learners, nor is it related to the introductory text content-wise. The only purpose of those exercises is to practise the present perfect structure. This approach is not really far away from the audio-lingual approach discussed in Chapter 3 of this book. Of course, learners do need practice phases in order to become more familiar with grammatical structures. However, in

5 | Check-in | Language 2 | Story | Wordwise | Check-out

A present for Sam

Lisa, Emma and Terry are shopping in town. They are looking for Sam's present now.

At the moment Emma and Lisa are looking at T-shirts in the sports shop. The name of the shop is All Sports. But they are not buying a T-shirt. They are too expensive.

The friends go to the newsagent's. Emma is reading the cards. But Terry and Lisa are not looking at the cards. They are leaving. They want to find a present first.

Emma and Lisa are running to the bus stop. They want to go to the department store. Where is Terry? He is not running. Is he going, too?

1 What is happening?

Finish these sentences with information from the pictures and text.

1. The three friends are looking for … .
2. They are not buying a … .
3. Emma is reading the … .
4. She is looking for a … .
5. But Terry and Lisa are leaving the … .
6. The two girls are running to the … .

GRAMMAR

I	am	looking
You	are	buying
He / She / It	is	listening
We	are	shopping
They	are	leaving

→ G 33

2 In a department store

Lisa is in a department store. Terry calls her.

Example:

Terry: Hi, Lisa. Where are you?
Lisa: I'm in the department store.
I'm [looking for] a [sweatshirt] now.

sweatshirt • bags • a computer game • a magazine • TV • a present for my …

playing • buying • looking for • trying on • looking at • watching

76 seventy-six

Figure 41: Example of a grammar introduction (here: present progressive) in a recent textbook (taken from Haß 2006b: 76f)

What's happening? | Language 2 | 5

3 New forms

Write these sentences with the right forms.

1. Wow! You (buy) a lot of things in this shop.
2. I (look) for a special present.
3. The bus (leave) now.
4. They (run) to the bus stop.
5. She (put) the things in her bag now.
6. The department store (close) now.

GRAMMAR

buy + ing → buying
dance + ing → dancing
run + n + ing → running

→ G34

4 In town

Example: Lisa and Emma aren't playing football in the sports shop.

Lisa and Emma The shop assistant Terry	**isn't** **aren't**	playing football in the sports shop. playing a computer game. buying a TV. talking on a mobile. writing an e-mail.

→ G33

5 What are they doing?

a) *Look at the pictures on page 76. Ask and answer questions about the pictures.*

Examples:

Lisa and Emma – look for Sam now? → **Are** Lisa and Emma **looking** for Sam now? – No, they **aren't**.

the bus – leave now? → **Is** the bus **leaving** now? – Yes, it **is**.

1. Emma • buy a T-shirt for Sam?
2. the girls • look at books?
3. Terry • buy shoes?
4. Terry and Lisa • leave the store?
5. Emma • still read the cards?
6. the friends • go to the CD shop?

→ G35

✱ b) *Make more questions about the pictures for your partner.*

⟨ ⟩ 6 A game: What are you doing?

What are you doing? Can the others guess?

A: What am I doing?
B: Are you playing basketball?
A: No, I'm not.
C: Are you dancing?
A: Yes, I am.

seventy-seven 77

our section on TBLT in Chapter 12 we put forward the view that a task-based approach that offers learning arrangements provides the learners with vast opportunities of implicit learning of grammar structures. Exercises like the ones in the example from the textbook form the weakest part of the task continuum (cf. figure 34 in Chapter 12). These exercises address the explicit learning of grammar and thus rather contribute to the growth of declarative knowledge by the learners. How easily this knowledge can be transferred into procedural knowledge without any work on more open tasks is subject to various factors.

Another problem with the presentation of grammar structures in textbooks is that the presentation of structures in isolation without authentic backgrounds is hardly learner-oriented. This may be counter-productive for the learners' motivation to deal with those structures. Why should a learner want to learn how to produce sentences like the ones in the exercises? As there is neither any relevant information gap that the learners might close to by doing the exercise nor a communicative need to use those structures teachers ought not be surprised if their learners do not feel the need to work on those exercises. With only a few "tricks" the teacher can transfer exercises like the ones presented in the textbook and create more learner-centred approaches that "force" the learners into using the present progressive structure in a task.

Ziégesars' model

In another approach to grammar teaching Ziégesar & Ziégesar (2009) suggest the following phases to introduce new grammatical structures:

1. Demonstration (→ "don't talk about language, use it")
2. Understanding & Reacting (→ "provide additional input")
3. Reproduction (→ "learners reproduce sample structures and may make mistakes")
4. Clarification & Focusing (→ "explicitly clarify the rule")
5. Production (→ "use the new structure productively")

In their acquisition-based model, Ziégesar & Ziégesar suggest that the target structure must be presented in a communicative context which is absolutely typical for the use of the structure. The examples provided for the use of the target structure should address the various learner and learning types. In contrast to TBLT approaches the next phase then offers learning opportunities that only focus on the target structure and ask the learners

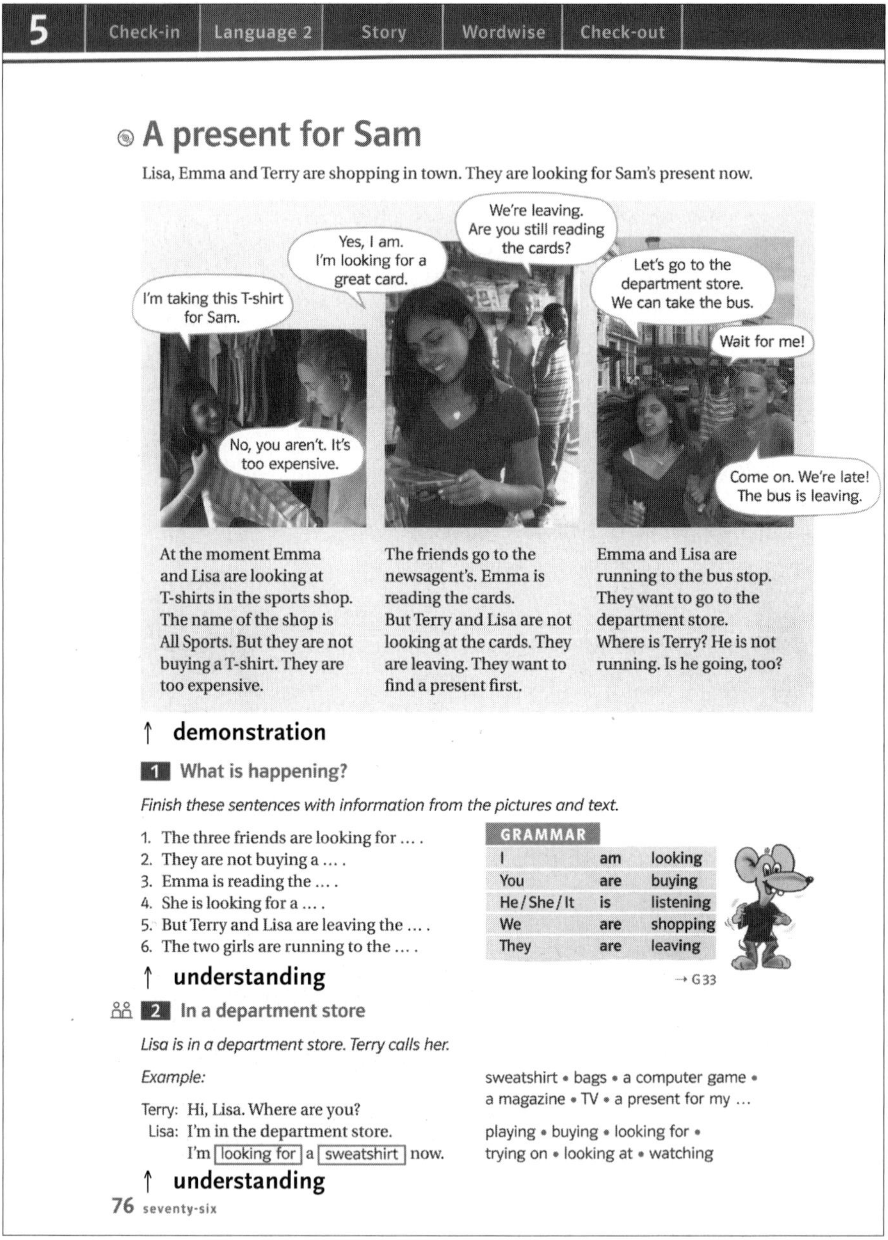

5 | Check-in | Language 2 | Story | Wordwise | Check-out

A present for Sam

Lisa, Emma and Terry are shopping in town. They are looking for Sam's present now.

At the moment Emma and Lisa are looking at T-shirts in the sports shop. The name of the shop is All Sports. But they are not buying a T-shirt. They are too expensive.

The friends go to the newsagent's. Emma is reading the cards. But Terry and Lisa are not looking at the cards. They are leaving. They want to find a present first.

Emma and Lisa are running to the bus stop. They want to go to the department store. Where is Terry? He is not running. Is he going, too?

↑ **demonstration**

1 What is happening?

Finish these sentences with information from the pictures and text.

1. The three friends are looking for … .
2. They are not buying a … .
3. Emma is reading the … .
4. She is looking for a … .
5. But Terry and Lisa are leaving the … .
6. The two girls are running to the … .

GRAMMAR		
I	am	looking
You	are	buying
He / She / It	is	listening
We	are	shopping
They	are	leaving

→ G33

↑ **understanding**

2 In a department store

Lisa is in a department store. Terry calls her.

Example:

Terry: Hi, Lisa. Where are you?
Lisa: I'm in the department store.
I'm [looking for] a [sweatshirt] now.

sweatshirt • bags • a computer game • a magazine • TV • a present for my …

playing • buying • looking for • trying on • looking at • watching

↑ **understanding**

76 seventy-six

Figure 42: Ziégesars' model applied to the textbook (illustration by Schuldt & Schröter 2009)

What's happening? | Language 2 | 5

3 New forms

Write these sentences with the right forms.

1. Wow! You (buy) a lot of things in this shop.
2. I (look) for a special present.
3. The bus (leave) now.
4. They (run) to the bus stop.
5. She (put) the things in her bag now.
6. The department store (close) now.

GRAMMAR

buy + ing → buying
dance + ing → dancing
run + n + ing → running

→ G34

↑ reproduction

4 In town

Example: Lisa and Emma aren't playing football in the sports shop.

Lisa and Emma The shop assistant Terry	+	isn't aren't	+	playing football in the sports shop. playing a computer game. buying a TV. talking on a mobile. writing an e-mail.

→ G33

↑ clarification ↓

5 What are they doing?

a) *Look at the pictures on page 76. Ask and answer questions about the pictures.*

Examples:

Lisa and Emma – look for Sam now? → **Are** Lisa and Emma **looking** for Sam now? – No, they **aren't**.

the bus – leave now? → **Is** the bus **leaving** now? – Yes, it **is**.

1. Emma • buy a T-shirt for Sam?
2. the girls • look at books?
3. Terry • buy shoes?
4. Terry and Lisa • leave the store?
5. Emma • still read the cards?
6. the friends • go to the CD shop?

→ G35

* b) *Make more questions about the pictures for your partner.*

⟨ ⟩ 6 A game: What are you doing?

What are you doing? Can the others guess?

A: What am I doing?
B: Are you playing basketball?
A: No, I'm not.
C: Are you dancing?
A: Yes, I am.

↑ production

seventy-seven 77

only to reproduce the structure. The underlying idea of this phase is that the learners first ought to internalize both form and function of the structure before they start using it in a productive way.

Although this approach wrongly implies that – in general – any grammatical structure can be learned at any time, this approach to grammar teaching may be successful if the learners are ready to acquire the structure in question. This approach is to be found in many current textbooks and can also be applied to the sample pages illustrated in figure 41. Applied to the sample of present progressive, we find all the above phases in the textbook. Figure 40 illustrates how the Ziégesars' model is applied to the textbook. Whether the model has actually been fully applied to the textbook and supports communicative grammar learning may be decided by the reader.

We acknowledge that the Ziégesars' model has been quite influential. As can be seen from figure 42 it has been a role model for current textbooks. We certainly do not dismiss the model completely. However, it must be realised that even the best model will not support implicit grammar learning if it does not take into account that foreign language acquisition happens along a developmental path (i.e. some grammatical structures are the prerequisite of the next structures within the developmental hierarchy).

We have discussed some of the limitations of textbooks in terms of grammar teaching. This does not imply, however, that we reject textbooks all together. Clearly, textbooks are the most important and well established foundation of instructed foreign language teaching. Nevertheless, if textbooks provided more authentic language learning tasks grammar and its teaching would become easier and more beneficial for both teachers and learners. Until more real-world tasks have been incorporated into textbooks teachers might want to invent and include some more of those tasks into their lessons. This is why we will now show how the *Interlanguage Approach* can be practically applied in the foreign language classroom.

Further Reading

Lenzing, A. (2008): "Teachability and Learnability: An Analysis of Primary School Textbooks." In: Keßler, J.-U. (ed.) (2008); pp. 221-241.

Kieweg, W. (1996): Alternative Konzepte zur Vermittlung von Grammatik. In: Der fremdsprachliche Unterricht Englisch 25; pp. 4-11.

Ziegésar v., D. & M. v. Ziegésar (2009): Einführung von Grammatik im Englischunterricht/ Materialien und Modelle. Nachdruck der 2. Auflage. München: Oldenbourg.

Study Questions:

1. List some of the limitations of textbooks regarding grammar and its teaching. Choose one those limitations and discuss its relevance for grammar teaching.
2. How can grammar be introduced in a more authentic way?
3. Textbooks are vital for foreign language teaching in many school settings. Think of some ideas of how to use your textbook and yet overcome some of the limitations discussed in this section.

Beyond Course Books – Grammar Learning Tasks

> For teaching purposes, however, [...] tasks have to be designed in a way that puts the learners into a position of having a real communicative need to interact with one another. This means that language learning tasks ought to be designed as focusing a communicative goal but allowing for a certain leeway for the learner to 'choose' a personalized approach to tackling the communicative problem set by the task according to his/her current linguistic abilities.
>
> Keßler (2008b: 302)

In the previous section we have illustrated and discussed some of the limitations of textbooks in terms of grammar teaching. It became clear that instructed grammar learning also needs to cater for the underlying principles of Interlanguage development by the learners. As the foreign language classrooms consist of a rather heterogeneous group of learners on their way to the target language, grammar teaching would have to be adapted to the communicative and linguistic needs of individual learners. From this perspective it would make more sense to look at grammar teaching tasks from a learner's perspective. The learners will have to take the active part in the learning process; as stated above, the teacher's role is rather to be the facilitator of the learning process. This is why in this section we will now take a closer look at tasks that enable individual learners in heterogeneous classrooms to acquire the target language grammar according to their individual state of Interlanguage development. Henceforward, we will address the grammar teaching tasks as grammar learning tasks.

In Chapter 12 we introduced TBLT as one promising approach to grammar teaching. In this section we will now apply the TBLT approach to teaching practice and introduce two sample tasks that cater for individual grammar learning within the language classroom. Figure 43 illustrates the rationale of grammar learning tasks as we consider them to be most suitable in an *Interlanguage Approach*.

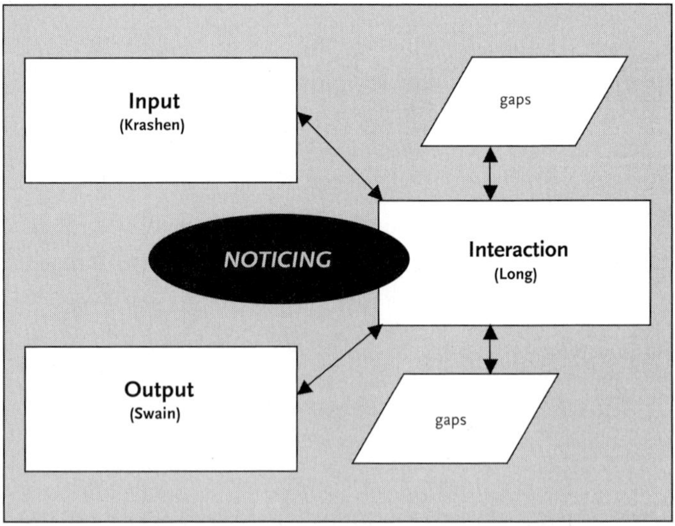

Figure 43: Rationale of Grammar Learning Tasks: The Role of Gaps in TBLT

As can be seen in figure 43 a variety of factors contribute to grammar learning tasks. Based on the concept of noticing (cf. Chapter 11), grammar learning tasks as put forward in this chapter draw from the Interaction Hypothesis (Long 1985, 1996). It has been put forward as an alternative to Krashen's Input Hypothesis (Krashen 1982, 1985) and Swain's Output Hypothesis (Swain, 2005). The Interaction Hypothesis claims that interaction between a native speaker and a non-native speaker or between two non-native speakers who are differently advanced in their Interlanguage grammar is most beneficial to foreign language acquisition. This is why we consider the interaction approach particularly useful for heterogeneous classrooms. According to Gass (2003: 234) classroom-based conversation in the target language is not only "a medium of practice but also the means by which learning takes place". Conversation is then the key to negotiation of meaning.

gaps in TBLT

In our rationale of grammar learning tasks gaps play a major role both for interaction as well as for noticing. These gaps have nothing in common with gap-filling exercises that can be found in most textbooks. Gaps in TBLT are meant to be

- information gaps
- opinion gaps
- etc.

These gaps between two or more interlocutors may occur due to different levels of pre-knowledge on the part of the learners, different amounts of information that the learners have, different individual experiences, opinions, or cultural backgrounds. Once, any of the gaps mentioned above have been established in the language classroom they create an authentic need for negotiation of meaning. If the teacher develops and manipulates grammar learning tasks in such a way that two or more learners with differently developed Interlanguage have to communicate in order to close the gaps, active language use happens automatically as a by-product of the negotiation process.

In Chapter 12 we explained the task cycle. According to Willis (1996) tasks organised in such a way would consist of components such as "pre-task", "task cycle" and "language focus. Figure 44 is taken from Willis (1996: 38) and summarises the underlying concepts for each of those components.

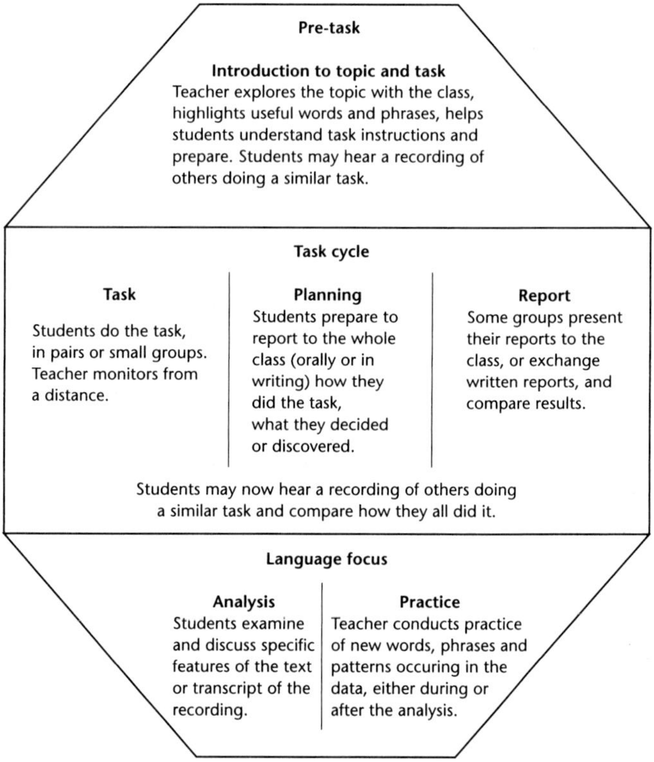

Figure 44: Task-based language learning (Willis 1996: 38)

Let us now look at two examples of grammar learning tasks from the EFL classroom. The first example has been introduced as the *Bike Task* (Keßler 2005 and 2008b) and can be administered in lower intermediate EFL classrooms. The second example is taken from Keßler & Liebner (in press) and combines media-based and task-based language learning in upper intermediate EFL classrooms. We have decided to use these two examples for the purpose of this book because both tasks have been administered and tested in various classrooms. Further examples can be found in Duran & Ramaut (2006) for primary school classrooms, in Van Gorp et al. (2006) and Keßler (2006a) for secondary school classrooms, and in Bogaert et al. (2006) for CLIL classrooms.

Example: Bike Task

The Bike Task (Keßler 2008b)

The task in our first example has been designed to create opportunities for authentic and meaningful language use. The goal of this extended 'spot-the-difference' task is twofold: first it aims at supporting the learners' communicative competence by providing them with a topic that is closely related to their everyday lives. Second, by focusing on those linguistic forms that have been identified in the profile analysis with Rapid Profile as the ones the learners are developmentally ready to acquire, tasks like this enable learners and teachers to enhance instructed Interlanguage development.

Pre-task activities: Providing the necessary vocabulary

Before the actual task can be administered the teacher as input provider has to make sure the learners are familiar with the word field of biking (cf. figure 44: pre-task activity). EFL methodology provides a variety of possible approaches to ensure that the learners are familiar with the vocabulary needed to perform the actual task. I would like to introduce a procedure that could be summarised as a Think – Pair – (Square) – Share activity: in the first step [Think] the individual learners have to work on a bike word search (see figure 45).

Bike – Word Search

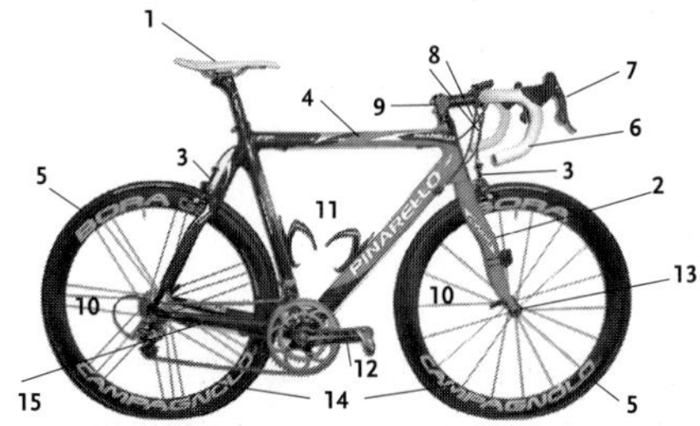

Please use your picture dictionary and name (at least) eight parts of the bike. Use the numbers from the picture:

1 saddle
2
3
4 frame
5 wheels + tyres
6
7 brakes
8 shifters
9 handlebars
10
11
12 pedals
13
14 ~~ventil~~ valve
15 derailleurs

word, words, words

This learner has just named nine parts of the bike during the *Think* phase. By doing so he fulfilled the assignment on the worksheet. Quicker learners might have named more parts during the same time. This approach of asking a reasonable minimum of words to be found caters for the heterogenous setting of the EFL classroom which can even be found in selective high schools. During the pair- and share phase this learner can complete his list before working on the actual bike task.

Figure 45: Bike Word Search and Picture Dictionary (taken from Keßler 2008b: 303)

Interaction & Negotiation of meaning

This is the silent phase of the pre-task activity when the learners can use a picture dictionary to find as many bike words as possible. To encourage self-directed learning in the EFL classroom the second phase of the pre-task work is to compare and discuss the individual worksheets with a classmate. During this [Pair] phase of the activity the learners can complete their own worksheet with more bike words. Now two learners can interact and a first negotiation of meaning can take place in discussing different solutions for the same missing word. In figure 45 (word # 14) the learner first used the German word "Ventil" and was corrected by his partner who had used an additional dictionary. This is one example of how learner interaction and negotiation of meaning can trigger foreign language use among learners in the classroom. If there is

Spot the Difference: Partner A

Look at your picture. Your partner has got a similar picture but there are some differences in the two pictures. Please ask questions about your partner's picture. Find out as many differences as you can.

Words:

______________________ __________

______________________ __________

______________________ __________

Differences:

______________________ __________

______________________ __________

______________________ __________

Spot the Difference: Partner B

Look at your picture. Your partner has got a similar picture but there are some differences in the two pictures. Please ask questions about your partner's picture. Find out as many differences as you can.

Words:

______________________ __________

______________________ __________

______________________ __________

Differences:

______________________ __________

______________________ __________

______________________ __________

Figure 46: The bike task – worksheets for learners (taken from Keßler 2008b: 304)

further need for small group interaction on the bike words two pairs can form a [Square] and again discuss and maybe complete their own lists. As this phase is optional within the activity and can be skipped we put "Square" in brackets when introducing this pre-task activity. The last part of this activity is the [Share] phase where all learners get another chance to compare and discuss their own worksheet with the rest of the class and may fill in remaining gaps.

After a sound lexical basis has been established through this pre-task activity the class can then move on to the actual task (cf. figure 46). This task has been set up as a 'spot-the-difference' task, which can eventually be extended to an opinion gap task once the learners have found the differences by asking their partners questions in order to find out as many differences between the two bike pictures as possible. Before the learners proceed to the opinion gap tasks where they are asked to discuss their personal experience with biking (post-task activities, cf. figure 44), however, they have to produce a whole range of questions about their partner's bike picture (cf. figure 46).

Interlanguage development

At earlier Stages of this book (Chapters 5 and 6) we explained that question formation by learners plays a major role in Interlanguage development. The learners can ask their questions according to their individual current state of Interlanguage grammar:

Stage 2: SVO-?	Your bike has (a) basket on the carrier?
Stage 3: Wh/Do/Aux-SVO?	Where the helmet is?
Stage 4: (Wh)Copula S(x)	Is there a lock on your bike?/What colour is your bike?
Stage 5: Aux-2nd-?	What does the background of your picture look like ?
Stage 6: Cancel Aux-2nd	I wonder where the helmet is.

A task design for the EFL classroom as introduced here focuses on a whole cluster of features (namely question formation according to the learners' developmental readiness) rather than focusing on a particular structure (e.g. questions with do-fronting). This is in line with Skehan's (1998: 130) claim that the "power of internal processing factors is simply too strong" to allow teachers to focus on any particular structure. This refers to the learnability problem (cf. Pienemann, 1989) as also discussed in Ellis (2003). Though both Skehan (1998) and Ellis (2003) acknowledge the necessity of "some method for keeping track of

Interlanguage development" (Ellis, 2003: 231) they do not explain, what such a method could look like. Rapid Profile, as introduced in Chapter 15 of this book offers a feasible solution to this problem (Keßler 2006; Keßler & Keatinge 2008).

Obviously it would be far too restricted to limit the scope of the tasks administered for language learning to focusing on a single linguistic structure. This is why the task-as-workplan (Seedhouse 2005; also see chapter 12) for the EFL classroom addresses question formation in general and thus allows for a cluster of features (cf. Skehan, 1998) to be taken into consideration.

post-task

After the differences have successfully been spotted the learners can proceed to the next Stage of the diagnostic task circle (cf. figure 44: post-task activity). This is the Stage that goes beyond question formation and focuses on further negotiation of meaning and communication. To indicate the start of the next task Stage the class listens to a song by the rock group Queen (Bicycle Race). Playing this song in the classroom not only provides some authentic (language) material and can be used as an excellent listening comprehension exercise, but can also introduce a discussion on what the learners in this particular classroom use their bikes for in their free time.

Discussing the various ideas of how to use a bike that derive from the learners' personal experience allows for considerable learner interaction and meaningful language production which opens further opportunities for negotiation of meaning and thus goes beyond addressing the learners' linguistic needs alone. This post-task Stage addresses the learners' communicative needs as it focuses on meaning rather than form and leaves leeway for open discussions. Here learners can discuss what they use their bikes for and what their own bikes look like.

Media in the EFL Classroom – Grammar Learning Tasks

> In conclusion, podcasts meet the need for oral activities that are often otherwise neglected in the EFL classroom. Teachers may not realize that using podcasts actively can start in a low risk way that can be developed further if students show an interest. [...] podcasts offer the pedagogical potential for varying degrees of involvement in interaction and proffer student engagement that promotes effective and deep learning according to currently accepted cognitive theories.
>
> Fox (2008, taken from website)

podcasts and grammar learning tasks: Killing Mr Griffin

The following example shows how literature, TBLT and new media can work together and create learning-centred opportunities for grammar teaching. The original idea of this task-based and media-based approach to the EFL classroom was introduced by Keßler & Liebner (2009 and in press). The goal of this task is twofold: first, tasks are administered to summarize and discuss a novel read in class. In a second step tasks are provided that help the teacher to diagnose the learners' individual current state of Interlanguage development. Once the teacher knows about the individual learners' developmental readiness s/he can administer various tasks that focus on question formation as well as third-person singular-s-structures. The basic advantage of this set of (diagnostic) tasks is that the learners can produce spontaneous oral speech samples as podcasts at home and upload them onto an intranet or internet platform. At a later Stage the teacher then can download the learners' products whenever s/he has time to do so and go back to each of his/her learners' speech production. Additionally, the learners can also listen to their classmates' audio-samples and replay them in order to discuss their content in more detail.

In this section we would like to exemplify how easily traditional approaches to literature teaching can be well combined with TBLT and lead into a media-supported new learning situation that contributes to grammar learning in a rather implicit way. "The class (year 9) has read the novel "Killing Mr Griffin" by Lois Duncan. Figure 47 provides a short summary of the plot; actually this summary is taken from one of the learners' podcasts after it was discussed in the EFL classroom.

Lois Duncan: Killing Mr Griffin

Brian Griffin is a strict and proper high school English teacher who is extremely tough on students His students want revenge, so a group of them decide to kidnap him. Mark and his friends, David, Jeff and Betsy decide to kidnap Mr. Griffin and "teach him a lesson."

Susan is a good student in Mr. Griffin's class. She engages him in conversation and walks with him to the school parking lot, where Mark, David, and Jeff kidnap Griffin. They drive him to a secret place in the mountains and Mark abandons him there, blindfolded and bound. When Susan and David return to check up on Mr. Griffin, they find him dead. They learn that Mr. Griffin had a heart problem. Usually, he would have taken a pill to deal with the condition, but was unable to, being bound and having his pills destroyed by his captors, who did not know what they were for.

The conspiracy unravels, and the police are contacted, with all of those involved other than Susan facing varying degrees of criminal charges. The novel ends with Susan's family telling her that Mark should be blamed for manipulating her along with the other students, because he is psychopathic.

Figure 47: Short summary of the plot of "Killing Mr. Griffin"

At first sight the whole teaching unit did not deal with grammar teaching at all. The entire focus was on reading and discussing the novel. Only after the novel had been read and discussed in the classroom did the teacher introduce the idea of podcasts to the class. First of all he explained how podcasts can be produced, recorded and uploaded onto the intranet platform. Figure 48 shows part of the worksheet of that session.

How to produce Your Own Podcasts

1. Find informations on **Podcasts**. Be able to give a definition and tell your classmates why they have become famous.

2. Go to the following websites and download *Audacity* and *Podcaster*. Make sure that you download the correct version for your operating system. *Audacity* allows you to record your Podcasts. *Podcaster* will help to publish them.
   - http://audacity.sourceforge.net/download/
   - http://www.kudlian.net/products/podcaster/download

Figure 48: Worksheet: How to Produce your own Podcast

pre-task

Once the learners were familiar with the production of their own podcasts the actual pre-task activity was initiated. As the focus of the (implicit) grammar learning unit was on question formation along the Interlanguage continuum introduced in part III of this book, the learners were asked to work on an activity where they had to use their understanding of the novel in a creative way. The idea of this pre-task was to identify with one of the protagonists more deeply and to think of how the storyline could have continued. This activity also prepared the learners for the main task where they then had to play a police interview. During this interview, two police officers had to question two of the subjects who were isolated from each other so that the police could establish any contradictions in their alibis. Figure 49 shows the worksheet of the pre-task activity.

Killing Mr. Griffin – What happened afterward?

Activity 1

- You have read Lois Duncan's "Killing Mr. Griffin". The ending of the story was quite abrupt. We still do not know how the students were punished. Here is how the story might go on:
  A few days after the police arrested the students Susan and David are interviewed by the police.

Now it's your turn.

Decide who is going to be Susan, David, Detective Baca and Detective Robinson.
Pick your role card and take ten minutes of preparation time. Try to find a solution for your situation.
Do not take notes in advance or look at the other role cards.

Figure 49: Worksheet: Pre-task activity – preparing for spontaneous speech production

The reason why the learners were asked not to take any notes or look at the other role cards was that after they had prepared their ideas on their role they would be asked to act out and record the alibis or the questions that the police officers had prepared for the questioning in a spontaneous way. This spontaneous speech production can either be used as a basis for a diagnostic linguistic profile (see Chapter 15 – *Rapid Profile* for details) or just as the basis for the main task.

main task

In the main task the learners had to act out the questioning itself. Here the main focus was on question formation. The police officers had to ask their questions to the suspects in order to find out whether the alibis were true or not. This phase included a differentiated approach to a heterogeneous classroom: those learners who either were more familiar with question formation or those who needed more practice in asking questions were asked to play one of the police officers, while the other learners were asked to react to the questions asked by those officers. Again, because of the spontaneous speech production the results of the podcasts could either be used for further diagnostic purposes or simply as additional practice time in the classroom. In both cases the learners had to produce a whole range of questions. This phase of the teaching unit contributed first of all to an increase in speaking time for each learner and secondly it provided a well-grounded training area for implicit grammar learning. Figure 50 illustrates what the worksheet for the main task looked like.

Killing Mr. Griffin – What happened afterwards?

2. Now press the record button and record your scene as a *Podcast*.

   Make sure that you have two rooms, one for Detective Baca and David and the other one for Detective Robinson and Susan.

   As in a real crime investigation Susan and David are not allowed to talk to each other after the interviews.

3. After that, please record two more Podcasts:

   David and Susan have the chance to talk about the police interviews and they want to find out about the other person's interview. Please record the conversation.

   The detectives have the task to find out whether Susan and David told the truth. Please record a conversation between the two detectives about the interviews.

Please upload your *Podcasts* to our platform.

Figure 50: Worksheet: Main task – asking and recording questions

As can be seen from figure 50, after the main task was completed two more tasks were administered to the learners; both aimed at a deeper understanding of the novel as well as a creative elaboration of pupils' own ideas and possible alterations of the learners' attitudes towards the protagonists and the plot of the book.

The last two podcasts also served a more communicative purpose for the whole class. While the previous podcasts were mainly utilized to record spontaneous learner speech for diagnostic purposes as well as individual feedback for the learners the last set of podcasts was aimed at presenting them to the whole class. Now the learners had to present and discuss their ideas before the whole class. This step deepened the discussion and provided a basis for authentic criticism of the quality both of media production and content matters by all the learners in the classroom.

post-task activity

The post-task activity led to a process of creative writing and a contribution to further media literacy by the learners. Now they were asked to think of actors who they would think most suitable to play the characters from the novel. The idea behind this task was not only to find a motivating approach to post reading/ post-task activities but also to change the medium of instruction as well as the language skill. Now the learners had to write a script for a possible cast of a movie based on the novel (cf. figure 51). They were allowed to use the internet as their resource. By searching the web for suitable actors the learners not only practised their media skills but also their critical thinking skill when they had to decide which websites to visit. By transferring the information from the websites into their own coherent text the learners changed their perspective towards the protagonists and the novel and by explaining the reasons for their choice of cast in writing, again implicitly, they also trained their grammar knowledge. Additionally, the texts created by the learners instigated a new round of classroom discussion that lead into the next round of feedback both from fellow learners as well as from the teacher. This feedback related to both content and grammar issues.

Betsy: Lucy Griffith

Because I think, that she could play a person, who is a bit nasty. Betsy doesn't hav a problem with Mark's plan at all, and she doesn't matter when Mr. Griffin dies. I think it isn't an easy role, but Lucy Griffith could do it. Also I imagined that Betsy had brown hair and well, in my Imagination it was her I saw, when I thought about Betsy.

Jeff Garett: Jackson Rathbone

I think he looks like a basketball player an Jeff is one. He is very tall and well – he is Jeff Garett

Brian Griffin: George Clooney

I think it's really hard to find a good actor for Mr. Griffin. Maybe George Clooney doesn't look like a strict teacher with heart-problems, but he could do it, I'm sure. It depends of his acting talent, and I think he has a big one.

Figure 51: Example of the Writing task (uncorrected pupil's work)

Teaching Unit 2: Podcasts and Grammar Learning Tasks – Killing Mr. Griffin

Teaching Unit

Topic:	Killing Mr. Griffin – Grammar Learning Tasks
Aims:	podcasting, researching, presenting, discussing, integrated skills
Level:	from grade 8
Time:	four 45-minute lessons

Procedure:	• 1st lesson: introduction, podcasting, extended discussion of the novel (→ pre-task) • 2nd and 3rd lesson: creating interviews and recording alibis and police quesionings (→ task cycle, part I) • 4th lesson: FonF: (individual) feedback on question formation and other structures needed during the task cycle (→ language focus) • 5th and 6th lesson: follow-up podcasts and creative writing activities: presentation of podcasts in the classroom; discussion of various solutions of the interviews; writing a script (→ task cycle, part II)
Materials:	• Novel "Killing Mr. Griffin" • Podcasting software/recorders (e.g. mobile phones) • Worksheets/Role Cards • related websites • projector for class discussions
Internet links	http://audacity.sourceforge.net/download/ (Podcasting) http://www.kudlian.net/products/podcaster/download/ (Podcasting) http://www.imdb.com/title/tt0119461/ (Killing Mr. Griffin) http://loisduncan.arquettes.com/ (Lois Duncan)

Summary

In this section we illustrated and exemplified how grammar learning tasks can easily be created and administered by the teacher in the foreign language classroom. Our aim was to prove that it is the interaction both between different learners and between the teacher and the learners that supports grammar learning in an activity-based way. This approach goes far beyond the historical approaches to grammar teaching (cf. Chapter 3) and even the rather traditional presentations of grammatical structures in recent textbooks. The merits of tackling grammar in a way such as the one discussed in this section is that grammar does not play the main role during the lessons. Grammar is rather introduced and practised implicitly, "hidden" by plenty of communicative activities in the foreign language classroom. Nevertheless, a teaching framework like this allows for occasional and well-grounded presentations of Focus on Form (cf. Chapter 11) with the purpose of enhancing and fostering the grammatical (Interlanguage) development of all the learners in the heterogeneous classroom.

Further Reading:

Fox, A. (2008): "Using Podcasts in the EFL Classroom." In: TESL-EJ Volume 11/4 (http://tesl-ej.org/ej44/a4.html, 16/03/2010).

Keßler, J.-U. (2008b): "Communicative Tasks and Second Language Profiling: Linguistic and Pedagogical Implications." In: Eckerth, J. & S. Siepmann (eds) (2008): pp. 291-310.

Keßler, J.-U. & M. Liebner (im Druck): „Medienbasierte Lernstandsdiagnostik und individuelle Lernerförderung – Neokommunikativer Fremdsprachenunterrich in heterogenen Lerngruppen." In: Reinfried, M. & L. Volkmann (Hrsg.): Medien im neokommunikativen Fremdsprachenunterricht. Einsatzformen, Inhalte, Lernerkompetenzen. Frankfurt und New York: Peter Lang.

Lenzing, A. (2008): "Teachability and Learnability: An Analysis of Primary School Textbooks." In: Keßler, J.-U. (ed.) (2008); pp. 221-241.

Willis, J. & D. Willis (eds.) (1996): Challenge and Change in Language Teaching. Oxford: Heinemann.

Study Questions:

1. Look at the quotation by Lenzing (2008) at the beginning of this chapter. Do you think a sequenced curriculum is feasible for classroom practice? Make a list of pros and cons for a sequenced curriculum in grammar teaching. What might such a curriculum look like?
2. Look at the quotation by Fox (2008) at the beginning of this section. In what way do podcasts offer "the pedagogical potential for varying degrees of involvement in interaction and proffer student engagement that promotes effective and deep learning according to currently accepted cognitive theories"?
3. Why would it make more sense to speak about grammar learning tasks rather than grammar teaching tasks?
4. Design your own grammar learning task and explain its rationale to your fellow students.
5. Discuss how grammar learning tasks can be implemented into everyday work in the EFL classroom.

15 Diagnosing Learner Progress

> Every language educator who has ever attempted to measure a student's communicative language ability has wondered: 'what exactly does a student need to "know" in terms of grammar to be able to use it well enough for some real-world purpose?'
>
> Purpura (2004: 51)

So far we have looked at grammar from various perspectives. We first have discussed what "grammar" is and why it is rather difficult to define. This led us to investigate several kinds of grammars. After a short summary of some historical approaches to grammar teaching we turned to SLA theory and discussed in more detail how knowing about SLA contributes to more professional grammar teaching. We demonstrated that teachers who know about basic concepts of SLA can support their learners in acquiring the target language and its grammar in the foreign language classroom.

In chapters 7 and 12 of this book we illustrated how a combination of theoretical foundations on the one hand and language pedagogy on the other hand can address the communicative as well as the linguistic needs of learners. In the previous chapter, we investigated how textbooks can support or impede grammar learning in instruction. Now we will turn to another essential aspect of instructed foreign language learning. Whenever teachers teach they want to know how successful their teaching is. In other words, language learners are tested in various ways for a number of reasons. This accounts also for the communicative classroom. As Purpura (2004) put it (cf. quotation above) without at least some grammar knowledge the learner would not be in a position to utilize his/her language skills to communicate successfully in real-world tasks.

This is why in this last chapter of our book we will now address some "fundamental considerations in language testing" (Bachman 1990). First of all it needs to be clear to teachers what exactly they want to diagnose when assessing learners' progress in grammar learning. Purpura (2004: 5ff) distinguishes various "notions of 'grammar' for assessment. He lists the following per-

different notions of grammar

spectives which all imply a slightly different approach towards grammar:

1. Grammar and linguistics (formal grammar)
2. Form-based perspectives of language
3. Form- and use-based perspectives of language
4. Communication-based perspectives of language

Depending on which perspective is taken in the foreign language classroom, different measures need to be applied in terms of assessing grammatical knowledge. In this chapter we will take a closer look at why and how grammatical knowledge in classroom-based acquisition should be assessed. In this chapter, two alternative approaches to assessing grammatical knowledge will be discussed. First we will briefly illustrate one of the most common approaches to grammar assessment, namely proficiency testing (Chapter 15.1). Here, the main emphasis will be laid on discussing the Common European Framework of Reference (CEFR). The chapter will then be concluded by the introduction and discussion of an alternative diagnostic approach that is in line with the *Interlanguage Approach* as taken throughout this book. Profile analyses form an SLA-based alternative to proficiency testing (Chapter 15.2). It will become clear that these two approaches are not – as one might think at first sight – in competition with one another but are essentially complementary approaches.

scope-precision dilemma

Let us first briefly look at a more general issue concerning the assessment of grammatical knowledge. Whenever one wants to assess grammatical knowledge one has to decide what exactly one wants to look at. There are plenty of approaches to language testing and assessment (cf. Bachman 1990, Hughes 2006). As they aim at different perspectives of grammar as well as different skills acquired by the learners they should rather been seen as complementary approaches. Figure 52 illustrates what Pienemann & Keßler (2007) have introduced as the scope-precision dilemma in any L2 measurement:

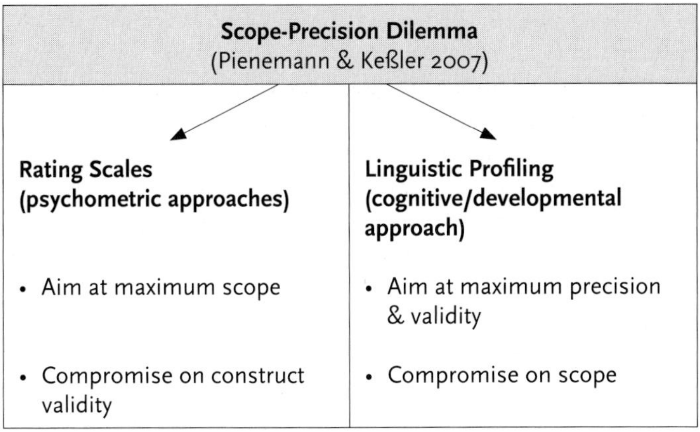

Figure 52: Scope-Precision Dilemma in L2 measurement

quality criteria

However, no matter which approach a teacher favours for his/her assessment of grammatical knowledge in the foreign language classroom, any approach must be well-grounded within a theoretical framework. Furthermore, any such approach must meet the basic quality criteria such as validity, reliability and objectivity. It would be beyond the scope of this chapter to discuss those quality criteria in detail. For a full discussion see Hughes (2006), McNamara (2007) or Bachman & Palmer (2008).

Proficiency Testing

In terms of assessing an L2 learner's proficiency, so-called 'rating scales' emerged in the field of proficiency testing throughout the last two decades. Rating scales describe different language ability levels from very basic to advanced proficiency in one or more of the four skills: reading, listening, writing and speaking. These descriptions are usually linked to some kind of communicative goal that is to be achieved or the degree of complexity of language structures which a learner can deal with. To gain a more precise overview of rating scales in proficiency testing, let us first turn to the functions proficiency testing can fulfil and then turn to a well-known rating scale in language assessment, namely the *Common European Framework of Reference.*

key functions of proficiency testing

Brindley (cf. 1998: 15) summarised four key functions, referring to Alderson (1997) and Pollitt and Murray (1996):

1. *user-oriented function:* the primary purpose is to serve as a guideline as to language proficiency for the learners themselves (e.g. the European Language Portfolio)
2. *assessor-oriented function*: the primary purpose is to assess a learner's performance by, e.g. a language instructor.
3. *constructor-oriented function:* the primary purpose is to give feedback about the validity and feasibility of the test itself to the test constructor(s)
4. ***diagnosis-oriented function:*** the primary purpose is to diagnose a learner's current developmental state in order for teachers and learners to know at which point in the developmental process s/he currently is (see chapter 15.2)

As the above functions demonstrate, proficiency testing aims at providing a guideline for curriculum development and at the corresponding structuring of language courses. In this way, it supports teachers in selecting and compiling learner- and learning-oriented instructional and test materials. In fact, language assessment, and thus rating scales provide feedback to each person involved in the field of language learning, i.e. the learners, teachers and further professionals. One such very popular rating scale dedicated to the aims summarised is the Common European Framework of Reference for Languages: Learning, Teaching, Assessment, abbreviated as CEFR. A particular objective of the CEFR is to provide a guideline to describe achievements of learners of foreign languages across Europe. In this concern, the CEFR is a professional tool for setting clear, attainable standards at different levels of language learning for European languages. This allows for standards to be easily comparable at an international level facilitating educational and occupational mobility. The CEFR was adopted by the Council of Europe between 1989 and 1996 when it was planned as the key element of the project "Language Learning for European Citizenship". In November 2001 then, a European Union Council Resolution recommended using the CEFR to set up systems of validation of language ability. The Common European Framework provides a common basis for the elaboration of language syllabuses, curriculum guidelines, examinations, textbooks, etc. across Europe. It describes in a comprehensive way what language learners have to do in order to use

Common European Framework of Reference (CEFR)

a language for communication and what knowledge and skills they have to develop so as to be able to act effectively. The description also covers the cultural context in which language is set. The Framework also defines levels of proficiency which allow learners' progress to be measured at each Stage of learning and on a life-long basis. (CEFR: 1)

The six reference levels (see tables 9 and 10) are becoming widely accepted as the European standard for grading an individual's language proficiency.

C2	*Conveys finer shades of meaning precisely and naturally.* Can express him/herself spontaneously and very fluently, interacting with ease and skill and differentiating finer shades of meaning precisely. Can produce clear, smoothly-flowing, well-structured descriptions.
C1	*Shows fluent, spontaneous expression in clear, well-structured speech.* Can express him/herself fluently and spontaneously, almost effortlessly, with a smooth flow of language. Can give clear, detailed descriptions of complex subjects. High degree of accuracy, errors are rare.
B2+	
B2	*Expresses points of view without noticeable strain.* Can interact o a wide range of topics and produce stretches of language with a fairly even tempo. Can give clear, detailed descriptions on a wide range of subjects related to his/her field of interest. Reasonably accurate use of main repertoire associated with more predictable situations.
B1+	
B1	*Relates comprehensibly the main points he/she wants to make.* Can keep going comprehensibly, even though pausing for grammatical and lexical planning and repair may be very evident. Can link discrete, simple elements into a connected sequence to give straightforward descriptions on a variety of familiar subjects within his/her field of interest. Reasonably accurate use of main repertoire associated with more predictable situations.
A2+	
A2	*Relates basic information on, e.g. work, family, free time etc.* Can communicate in a simple and direct exchange of information on familiar matters. Can make him/herself understood in very short utterances, even though pauses, false starts and reformulation are very evident. Can describe in simple terms family, living conditions, educational background, present or most recent job. Uses some simple structures correctly, but may systematically make basic mistakes.

A1	*Makes simple statements on personal details and very familiar topics.* Can make him/herself understood in a simple way, asking and answering questions about personal details, provided the other person talks slowly and clearly and is prepared to help. Can manage very short, isolated, mainly pre-packaged utterances. Much pausing to search for expressions, to articulate less familiar words.

Table 11: Global oral assessment scale (CEFR) (Council of Europe 2009)

	RANGE	ACCURACY	FLUENCY	INTER-ACTION	COHERENCE
C2	Shows great flexibility reformulating ideas in differing linguistic forma to convey finer shades of meaning precisely, to give emphasis, to differentiate and to eliminate ambiguity. Also has a good command of idiomatic expressions and colloquialisms.	Maintains consistent grammatical control of complex language, even while attention is otherwise engaged (e.g. in forward planning, in monitoring others' reactions).	Can express him/herself spontaneously at length with a natural colloquial flow, avoiding or backtracking around any difficulty so smoothly that the interlocutor is hardly aware of it..	Can interact with ease and skill, picking up and using non-verbal and intonational cues apparently effortlessly. Can interweave his/her contribution into the joined discourse with a fully natural tumtaking, referencing, allusion making etc.	Can create cohesive and coherent discourse making full and appropriate use of a variety of organisational patterns and a wide range of connectors and other cohesive devices.
C1	Has a good command of a broad range of language allowing him/her to select a formulation to express him/her clearly in an appropriate	Consistently contains a high degree of grammatical accuracy; errors are rare, difficult to spot and generally connected when they do occur.	Can express him- or herself fluently and spontaneously, almost effortlessly. Only a conceptually difficult subject can hinder a natu	Can select a suitable phrase from a readily available range of discourse functions to preface his remarks in order to get or to keep the	Can produce clear, smoothly flowing, well-srtuctured speech, showing con trolled use of organisational patterns, connectors

	RANGE	ACCURACY	FLUENCY	INTER-ACTION	COHERENCE
	style on a wide range of general, academic, professional or leisure topics without having to restrict what he/she wants to say.		ral, smooth flow of language	floor and to relate his/her contributions skilfully to those of other speakers.	and cohesive devices.
B2+					
B2	Has a sufficient range of language to be able to give clear descriptions, express viewpoints on most general topics, without much conspicuous searching for words, using some complex sentence forms to do so.	Shows a relatively high degree of grammatical control. Does not make errors which cause misunderstanding, and can correct most of his/her mistakes.	Can produce stretches of language with a fairly even tempo although he/she can be hesitant as he or she searches for patterns and expressions, there are few noticeably long pauses.	Can initiate discourse, take his/her turn when appropriate and end conversation when he/she may not always do this elegantly. Can help the discussion along on familiar ground confirming comprehension, inviting others in, etc.	Can use a limited number of cohesive devices to link his/her utterances into clear, coherent discourse, though there may be some "jumpiness" in a long contribution.
B1+					
B1	Has enough language to get by, with sufficient vocabulary to express him-/herself with some hesitation and cir	Uses reasonably accurately a repertoire of frequently used 'routines' and patterns associated with more	Can keep going comprehensibly, even though pausing for grammatical and lexical planning and repair i	Can initiate, maintain and close simple face-to-face conversation on topics that are familiar or of personal interest. Can	Can link a series of shorter, discrete simple elements into a connected, linear sequence of points.

	RANGE	ACCURACY	FLUENCY	INTER-ACTION	COHERENCE
	cumlocutions on topics such as family, hobbies and interests, work, travel, and current events.	predictable situations.	s evident, especially in longer stretches of free production.	repeat back part of what someone has said to confirm mutual understanding.	
A2+					
A2	Uses basic sentence patterns with memorised phrases, groups of a few words and formulae in order to communicate limited information in simple everyday situations.	Uses some simple structures correctly, but still systematically makes basic mistakes.	Can make him/herself understood in very short utterances , even though pauses, false starts and reformulation are very evident.	Can ask and answer questions and respond to simple statements. Can indicate when he/she is following but is rarely able to understand enough to keep conversation going of his/her own accord.	Can link groups of words with simple connectors like „and, „but", „because".
A1	Has a very basic repertoire of words and simple phrases related to personal details and particular concrete situations.	Shows limited control of a few simple grammatical structures and sentence patterns in a memorised repertoire.	Can manage very short, isolated prepackaged utterances, with much pausing to search for expression, to articulate less familiar words, and to repair communication.	Can ask and answer questions about personal details. Can interact in a simple way, but communication is totally dependent on repetition, rephrasing and repair.	Can link words or groups of words with very basic linear connectors like „and" or „then."

Table 12: Oral assessment criteria grid (CEFR) (Council of Europe 2009)

European Language Portfolio (ELP)

> The development of a European Language Portfolio (ELP) enabling an individual to record and present different aspects of his or her language biography [...] is designed to include not only any officially awarded recognition obtained in the course of learning a particular language but also record of more informal experiences involving contacts with languages and other cultures.
>
> (CEFR 2001: 175)

The European Language Portfolio is a form of self-evaluation which was established by the Council of Europe in the CEFR. The portfolio thus also serves as an assessment tool for implementing the EU language policy in European societies and education that are increasingly becoming plurilingual. The ELP was developed and piloted by the Language Policy Division of the Council of Europe, Strasbourg, between 1998 and 2000.

The ELP is a document in which L2 learners – either naturally acquiring the SLA in a foreign country or being formally instructed at school or any other institution – can record and reflect on their language learning and cultural experiences with the target language speech community(-ies).

ELP: 3 parts

The ELP consists of three parts.

1) The *Europass Language Passport* which the learner updates on a regular basis. A grid is provided where the learner's language competences can be described according to the skills and respective levels as defined in the CEFR scale which is accepted across Europe. This grid can serve as a complement to customary certificates. The passport records formal qualifications and describes language competencies and significant language and intercultural learning experiences; it allows for self-assessment, teacher assessment and assessment by educational institutions and examination boards; it requires that information entered in the passport states on what basis, when and by whom the assessment was carried out.
2) A *Language Biography* which facilitates the learner's involvement in planning, reflecting upon and assessing her/his learn-

ing process and progress; it encourages the learner to state what s/he can do in each language and to include information on linguistic and cultural experiences gained in and outside formal educational contexts; it is organised to promote plurilingualism i.e. the development of competencies in a number of languages.

3) A *Dossier* to select and keep materials to document and illustrate achievements or experiences recorded in the Language Biography or Passport.

(adopted from the Council of Europe 2009)

Portfolio models vary according to countries and educational contexts, but they are all examined by a European Validation Committee. Basically, the European Language Portfolio has to main objectives: a) from a pedagogic viewpoint: documenting one's progress by acknowledging their efforts can motivate learners to extend and diversify their language skills. The inherent reflection of one's learning progress can help to structure future planning of how to become more proficient. Thus, the learner is responsible for her/his progress in the TL and autonomous in planning. b) The value of the record in higher education or a future job: to provide a record of the linguistic and cultural skills can serve as a point of departure when learners are moving to a higher learning level or apply for a job at home or in a foreign country. The holding of such a record makes one's L2 proficiency internationally comparable as it is based on the CEFR.

Some Problems with rating scales

At face value, rating scales are well-defined, hierarchically organised and transparent. As most rating scales, the CEFR scale describes what the test constructors assume learners should be able to do at a particular level rather than that it reflects the learner's current Stage of IL development related to sociocultural abilities. A problem which has been raised frequently in SLA and language testing research, however, is that each level of such a hierarchy has to be clearly spelled-out and refer to particular features that make up 'language proficiency'. That is to say, "for the purpose of measurement the notion 'language' would need to be operationalised at the phonological, lexical, semantic, morphological, syntactic, discourse and interactional level (...)." (Pienemann & Keßler 2007: 247) On the basis of such an operationalised concept of language and its levels as listed by Pienemann and Keßler, one could spell out a 'proficiency hierarchy', as it were. To make a case in point referring to the CEFR, it would be very helpful in terms of validity and comparability to complement the "can-do" descriptive levels ranging from A1 to C2 by referring to particular features from at least some or all of the linguistic levels. As to vocabulary and morphosyntax, for example, it remains rather vague what the following description actually refers to: "shows a relatively high degree of grammatical control.(...) Can initiate, maintain and close simple face-to-face conversation on topics that are familiar or of personal interest. (...) "Has enough language to get by, with sufficient vocabulary to express him/herself with some hesitation and some circumlocutions." (cf. oral assessment criteria grid, level B1, emphasis added). 'Familiar topics' or 'personal interests' may, in fact, vary among each individual speaker and, moreover, among instruction programmes. In instructed SLA, learners are provided with vocabulary pre-selected by the teacher as a result of which the learned words do not necessarily mirror their particular field(s) of interest. Moreover, one of the CEFR's key characteristics is that it can be applied cross-linguistically.

In this concern, Little 2007 and Rimmer 2006 summarise the above sketched issues in pointing to the fat that the CEFR in not being language specific does not provide any detailed information as to which syntactic, morphological or lexical structures[30] should be acquired at a particular level. Despite the lack of an underlying SLA theory, the CEFR clearly has a strong basis as to pragmatics, in particular sociocultural language behaviour. The potential inherent in a clearly spelled-out rating scale is, however, not fully exhausted, since proficiency rating relies on morphosyntax (Pienemann & Keßler 2007), in the first place.

[30] In the meantime the Council of Europe established a long-term collaborative research programme, known as English Profile (English Profile. 13/09/09) which aims at developing a set of Reference Level Descriptions (RLD) for English, which can be used complementary to the CEFR to make the assessment more language specific. These will provide detailed descriptions of the grammar, vocabulary and functions necessary to master language levels

This sketch of problems occurring with rating scales narrows down to one fundamental flaw, namely that scale developers do not always reveal the theoretical basis of their level descriptors or make explicit claims concerning the universality of the developmental phenomena described in the scales" (cf. Brindley 1998: 115) This mainly results from the fact that it is unclear as to how 'language proficiency' and 'IL development' are related. This, in turn, leads to the scope-precision dilemma sketched in VII. Proficiency testing as the CEFR aims at providing a global picture of learner development whereas linguistic profiling aims at providing a precise picture of grammatical development being an essential part of 'linguistic proficiency'. Do these opposing strengths of assessment tools, then, exclude each other?

As will be shown throughout this chapter, this is clearly not the case. The two kinds of linguistic measurement, i.e. rating scales and diagnostic tools, should rather scope or precision. Why not integrate a diagnostic tool of profile analysis (VII.2) in such a framework as the CEFR? Through combining both approaches to linguistic measurement, two basic goals could be achieved (Pienemann & Mackey 1992: 135):

1. A comprehensive [global] assessment of a wide [scope] of components of language in use
2. An [precise] overview of the learner's grammatical development at a particular point in time which, moreover, predicts which grammatical structures will be learnable next.

This complementary analysis of a learner's L2 performance could serve as a guideline for (future) language teachers for developmentally guided form-focused instruction as explained in chapter 11. In the following section we will now spell out one approach to linguistic profiling in more detail.

Profile Analysis

As one can see, communicative tasks play an important role both as a teaching tool in second language pedagogy and as a means of data elicitation in SLA research. Both functions complement each other [...] Interlanguage data yielded by the use of tasks for SLA research can also be used to create valid

> linguistic profiles of the learners. These profiles provide the diagnostic basis for a learner-oriented task based approach to instructed language learning. [...] One of the purposes Rapid Profile has been designed for is to provide teachers with a diagnostic tool that can be applied in formal EFL settings.
>
> (Keßler 2008b: 296f)

Profile analysis is far from being a new approach to diagnosing language progress. It was first introduced by Crystal, Fletcher & Garman (1976) who developed it to analyse language disorders in first language acquisition. Clahsen (1985) developed an approach to profile analysis that catered for the special needs in second language learning. To date, profile analyses are carried out for various second languages, acquired both in natural and in instructed settings (cf. Grieshaber 2006, Keßler, 2006 and 2008b, Pienemann, 2006). In the following section we will focus on Rapid Profile, a recent and well researched shorthand version of profile analyses. Rapid Profile has been tried and tested in various types of schools in Australia and Germany. It has also been utilised as a research tool when large amounts of data had to be scanned for levels of acquisition (cf. Eckerth, Schramm & Tschirner 2009).

Rapid Profile is a computer-assisted procedure for screening speech samples collected from language learners to assess their level of language development as compared to standard patterns in the acquisition of the target language. Based on standard Profile Analysis (Crystal, Fletcher & Garman 1976), Rapid Profile is a shorthand version of this original procedure and was developed by Manfred Pienemann from the suggestions made by Clahsen (1985) and by Pienemann, Johnston & Brindley (1988). Since then, a lot of research has been conducted and invested in making Rapid Profile a strong and applicable tool for online-assessment of learner language and the diagnosis of Interlanguage development.

The current version of Rapid Profile utilises this developmental schedule for English as a second language and compares the structures found in speech samples collected from English L2 learners. The analyst then has to locate the patterns found in the sample within the overall regularities of the standard developmental schedule.

Rapid Profile limits itself to the analysis of a number of well established morpho-syntactic features to be found in EFL learners' Interlanguage (cf. Pienemann 1998). The linguistic features being focused on may not. Immediately resemble the full picture of human language, however, they do in fact reflect far more of what we know of learner language development as a whole than is immediately apparent. This developmental path of learner language has been substantiated by many empirical findings (e.g. Pienemann 1884 and 1998, Johnston 1997, DiBiase 2002, Mansouri & Duffy 2005, Keßler 2006).

The Rationale of Rapid Profile

A learner does not necessarily produce a simplified or pidgin-like variety of the target language and then gradually develop a more standard-like Interlanguage. Based on a corpus of GSL speech production by migrant workers in Germany, the research group ZISA determined a developmental sequence for German as a second language which reflects a processing hierarchy. The acquisition of a new rule requires more complex language processing and causes a qualitative change in the Interlanguage. For this reason, "emergence" rather than the "mastery" of a given structure (Pienemann, Johnston and Brindley 1988) is taken as evidence for a change in the speaker's Interlanguage. A structure does not need to occur in the speech sample with an arbitrary accuracy rate in order to be acquired. Pienemann and Johnston (1987) applied the processing approach to a range of morphosyntactic phenomena in the acquisition of ESL and predicted a developmental sequence for the acquisition of ESL. These studies first of all provided further empirical evidence for the claim there is an implicational and universal processing hierarchy. This hierarchy for the acquisition of ESL also provided the theoretical basis for the construction of an assessment procedure that would resolve the shortcomings of a standard profile analysis, a tool originally developed for the diagnosis of language impairment (cf. Crystal et. al 1976). Based on the notion that fixed Stages exist in language acquisition, the procedure comprises of an interview and a transcription and provides a statistical analysis of the speech sample. Clahsen (1985) adopted this approach for the assessment of German as a second language, claiming that the following requirements for a profile analysis in second language acquisition should be fulfilled:

A. The evaluation of oral speech production should be at the core of an assessment procedure which aims at identifying the general development of the learners Interlanguage
B. The assessment should be based on a representative example of spontaneous speech which is gathered in a natural communicative situation
C. The procedure should attempt to provide a comprehensive description of the learners' Interlanguage
D. The procedure should focus on the evaluation of syntax and morphology.
E. The procedure should grade the linguistic structures used by the learners in terms of the order of acquisition in natural L2 development.

(Clahsen 1985: 286-288)

However, Pienemann (1992: 2-3) points out two main disadvantages of the procedure: "in the original version of profile analysis, as well as that developed by Clahsen (1985), the analyst basically acts as a language acquisition researcher. That is, the analyst collects a speech sample, usually of about 60 minutes, transcribes that sample and analyses it according to certain criteria set out in profile analysis. (...) In real terms, standard profile analysis usually requires speech pathologists to spend 20 – 40 hours on the assessment of one individual, and it is obvious that it is impossible to spend this amount of time on each student in the classroom. Apart from that, profile analysis also requires a very high degree of specialised training in areas which teachers do not normally have expertise."

Hence, there was a potential interest in a procedure that would be more compatible with the needs of practitioners. The idea behind Rapid Profile – to create a "short- hand version of a full profile analysis" (Pienemann, Johnston and Brindley 1988: 233) – was motivated by a number of facts: the programme needed to be easy to understand and easy to use by language teachers and researchers alike and it needed to be highly valid and reliable at the same time. Rapid Profile was developed as a criterion-referenced screening procedure in order to condense the standard profile analysis to a 20 minute interview (cf. Pienemann

1992). Communicative tasks were used to elicit the respective morpho-syntactic structures of the developmental hierarchy and rather than fully transcribing the interview, an observation procedure was developed. The structures produced by the learner were then matched against the developmental schedule. This way, the developmental Stage of Interlanguage could be determined. The first feasibility study (cf. Pienemann, and Johnston 1986, Pienemann, Johnston and Brindley 1988) of the profiling procedure demonstrated a certain reliability of the procedure but also revealed a problematic aspect. Analysts applied an accuracy criterion rather than the "emergence" criterion. The study was nevertheless a starting point for further development and research (cf. Keßler 2007).

Linguistic Profiling using Rapid Profile for ESL Development

The current version of Rapid Profile is based on extensive second language acquisition research in formal and natural environments yielding a specific developmental schedule (see figure 53). Since Rapid Profile is criterion-referenced, it considers both what the learner can do as well as what he cannot do at a given point in the EFL learning process.

To use Rapid Profile in practice, one first needs to collect a speech sample from the informant. For this purpose a communicative task is administered to elicit data that will serve as linguistic indicators of second language development. The speech sample is then coded online with the Rapid Profile software. In order to do this, the analyst simply checks the boxes on the computer interface that mark the developmental feature found in the speech sample. Figure 53 shows the user interface of the Rapid Profile online feedback as produced during the screening procedure. The software stores the information entered by the analyst (including additional lexical information) and calculates – on this basis – the developmental level of the learner. The information is displayed on-line in the feedback screen (cf. figure 53). This online feedback permits the analyst to select appropriate communicative tasks that elicit further developmental features that may have been under-determined in the sample – providing a rich and diverse speech sample.

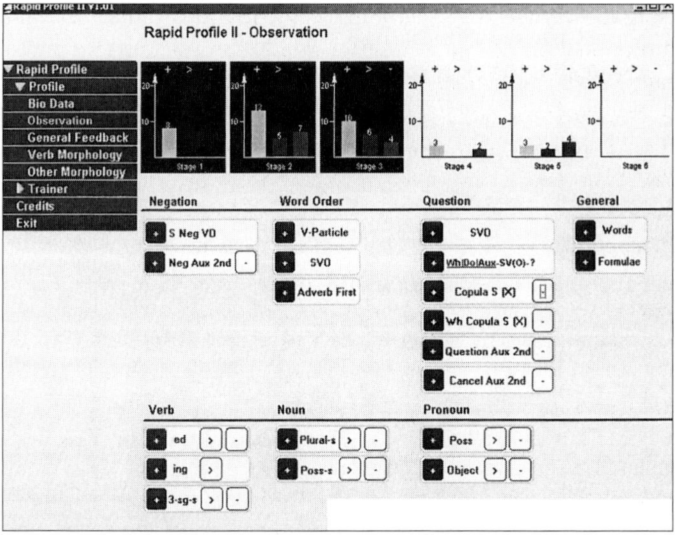

Figure 53: Rapid Profile: online feedback – observation

Various reporting functions allow a more detailed insight into the current state of the learner language. The "General Feedback" (figure 54) distinguishes between syntactic and morphological structures produced by the learner and fed into the programme by the analyst. It can be stored digitally in various formats and can be printed out.

In addition to the two feedback screens shown in figures 53 and 54 Rapid Profile provides two more screens completing the online feedback. These two screens feature the morphological development of the learner language screened by the analyst in more detail. This is particularly important in getting a better understanding of the underlying emergence criterion (Pienemann 1998: 144ff) for morphology.

Within about 15 minutes, the sample collected and analysed using Rapid Profile renders a reliable conclusion about the learner's level of acquisition (Keßler 2006). The analysis provided by the system also allows the user to assess aspects of the lexicon and of variational features.

The developmental profile yielded by this procedure permits the teacher in the EFL classroom to identify developmental features that are learnable at the given point in time. Thus the teacher is able to decide which underlying structures can beneficially be focused on next in what we would like to refer to as a developmentally moderated syllabus (Keßler, 2006 and 2008b).

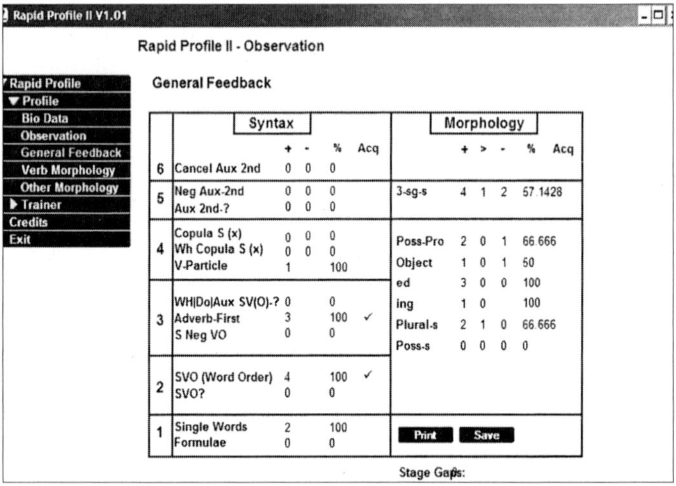

Figure 54: Rapid Profile: general feedback (learner profile)

The feasibility of Rapid Profile in the foreign language classroom

Rapid Profile can diagnose learner language development online. For this, the analyst has to collect the learner's speech samples. These samples have to comprise a sufficiently high data density to validly diagnose the current state of Interlanguage development of the learner in a short span of time.

Keßler (2006) carried out a study to test whether an online-speech sample of approximately 15 minutes really can elicit sufficient relevant data for the analyst to be able to screen the current state of Interlanguage of an EFL learner and furthermore to test whether such speech samples can be used to conduct Rapid Profile online screenings to assess the current state of learner language development. The author collected speech samples from four EFL learners from four different EFL classrooms in three different schools. Two of the learners were about to finish an early start programme at primary school. They had started learning English in formal classroom settings at the age of eight. Their total EFL input was 145 lessons with two lessons per week. The other two learners started learning English at the age of ten and did not have any EFL instruction in primary school. They attended different secondary schools which both followed a more traditional EFL programme. Their total EFL input also was 145 lessons but it had been provided in a more intensive programme of 5 lessons a week. All four learners were taught English by a different teacher. The L1 of all four learners was German.

Two undergraduate students who had undergone the assessor training collected the speech samples from these four learners. Thus, it could be shown that future analysts would not need to be experts in psycholinguistics to be able to conduct the online screening procedure using Rapid Profile.

For this purpose, one of them administered a range of communicative tasks especially designed to elicit linguistic indicators of the current EFL Interlanguage of the learners (cf. Keßler & Kohli 2006). Taking turns, each of the students elicited two speech samples while the other one conducted the Rapid Profile online-screening. The interviews for the data elicitation took an average of 12.5 minutes and ranged between seven and 17 minutes. All interviews were video- and audio-recorded. Each of the interviews was fully transcribed from the recordings. These transcripts were then checked according to the underlying structures needed for the online assessment using Rapid Profile. The data density (Pienemann 1998) in all the interviews proved to be sufficiently high as each interview contained a large variety of underlying structures for each of the Stages reached by the individual learners. On the basis of a full transcript for each of the four learners the traditional linguistic profiling confirmed the current profile of L2-development for all the learners involved. The elicited Stages of acquisition attained by the learners ranged between Stage 1 and Stage 2 (primary school learners) and Stage 4 and an early Stage 5 for the learners who had started learning English at secondary school.

What happens after the diagnosis?

For language teachers it is essential not only to know exactly about their learners' current state of Interlanguage development. In order to support each learner individually according to his/her linguistic and communicative needs, it is also vital to utilize the linguistic profile yielded by Rapid Profile for (individual) treatment in the foreign language classroom. To this end, we would like to suggest extending the task cycle (Willis & Willis 1996) discussed in chapter 12 into a "diagnostic task cycle" (Keßler 2008b). Once the teacher knows about the individual states of Interlanguage development of his/her learners s/he can administer communicative tasks (cf. Chapters 12 and 14) that match the developmental readiness of all the learners in the classroom. Figure 55 provides an outline of the diagnostic task cycle:

Diagnostic Task Cycle

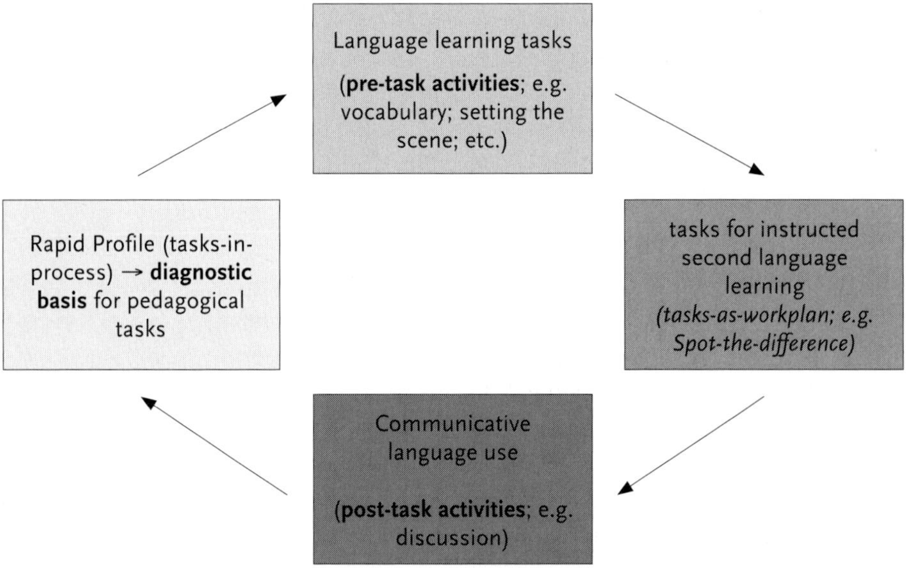

Figure 55: Diagnostic Task Cycle (Keßler 2008b: 301)

Obviously, different learners will then tackle the tasks in different ways according to their individual state of Interlanguage development. If the learners work on a "spot the difference task" the emphasis would be on question formation. In various sections of this book we have explained and discussed the developmental path of question formation (cf. Chapter 6). We have pointed out that question formation develops along the Interlanguage continuum. This continuum contains valid Interlanguage structures for questions that are not target-like. However, they are a necessary step in the learners' Interlanguage development. Here again, it is important that the teacher knows about the different Stages of Interlanguage development as introduced, explained and discussed throughout this book. A teacher who is familiar with both the development as well as the variation of Interlanguage is then in a position to decide effectively which learner errors during the task work need to be addressed and corrected (because they are examples of variational errors) and which ones can rather be neglected (as they are examples of developmental errors). The distinction between those two error types and its relevance for teaching and error correction was discussed in detail in Chapter 9. The two examples for grammar learning tasks in Chapter 14 are also based on this diagnostic task cycle.

complementary: SLA (diagnostic tools) and rating scales

Having presented different approaches to assessment, we will now take a closer look as to how these can be effectively combined and complement each other. SLA can support testers in providing a principled basis for:

- theoretical role: defining acquisition in terms of developmental sequences and Stages
- diagnostic role: selecting grammatical elements that are relevant to each Stage
- curricular role: selecting grammatical elements that need to be assessed

(adapted from Ferrari & Nuzzo 2009)

Comparing the CEFR and Rapid Profile

In a recent study Michalska (2010) compared the inter-rater-reliability as well as the correlation of diagnosing learner progress using the CEFR and Rapid Profile. As can be seen from table 13 her study revealed that both approaches to diagnosing learner progress led – in general – to comparable results.

Partici-pant	CEFR Rater 1	CEFR Rater 2	CEFR Rater 3	CEFR Rater 4	CEFR Levels	RP Rater 1	RP Rater 2	RP PT-Stages
1	B2	B2	B2	B2	B2	5	5	5
2	B2	B2	C1	C1	**B2;C1**	6	6	6
3	B2	B1	B1	B1	**B1;B2**	5	5	5
4	C1	C1	B2	C1	**B2;C1**	5	5	5
5	B1	B1	A2	B1	**A2;B1**	3	3	3
6	B2	B2	B2	B1	**B1;B2**	5	5	5
7	C1	C1	C1	B1	**B1;C1**	5	5	5
8	B1	B2	B1	A2	**A2;B1;B2**	5	5	5
9	B1	B1	B2	B2	**B1;B2**	4	5	**4;5**
10	B2	B1	B1	B1	**B1;B2**	3	3	3
11	A2	A2	A1	A1	**A1;A2**	3	3	3
12	B1	B1	B1	A2	**A2;B1**	4	4	4

Table 13: Results of a comparative study of the CEFR and Rapid Profile (adapted from Michalska, 2010)

However, Rapid Profile scored considerably higher in terms of inter-rater-reliability as only one learner was rated differently by two raters using Rapid Profile as compared to 12 varying ratings conducted by the raters when using the CEFR. Michalska's study supports the point we made in the beginning of this chapter: both diagnostic tools enjoy quite some correlation in their results. This may be due to the fact that even when rating more communicative skills of the learners as aimed at by the CEFR, raters are not completely free of the underlying grammatical structures produced by the learners. This reinforces the case we made for grammar and its teaching throughout this whole book.

Further Reading:

Brindley, G. (1998). "Describing language development?" In Bachman, L. F. & Cohen, A. D. (eds.) *Interfaces between second language acquisition and language testing research*. Cambridge: CUP.

Keßler, J.-U. (2006): *Englischerwerb im Anfangsunterricht diagnostizieren. Linguistische Profilanalysen am Übergang von der Primarstufe in die Sekundarstufe I*. Tübingen: Narr.

Keßler, J-U. & D. Keatinge (2008): "Profiling Oral Second Language Development." In: Keßler, J.-U. (ed.) (2008): *Processability Approaches to Second Language Development and Second Language Learning*. Newcastle upon Tyne: Cambridge Scholars Publishing; pp. 167-197.

Michalska, B. (2010). *Interface between language testing and SLA research: Investigating correlations between proficiency rating scales of the Common European Framework and developmental Stages of Rapid Profile*. Unpublished Thesis, Newcastle University, 2010.

Plesser, A. & A. Lenzing. (in progress). "The Common European Framework – Linguistic Profiling. A complementary relationship?"

Study Questions:

1. Why is it important do diagnose learner progress in the EFL classroom?
2. Explain the "Scope-Precision-Dilemma".
3. Discuss when to apply the CEFR and when to make use of linguistic profiles as can be yielded by Rapid Profile.
4. How can grammar teaching be adopted to individual learners' needs?

Service Section | IV

Glossary

accuracy criterion: criterion used in SLA research to measure L2 grammatical development; establishes the acquisition of L2 forms on the basis of the degree of grammatical correctness with which they are produced.

argument structure: level of linguistic representation proposed in Lexical Functional Grammar (LFG); it specifies the arguments which verbal predicates take and assume a particular role in the meaning of a predicate. For example, the verbal predicate 'hit' requires two arguments, one of which assumes the role of AGENT and the other one the role of PATIENT.

Behaviourism: theory of learning that assumes that learners of an L2 learn language through imitation,practice, and pattern drills only.

Communicative Competence: includes the grammatical, sociolinguistic, and pragmatic competence of a language learner; according to many SLA theories, Communicative Competence is the aim of language learning.

constituent structure: level of linguistic representation; it specifies the hierarchical and linear arrangement of words and phrases in a sentence.

corrective feedback: if a learner receives corrective feedback (e.g. by the teacher) s/he is made aware of an error/mistake. If a learner says: "He like cakes" the teacher could provide corrective feedback by responding: "Yes, he likes cakes", which is a form of implicit corrective feedback, or "No, you have to say he like**s** cakes", which is a form of explicit corrective feedback.

deductive teaching and learning: in deductive teaching the teacher states a rule and presents some examples. After that, the learners apply the rule in an exercise.

descriptive grammar: a type of grammar which focuses on describing the actual use of a language by its respective speech community.

developmental error: an error that occurs in a learner's Interlanguage and shows that a developmental feature has not been acquired (e.g. as indicated by a missing 3rd–SG-s).

developmental path: predictable sequence L2 learners follow in the acquisition of L2 morphosyntactic structures.

developmental problem: key issue in SLA which is concerned with the question why learners follow a predictable sequence of stages of acquisition.

developmental readiness: this term indicates that learners minds have to be developmentally ready to process a grammatical structure before it can be learned and thus produced.

Diagnostic Task Cycle: extended version of the task cycle as proposed by Willis & Willis 1996. The D.T.C. as put forward by Keßler is based on the Rapid Profile analysis of a learner's Interlanguage; once the teacher knows about the individual states of Interlanguage development of his/her learners s/he can administer communicative tasks which match the developmental readiness of all the learners in one classroom.

Direct Method: also: Natural Method; a way of teaching an L2 with focus on oral communication; only the target language is used during the lessons.

Emergence Criterion: Criterion used in SLA research to measure the acquisition of L2 grammatical forms; takes emergence in production, i. e. the productive (non-formulaic) use of these forms as indicative of their acquisition.

empirical research: this type of research is based on observations and/or experiments.

error treatment: the way a teacher deals with errors occurring in both written and spoken Interlanguage.

exercise: this special type of activity usually has a restrictive focus and there is normally just one correct solution. Example: gap-texts

explicit memory: (also declarative memory) in e.m. of the human mind that type of knowledge is stored which is consciously accessible; contains our factual knowledge (e. g. that the word 'dog' refers to a hairy four-legged animal) and events (e. g. what we ate for breakfast).
In terms of language, explicit knowledge may enable a learner to express the rule "He/She/It, -s muss mit!" At the same time, the learner is not able to apply the rule until s/he has reached Stage 5, because the necessary processing procedure is part of implicit memory.

feature unification: formalism used in a variety of syntactic theories, including Lexical Functional Grammar (LFG); it allows the merging of features which belong to different places a sentence but are associated with the same conceptual unit. For example, in the sentence 'Many visitors came to see us' both the determiner 'many' and the noun 'visitors' carry the feature information 'number = plural'. The unification of both features ensures that these part of the sentence actually fit together (*'Many visitor came to see us').

Focus on Form (FonF): FonF is somehow between focus on meaning and focus on forms. In a FonF setting, there is a certain focus on grammatical structures which is connected to tasks that still focus on meaningful and authentic communication.

focused task: in contrast to unfocused tasks, focused tasks focus on language structures that the students have to use in order to complete the task (e.g. the 3rd –SG-s).

formula: language chunk, i.e. a sequence of words which is mentally stored and retrieved either as a whole unit ('How are you?') or as a partially analysed unit ('Do you have a ___?'). Formulaic language is considered the opposite of creative and productive language use which, however, still constitutes an important phase in the SLA process.

functional structure: level of linguistic representation (proposed in Lexical Functional Grammar); it specifies functional information in terms of grammatical functions (subject, object, etc.) and abstract features (number, tense, etc.).

Grammar Translation Method: an outdated way of teaching grammar with little focus on speaking; students translate texts from the L2 into their L1 concentrating on grammar rules and vocabulary.

Hypothesis Space: specifies the structural hypotheses learners can draw upon at each stage of development, i.e. which morpho-syntactic structures they can produce on the basis of already acquired processing procedures as well as the variational dimensions these procedures allow for.

Immersion: in Immersion Programmes, learners 'take a bath' in the target language. That means learners learn subjects such as mathematics or biology in the target language.

implicational hierarchy: a hierarchy of elements (here: processing procedures) in which a higher step requires the presence of all possible further steps. Due to the architecture of the human language processing system, the activation of lower-level resources are a necessary prerequisite for the functioning of higher-level resources. Thanks to the SLA process being implicationally ordered, linguists and applied linguists can predict which linguistic structure occurs next in a learner's Interlanguage, which facilitates L2 instruction.

implicit knowledge: type knowledge stored in the human mind which is not consciously accessible; implicit knowledge enables us to, e.g. walk, ride a bike, use a language productively.

inductive teaching and learning: in inductive teaching, L2 learners can discover the rules in the L2 input or presented examples presented by the teacher in contrast to deductive teaching.

initial state: starting point in the acquisition of L2 grammatical knowledge; the investigation what the initial state actually is, is one of the key issues dealt with in SLA research.

Input Enhancement: a method for foreign language teachers to provide input in a learner-centered fashion.

Interlanguage: a term coined by Larry Selinker in 1972; refers to the individual mental grammar each L2 learner. This internal linguistic system is neither the L1 nor the L2 of a learner.

Interlanguage variation: the Interlanguage is not the same among individual L2 learners (see target language variety), i.e. one learner may prefer a simplified version of the L2 from a more target like one.

learnability: l. means that L2 learners are only able to acquire a new grammatical form when they are cognitively ready for it and have already acquired its foundations (e.g. Stages 1-5 are the cognitive foundations of Stage 6).

learner grammar: see Interlanguage

lemma: mental representation of a lexical entry's meaning and syntax.

linearisation problem: in speech production, thoughts have to be mapped onto linguistic expressions. In this process, the speaker has to linearise, i.e. order the different pieces and types of information to express them in a way the interlocutor understands her/his message. For example, during message generation the speaker may linearise a sequence of events as 'Before Peter went to school, he ate a piece of cake' or 'After Peter ate a piece of cake, he went to school'.

logical problem: key issue in SLA which is concerned with the origins of an individual's linguistic knowledge.

Mapping (Lexical): correspondence or linking between different levels of linguistic representation. In LFG, lexical mapping refers to the correspondence between thematic structure, i.e. the representation of thematic roles such as AGENT, and argument structure, and between argument structure and functional structure.

memory: mental processes engaged in the acquisition, storage and retrieval of information; comprises explicit and implicit memory as particular mental memory stores.

mental representation: no physical entity, but mental structure that encodes knowledge of various types, such as phonological, morphological and syntactic information.

message generation: part of the speech production process; comprises the planning of what one wants to express, including the conception of a communicative intention and the selection of appropriate information for its realisation.

mistake: in contrast to an error, mistakes can be corrected by the learners themselves. They can be caused by tiredness or nervousness and are sometimes also called slips.

morphosyntax: term used to indicate that morphemes often exhibit syntactically-relevant information, such as whether an expression functions as the subject or object in a sentence. At the level of scientific study, the term refers to the investigation of these grammatical morphemes.

noticing: first proposed in the 1990s by Schmidt; refers to the moment when an L2 learner registers a particular linguistic form, e.g. the plural –s in ESL, in the output of a speaker or in the instructional material.

pattern drill: teaching technique applied in Audiolingualism which is characterized by frequent repetitions of grammatical patterns with the aim that students internalise the respective structure(s).

pedagogical grammar: this type of grammar describes a target language variety which facilitates the teaching and learning process.

prescriptive grammar: this type of grammar focuses on the structure of a language and how the language should be used.

procedural knowledge: see implicit knowledge.

Processability Theory: a psycholinguistic theory of SLA proposed by Pienemann (1998; 2005); explores in detail what happens in the mind of an L2 learner during the L2 acquisition process in that it accounts for processing mechanisms in SLA. PT spells out why certain grammatical features, such as 3rd-SG-s, are acquired later than, e.g. the plural-s in ESL.

processing procedure: psychological mechanism involved in the retrieval and assembly of linguistic information.

Profile Analysis: tool generated by Crystal et al. to assess language disorders; Rapid Profile was developed on its basis.

psychological constraint: a restriction that the architecture of the human language processing system imposes upon the learning of an L2.

Rapid Profile: computer-assisted program for screening speech samples collected from language learners to assess their level of language development as defined in Processability Theory.

rating scale: approach to evaluate and rate the language output of L2 learners (e.g. the Common European Framework of Reference).

Scope-Precision Dilemma: problem of researchers in the field of language testing whether to focus on either the language as a whole but superficially or a few aspects only but in a detailed way.

SLA research: concerned with the processes a learner undergoes while acquiring a foreign language; develops and deals with SLA theories.

stabilisation: temporary stagnation of particular Interlanguage features. S. can affect only certain linguistic features such as phonology or morphosyntax, while other parts of the Interlanguage system, such as vocabulary, are still developing.

Stage of acquisition: in Processability Theory, the Processing Hierarchy consists of six stages consisting of particular morphological and syntactic target language structures which are acquired successively.

Standard English: there is not just one Standard English. Among others there is American English, Australian English, British English, Canadian English and Indian English. Those varieties can differ in terms of phonology, grammar, vocabulary and spelling.

Steadiness Hypothesis: states that the Interlanguage and, thus, the learner's output remains steady in various communication-based tasks.

target language variety: individual L2 learners speak different varieties of a second language, which needs to be considered when teaching an L2 (cf. Hypothesis Space).

task: this special type of activity has an open outcome. There is more than just one correct solution to it.

Teachability Hypothesis: subset of Processability Theory which states that no Stage can be skipped or altered by instruction; the TH implies that foreign language teaching is most successful when its curriculum follows the stages of the Processing Hierarchy.

unfocused task: in comparison to focused tasks, unfocused tasks do not focus on any particular language structure.

Bibliography

Alderson, J. C. (1991). "Bands and Scores." In Alderson, J. C. and B. North (eds). *Language Testing in the 1990s*. London: Macmillan, pp. 71-86.

Alderson, J. C. (2007). "The CEFR and the Need for More Research." *The Modern Language Journal*, 91(4), pp. 659-663.

Allwright, R. L. (1984). "Why Don't Learners Learn What Teachers Teach? – The Interaction Hypothesis." In Singleton, D. M. and D. G. Little (eds). *Language Learning in Formal and Informal Contexts*. IRAAL: Dublin, pp. 3-18.

Azar, B. (2009). "The Final -S Problem: Does Teaching Grammar Help? Students Still Make Mistakes." At: teacher talk blog http://www.azargrammar.com/teacherTalk/blog/2009/04/final-s-problem-does-teaching-grammar.html (26/08/2009)

Bachman, L. (1990). *Fundamental Considerations in Language Testing*. Oxford: Oxford University Press.

Bachman, L. and A. S. Palmer (2008). *Language Testing in Practice: Designing and Developing Useful Language Tests*. Oxford: Oxford University Press.

Baddeley, A. D., S. E. Gathercole and C. Papagno (1998). "The Phonological Loop as a Language Learning Device." *Psychological Review*, 105, pp. 158-173.

Barnwell, D. (1987). "Oral Proficiency Resting in the United States." *British Journal of Language Teaching*, 25, pp. 35-42.

Bausch, K. R. and F. G. Königs (1983). "'Lernt' oder 'erwirbt' man Fremdsprachen im Unterricht? Zum Verhältnis von Sprachlehrforschung und Zweitsprachenerwerbsforschung." *Die Neueren* Sprachen, 82(4), pp. 308-336.

Bhabha, H. K. (1997). "Queen's English – Ebonics, Nonstandard Vernacular or Hybridized Order of Speech." In ArtForum. http://findarticles.com/p/articles/mi_m0268/is_n7_v35/ai_19290185/pg_3/?tag=content;col1 (24/08/2009).

Birdsong, D. (1992). "Ultimate Attainment in Second Language Acquisition." Language, *68*, pp. 706-705.

Bley-Vroman, R. (1989). "The Logical Problem of Foreign Language Learning." In Gass, S. and J. Schachter (eds). *Linguistic Perspectives on Second Language Acquisition*. Cambridge: Cambridge University Press, pp. 41-68.

Börner, W. and K. Vogel (eds) (2002). *Grammatik und Fremdsprachenerwerb. Kognitive, psycholinguistische und erwerbstheoretische Perspektiven.* Tübingen: Narr.

Bogaert, N., K. Van Gorp, K. Bultynckk, A. Lanssens and V. Depauw (2006). "Task-Based Language Teaching in Science Education and Vocational Training." In Van den Branden, K. (ed). *Task-Based Language Teaching. From Theory to Practice.* Cambridge: Cambridge University Press, pp. 106-128.

Breen, M. (1987). "Learner Contributions to Task Design." In Candlin, C. and D. F. Murphy (eds). *Language Learning Tasks.* London: Prentice Hall, pp. 23-46.

Bresnan, J. (2001). *Lexical Functional Syntax.* Malden, Mass.: Blackwell.

Brindley, G. (1998). "Describing language development?" In Bachman, L. F. and A. D. Cohen (eds). *Interfaces Between Second Language Acquisition and Language Testing Research.* Cambridge: Cambridge University Press, pp. 112-140.

Brumfit C. J. and J. T. Roberts (1983). *An Introduction to Language and Language Teaching.* London: Batsford Academic and Educational.

Burmeister, P. (2006). "Immersion und Sprachunterricht im Vergleich." In Pienemann, M., J.-U. Keßler and E. Roos (eds). *Englischerwerb in der Grundschule. Ein Studien- und Arbeitsbuch.* Paderborn: Schöningh/UTB, pp. 196-216.

Burmeister, P. and A. Daniel (2002). "How Successful Is Late Partial Immersion? Some Findings from a Secondary School Program in Germany." In Burmeister, P., T. Piske and A. Rohde (eds). *An Integrated View of Language Development. Papers in Honor of Henning Wode.* Trier: Wissenschaftlicher Verlag Trier, pp. 499-515.

Burt, M. and C. Kiparsky (1975). *The Gooficon: A Repair Manual for English.* Rowley: Newbury House.

Bygate, M., P. Skehan and M. Swain (eds) (2001). *Researching Pedagogic Tasks: Second Language Learning, Teaching and Testing.* Harlow: Longman.

Byram, M. (1997). *Teaching and Assessing Intercultural Communicative Competence.* Clevedon: Multilingual Matters

Canale, M. and M. Swain (1980). "Theoretical Bases of Communicative Approaches to Second Language Teaching and Testing." *Applied Linguistics,* 1(1), pp. 1-47.

Candlin, C. (1987). "Towards Task-Based Language Learning." In Candlin, C. and D. F. Murphy (eds). *Language Learning Tasks*. London: Prentice Hall, pp. 5-22.

Candlin, C. and D. F. Murphy (eds) (1987). *Language Learning Tasks*. London: Prentice Hall.

Carless, D. (2009). "Revisiting the TBLT versus P-P-P Debate: Voices from Hong Kong." *Asian Journal of English Language Teaching*, 19, pp. 49-66.

Celce-Murcia, M. (ed) (2001). *Teaching English as a Second or Foreign Language*. 3rd edition. Boston, MA: Heinle.

Cheshire, J. (1991). *English Around the World. Sociolinguistic Perspectives*. Cambridge: Cambridge University Press.

Christelli, G. (1994). *An Integrated, Contend-based Curriculum for Beginning Level English as a Second Language Learners of Middle School Age: Four Pilot Units*. An Independent Professional Project, School for International Training.

Chomsky, N. (1965). *Aspects of the Theory of Syntax*. Cambridge, Mass.: MIT Press.

Clahsen, H. (1985). "Profiling Second Language Development: A Procedure for Assessing L2 Proficiency." In Hyltenstam, K. and M. Pienemann (eds). *Modelling and Assessing Second Language Acquisition*. Clevedon: Multilingual Matters, pp. 283-331.

Cook, V. (2001). *Second Language Learning and Second Language Teaching*. 2nd edition. London: Arnold.

Corder, P. (1981). *Error Analysis and Interlanguage*. Oxford: Oxford University Press.

Cowan, R. (2008). *The Teacher's Grammar of English. A Course Book and Reference Guide*. Cambridge: Cambridge University Press.

Council of Europe (2001). *Common European Framework of Reference for Languages: Learning, Teaching, Assessment*. Cambridge: Cambridge University Press.

Council of Europe (2002). *Common European Framework of Reference for Languages: Learning, Teaching, Assessment. Case Studies*. Strasbourg: Council of Europe.

Council of Europe (2009). *Relating Language Examinations to the Common European Framework of Reference for Languages: Learning, Teaching, Assessment (CEFR). A Manual*. Strasbourg: Council of Europe.

Crookes, G. (1986). "Task Classifications: A Cross-Disciplinary Review." In *Technical Report No. 4*. Honolulu: Center for Second

Language Classroom Research, Social Science Research Institute, University of Hawaii.
Crowell, S. (2004). "The Neurobiology of Declarative Memory." In Schuhmann, J. H. et al. (eds). *The Neurobiology of Learning. Perspectives from Second Language Acquisition.* Mahwah, New Jersey: Erlbaum, pp. 67-98.
Crystal, D. (2002). *The English Language.* London: Penguin Books.
Crystal, D. (2004a). "In Word and Deed." *TES Teacher*, April 30, 2004.
Crystal, D. (2004b). *Rediscover Grammar.* 3rd edition. Harlow: Pearson and Longman.
Crystal, D., P. Fletcher and M. Garman (1976). *The Grammatical Analysis of Language Disability.* London: Arnold.
Cummins, J. (1976). "The Influence of Bilingualism on Cognitive Growth: A Synthesis of Research Findings and Explanatory Hypotheses." *Working Papers on Bilingualism*, 9, pp. 1-43.

DeKeyser, R. (2003). "Implicit and Explicit Learning." In Doughty, C. J. and M. H. Long (eds). *The Handbook of Second Language Acquisition.* Malden, MA: Blackwell, pp. 313-348.
Delanoy, W. and L. Volkmann (eds) (2006). *Cultural Studies in the EFL Classroom.* Heidelberg: Winter.
Desai, A. (1988). *Baumgartner's Bombay.* Portsmouth, NH: Heinemann.
DESI-Konsortium (2006). Unterricht und Kompetenzerwerb in Deutsch und Englisch. Zentrale Befunde der Studie Deutsch-Englisch-Schülerleistungen-International (DESI). Frankfurt a. M.: Deutsches Institut für Internationale Pädagogische Forschung. PDF-Datei bei: http://www.dipf.de/de/pdf-dokumente/projekte-materialien/desi-zentrale-befunde/view (19/02/2010).
Di Biase, B. (2002). "Focusing Strategies in Second Language Development: A Classroom-Based Study of Italian L2 in Primary School." In Di Biase, B. (ed). *Developing a Second Language: Acquisition, Processing and Pedagogy Issues in Arabic, Chinese, English, Italian, Japanese, Swedish.* Melbourne: Language Australia, pp. 95-120.
Di Biase, B. (2008). "Focus on Form and Development in L2 Learning." In Keßler, J.-U. (ed). *Processability Approaches to Second Language Development and Second Language Learning.* Newcastle upon Tyne: Cambridge Scholars Publishing, pp. 197-219.
Dirven R. (1990). "Pedagogical Grammar." *Language Teaching*, 13(1), pp. 1-18.

Doughty, C. J. (1991). "Second Language Instruction Does Make a Difference: Evidence from an Empirical Study of SL Relativization." *Studies in Second Language Acquisition, 13*, pp. 431-469.

Doughty, C. J. (2003). "Instructed SLA: Constraints, Compensation, and Enhancement." In Doughty, C. J. and M. H. Long (eds). *The Handbook of Second Language Acquisition*. Malden, MA: Blackwell, pp. 256-310.

Doughty, C. J. (2004). "Effects of Instruction on Learning a Second Language: A Critique of Instructed SLA Research." In VanPatten, B., J. Williams, S. Rott and M. Overstreet (eds). *Form-Meaning Connections in Second Language Acquisition*. New York: Routledge, Taylor & Francis, pp. 181-202.

Doughty, C. J. and J. Williams (eds) (1998). *Focus on Form in Classroom Second Language Acquisition*. Cambridge: Cambridge University Press.

Doughty, C. J. and M. H. Long (eds) (2003). *The Handbook of Second Language Acquisition*. Malden, MA: Blackwell.

Dulay, H. and M. Burt (1973). "Should We Teach Children Syntax?" *Language Learning, 23*(2), pp. 245-258.

Duncan, L. (2005). *Killing Mr. Griffin*. Egmont: Aschhoug/Alina.

Duran, G. and G. Ramaut (2006). "Tasks for Absolute Beginners and Beyond: Developing and Sequencing Tasks at Basic Proficiency Levels." In Van den Branden, K. (ed). *Task-Based Language Teaching. From Theory to Practice*. Cambridge: Cambridge University Press, pp. 47-75.

Eckerth, J. (2008). "Task-Based Language Learning and Teaching – Old Wine in New Bottles?" In Eckerth, J. and S. Siekmann (eds). *Task-Based Language Learning and Teaching. Theoretical, Methodological, and Pedagogical Perspectives*. Frankfurt and New York: Peter Lang, pp. 13-46.

Eckerth, J. and S. Siekmann (eds) (2008). *Task-Based Language Learning and Teaching. Theoretical, Methodological, and Pedagogical Perspectives*. Frankfurt and New York: Peter Lang.

Eckerth, J., K. Schramm and E. Tschirner (2009). "Recent Research (2002–2008) on Applied Linguistics and Language Teaching with Specific Reference to L2 German (Part 1)." *Language Teaching, 42*(1), pp. 41-66.

Edelenbos, P., R. Johnston and A. Kubanek (2006). "The Main Pedagogical Principles Underlying the Teaching of Languages to Very

Young Learners. Languages for the Children of Europe. Published Research, Good Practice and Main Principles." In: *Final Report of the EAC 89/04*, Lot 1 study.

Ellis, N. C. (ed) (1997). *Implicit and Explicit Learning of Languages.* London: Academic Press.

Ellis, R. (1985). *Understanding Second Language Acquisition.* Oxford: Oxford University Press.

Ellis, R. (1989). "Are Classroom and Naturalistic Acquisition the Same? A Study of the Classroom Acquisition of German Word Order Rules." *Studies in Second Language Acquisition*, 11, pp. 303-28.

Ellis, R. (1991). *Second Language Acquisition and Language Pedagogy.* Clevedon: Multilingual Matters.

Ellis, R. (1994). *The Study of Second Language Acquisition.* Oxford: Oxford University Press.

Ellis, R. (1997). *SLA Research and Language Teaching.* Oxford: Oxford University Press.

Ellis, R. (ed) (2001). *Form-Focused Instruction and Second Language Learning.* Malden, MA: Blackwell.

Ellis, R. (2003). *Task-Based Language Learning and Teaching.* Oxford: Oxford University Press.

Elsner, D. (2007). Hörverstehenstest "Zeig was du kannst"; online unter: http://www.fb10.uni-bremen.de/homepages/elsner/ (8/03/2010).

Estaire, S. and J. Zanón (1994). *Planning Classwork: A Task-Based Approach.* Oxford: Heinemann.

Felix, S. (1982). *Psycholinguistische Aspekte des Zweitspracherwerbs.* Tübingen: Narr.

Ferrari, S. & N. Nuzzo (2009): "Exploring Interfaces, between PT and SLA developmental measures." Paper read at the 9th International Symposium on Procerability, Bilingualism and SLA. Ludwigsburg, 16.7.2009.

Fotos, S. (2001). "Cognitive Approaches to Grammar Instruction." In Celce-Murcia, M. (ed). *Teaching English as a Second or Foreign Language.* 3rd edition. Boston, MA: Heinle, pp. 267-283.

Fox, A. (2008). "Using Podcasts in the EFL Classroom." In *TESL-EJ*, *11*(4) (http://tesl-ej.org/ej44/a4.html, 16/03/2010).

Gascoigne, C. (2006). "Toward an Understanding of Incidental Input Enhancement in Computerized L2 Environments." *CALICO Journal*, 24(1), pp. 147-162.

Gass, S. (2003). "Input and Interaction." In: Doughty, C. J. and M. H. Long (eds). *The Handbook of Second Language Acquisition.* Malden, MA: Blackwell, pp. 224-255.

Gazzaniga, M. S. (2002). *Cognitive Neuroscience.* New York: Norton.

Genesee, F. (1987). *Learning Through Two Languages. Studies of Immersion and Bilingual Education.* Cambridge, MA: Newbury House.

Genesee, F. (1994). *Integrating Language and Content: Lessons from Immersion* (Educational Practice Report No. 11). Santa Cruz, CA and Washington, DC: National Center for Research on Cultural Diversity and Second Language Learning.

Grießhaber, Wilhelm (2006). *Lernende unterstützen: die Profilanalyse als didaktisch nutzbares Werkzeug der Lernersprachenanalyse.* Münster: WWU Sprachenzentrum (online verfügbar unter: http://spzwww.uni-muenster.de/~griesha/pub/tlernendeunterstuetzen06.pdf, 18/3/2010)

Håkansson, G. and C. Norrby (2007). "Processability Theory Applied to Written and Oral Swedish." In Mansouri, F. (ed). *Bilingualism and Theory-Driven Second Language Acquisition Research.* Cambridge: Cambridge Scholar Press, pp. 81 – 94.

Haley, M. H. and P. Rentz (2002). "Applying SLA Research and Theory to Practice: What Can a Teacher Do?" *TESL-EJ*, 5(4), A-2. Retrieved 07/17/07 from: http://teslej.org/ej20/a2.html.

Han, Z.-H. (2004). *Fossilization in Adult Second Language Acquisition.* Clevedon, UK: Multilingual Matters.

Han, Z.-H. and T. Odlin (eds) (2004). *Studies of Fossilization in Second Language Acquisition.* Clevedon: Multilingual Matters.

Harrington, K. N. and T. Ware (eds) (2007). *Recipes for Success in Foreign Language Teaching: Ready-Made Activities for the L2 Classroom.* München: Lincom.

Haß, F. (2006). *Fachdidaktik Englisch. Tradition – Innovation – Praxis.* Stuttgart: Klett.

Haß, F. (ed) (2006a). *Red Line 1.* 2nd edition. Stuttgart: Klett.

Hollm, J., A. Hüttermann, J.-U. Keßler and G. Schlemminger (2010). *Zwischenbericht der wissenschaftlichen Begleitung des Schulversuchs „BiliReal2013" in Baden-Württemberg.* Stuttgart: Ministerium für Kultus, Jugend und Sport.

Huber, T. (2009). *Bilingualer Unterricht an Hauptschulen? Ein Bilinguales Modul im Fach Religion. Zulassungsarbeit an der Pädagogischen Hochschule Ludwigsburg.* Unveröffentlichtes Manuskript.

Hüllen, W. (1987). *Englisch als Fremdsprache.* Tübingen: Francke/UTB.

Hudson, R. (1992). *Teaching Grammar. A Guide for the National Curriculum.* Oxford: Blackwell.

Hughes, A. (2006). *Testing for Language Teachers.* 2nd edition. Cambridge: Cambridge University Press.

Hughes, A. and P. Trudgill (1987). *English Accents and Dialects.* London: Arnold.

Hyltenstam, K. and M. Pienemann (eds) (1985). *Modelling and Assessing Second Language Acquisition.* Clevedon: Multilingual Matters,

Issidorides, D. C. and J. Hulstijn (1992). "Comprehension of Grammatically Modified and Non-Modified Sentences by Second Language Learners." *Applied Psycholinguistics,* 13(2), pp. 147-164.

Jansen, L. (1991). "The Development of Word Order in Natural and Formal German Second Language Acquisition." *Australian Working Papers of Language Development,* 5, pp. 1-42.

Johnston, M. (1997). *Development and Variation in Learner Language.* PhD Dissertation. Canberra: Australian National University.

Johnson, K. (2003). *Designing Language Teaching Tasks.* Basingstoke, Hampshire: Palgrave MacMillan.

Johnson, K. and K. Morrow (1981). *Communication in the Classroom.* Harlow: Longman.

Kersten, K. (2009). "Profiling Child ESL Acquisition: Practical and Methodological Issues." In Keßler, J.-U. and D. Keatinge (eds). *Research in Second Language Acquisition: Empirical Evidence Across Languages.* Cambridge: Cambridge Scholars Press, pp. 267-293.

Kersten, K., U. Fischer, P. Burmeister and A. Lommel (2009). *Immersion in der Grundschule. Ein Leitfaden.* Kiel: Verein für Frühe Mehrsprachigkeit an Kindertagesstätten und Schulen e.V.; PDF-Datei zum Download unter: http://www.fmks-online.de/ (22/02/2010)

Keßler, J.-U. (2005). "Fachdidaktik meets Psycholinguistik – Heterogenität im Englischunterricht erkennen, verstehen und als Chance nutzen." In Bräu, K. and U. Schwerdt (eds). *Heterogenität als Chance. Vom Umgang mit Gleichheit und Differenz in der Schule.* Münster: LIT, pp. 263-284.

Keßler, J.-U. (2006). *Englischerwerb im Anfangsunterricht diagnostizieren. Linguistische Profilanalysen am Übergang von der Primarstufe in die Sekundarstufe I.* Tübingen: Narr.

Keßler, J.-U. (2006a). "Negotiation for Intercultural Meaning in Secondary School EFL-Classrooms: Australia – a Project." In Delanoy, W. and L. Volkmann (eds). *Cultural Studies in the EFL Classroom*. Heidelberg: Winter, pp. 183-194.

Keßler, J.-U. (2006b). "Frühbeginn und Lernersprache: Englischerwerb in der Primarstufe." In Schlüter, N. (ed). *Fortschritte im frühen Fremdsprachenunterricht*. Berlin: Cornelsen, pp. 101-108.

Keßler, J.-U. (ed) (2008). *Processability Approaches to Second Language Development and Second Language Learning*. Newcastle upon Tyne: Cambridge Scholars Publishing.

Keßler, J.-U. (2008a). "Processability Aspects of Second Language Development and Second Language Learning." In Keßler, J.-U. (ed). *Processability Approaches to Second Language Development and Second Language Learning*. Newcastle upon Tyne: Cambridge Scholars Publishing, pp. 67-86.

Keßler, J.-U. (2008b). "Communicative Tasks and Second Language Profiling: Linguistic and Pedagogical Implications." In Eckerth, J. and S. Siekmann (eds). *Task-Based Language Learning and Teaching. Theoretical, Methodological, and Pedagogical Perspectives*. Frankfurt and New York: Peter Lang, pp. 291-310.

Keßler, J.-U. (2009). "Englischdidaktik in 'Erklärungsnot': Implizites und explizites Wissen und die Rolle der Bewusshort-term memoryachung im schulischen Englischerwerb." In Vogt, R. (ed). *Erklären: Gesprächsanalytische und fachdidaktische Perspektiven*. Tübingen: Stauffenburg, pp. 93-107.

Keßler, J.-U. and V. Kohli (2006). "Erhebung von Sprachprofilen im frühen Englischerwerb: Kommunikative tasks in Forschung und Fremdsprachenunterricht." In Pienemann, M., J.-U. Keßler and E. Roos (eds). *Englischerwerb in der Grundschule. Ein Studien- und Arbeitsbuch*. Paderborn: Schöningh/UTB, pp. 89-96.

Keßler, J.-U. and D. Keatinge (2008). "Profiling Oral Second Language Development." In Keßler, J.-U. (ed). *Processability Approaches to Second Language Development and Second Language Learning*. Newcastle upon Tyne: Cambridge Scholars Publishing, pp. 167-197.

Keßler, J.-U. and A. Lenzing (2008). "The dog is grabing" – Englischunterricht in der Grundschule und den Übergang neu denken." In Heggen, T. and D. Götze (eds). *Grundschule neu denken. Beiträge des Paderborner Grundschultages 2006 zu Heterogenität, Medien und Ganztag*. Münster: LIT, pp. 99-111.

Keßler, J.-U. and M. Liebner (2009). "Diagnostic Task Cycle & Podcasts im Aufgabenorientierten Fremdsprachenunterricht." Paper presented at the 23rd DGFF Congress. Leipzig: 01/10/2009.

Keßler, J.-U. and M. Liebner (in press): "Medienbasierte Lernstandsdiagnostik und individuelle Lernerförderung – Neokommunikativer Fremdsprachenunterricht in heterogenen Lerngruppen." In Reinfried, M. and L. Volkmann (eds). *Medien im neokommunikativen Fremdsprachenunterricht. Einsatzformen, Inhalte, Lernerkompetenzen.* Frankfurt and New York: Peter Lang.

Keßler, J.-U., M. Liebner and F. Mansouri (in press). "Teaching." In Pienemann, M. and J.-U. Keßler (eds). *Studying Processability Theory. An Introductory Textbook.* Amsterdam: John Benjamins.

Kieweg, W. (1996). Alternative Konzepte zur Vermittlung von Grammatik. *Der fremdsprachliche Unterricht Englisch*, 25, pp. 4-11.

Ko, Heejong (2005). "Interlanguage Grammars in Second Language Acquisition." PowerPoint Presentation, MIT. http://ling.snu.ac.kr/ko/Publication.html (14/01/2010).

Kohli, D. (1989). "Indian English: A Khichri of Words." In *Times Literary Supplement*, December 1-7, p. 1322 and p. 1340.

Krahnke, K. (1987). *Approaches to Syllabus Design for Foreign Language Teaching.* New York: Prentice Hall.

Krashen, S. D. (1981). *Second Language Acquisition and Second Language Learning.* Oxford: Pergamon Press.

Krashen, S. D. (1984). "Immersion: Why It Works and What It Has Taught Us." *Language and Society*, 12, 61-64.

Krashen, S. D. (1985). *The Input Hypothesis: Issues and Implications.* London: Longman.

Krashen, S. D. and T. Terrel (1983). *The Natural Approach: Language Acquisition in the Classroom*. Hayward, CA: Alemy Press.

Lakshmanan, U. and L. Selinker (2001). "Analysing Interlanguage: How Do We Know What Learners Know?" *Second Language Research*, 17(4), pp. 393-420.

Larsen-Freeman, D. (1997). "Grammar and Its Teaching: Challenging the Myths." http://www.cal.org/resources/digest/larsen01.html (19/08/2009).

Larsen-Freeman, D. (2000). *Techniques and Principles in Language Teaching.* Oxford: Oxford University Press.

Larsen-Freeman, D. (2001). "Teaching Grammar." In Celce-Murcia, M. (ed). *Teaching English as a Second or Foreign Language.* 3rd edition. Boston, MA: Heinle, pp. 251-266.

Lee, N. (2004). "The Neurobiology of Procedural Memory." In Schuhmann, J. H. et al. (eds). *The Neurobiology of Learning. Perspectives from Second Language Acquisition.* Mahwah, New Jersey: Erlbaum, pp. 39-66.

Lee, J. (2000). *Tasks and Communicating in Language Classrooms.* Boston: McGraw-Hill.

Lenneberg, E. H. (1967a). *Biological Foundations of Language.* New York: Wiley.

Lenneberg, E. H. (ed) (1967b). *New Directions in the Study of Language.* Cambridge, Mass.: MIT Press.

Legutke, M., A. Müller-Hartmann and M. Schocker-v. Ditfurth (2009). *Teaching English in the Primary School.* Stuttgart: Klett.

Lenzing, A. (2004). *Textbooks and Teachability: An Analysis of Primary School Textbooks in Terms of Processability Theory.* Unpublished thesis at Paderborn University, Germany.

Lenzing, A. (2006). "Lehrwerke für den frühen Fremdsprachenunterricht. Eine sprachwissenschaftliche Analyse." In Pienemann, M., J.-U. Keßler and E. Roos (eds). *Englischerwerb in der Grundschule. Ein Studien- und Arbeitsbuch.* Paderborn: Schöningh/UTB, pp. 185-196.

Lenzing, A. (2008). "Teachability and Learnability: An Analysis of Primary School Textbooks." In Keßler, J.-U. (ed). *Processability Approaches to Second Language Development and Second Language Learning.* Newcastle upon Tyne: Cambridge Scholars Publishing, pp. 221-241.

Liebner, M. (2002). *Empirische Untersuchung des englischen Zweitspracherwerbs in verschiedenen Lernergruppen.* Unpublished thesis at Paderborn University, Germany.

Lenzing, A. (in progress). *The Development of the Grammatical System in Second Language Acquisition.*

Levelt, Willem J.M. (1989). *Speaking. From Intention to Articulation.* Cambridge, Mass: MIT Press.

Lightbown, P. (1985). "Can Language Acquisition be Altered by Instruction?" In Hyltenstam, K. and M. Pienemann (eds). *Modelling and Assessing Second Language Acquisition.* Clevedon: Multilingual Matters, pp. 101-112.

Lightbown, P. (1998). "The Importance of Timing in Focus on Form." In: Doughty, C. J. and J. Williams (eds). *Focus on Form in Classroom*

Second Language Acquisition. Cambridge: Cambridge University Press, pp. 177-196.

Lightbown, P. and N. Spada (2006). *How Languages Are Learned.* 3rd revised edition. Oxford: Oxford University Press.

Little, D. (2006). "The Common European Framework of Reference for Languages: Content, Purpose, Origin, Reception, and Impact." *Language Teaching, 39*, pp. 167-190.

Littlewood, L. (1984). *Foreign and Second Language Learning: Language Acquisition Research and Its Implication for the Classroom.* Cambridge: Cambridge University Press.

Littlewood, W. (2004). "The Task-Based Approach: Some Questions and Suggestions." *ELT Journal, 58*(4), pp. 319-326.

Long, M. H (1983). "Does Second Language Instruction Make a Difference? A Review of Research." *TESOL Quarterly, 17*, pp. 359-382.

Long, M. H. (1985). "A Role for Instruction in Second Language Acquisition: Task-Based Language Teaching." In Hyltenstam, K. and M. Pienemann (eds). *Modelling and Assessing Second Language Acquisition.* Clevedon: Multilingual Matters, pp. 77-99.

Long, M. H. (1991). "Focus-on-Form: A Design Feature in Language Teaching Methodology." In de Bot, K., R. Ginsberg and C. Kramsch (eds). *Foreign Language Research.* Amsterdam: John Benjamins, pp. 39-52.

Long, M. H. (1996). "The Role of Linguistic Environment in Second Language Acquisition." In Ritchie, W. and T. Bhatia (eds). *Handbook of Research on Second Language Acquisition.* New York: Academic, pp. 413-468.

Long, M. H. (1997) http://www.mhhe.com/socscience/foreignlang/conf/option3.htm. last accessed: Feb 14th, 2010.

Long, M. H. (2000). "Focus on Form in Task-Based Language Teaching." In Lambert, R. and E. Shohamy (eds). *Language Policy and Pedagogy.* Amsterdam: John Benjamins, pp. 179-192.

Long, M. H. (2003). "Stabilisation and Fossilization in Interlanguage Development." In Doughty, C. J. and M. H. Long (eds). *The Handbook of Second Language Acquisition.* Malden, MA: Blackwell, pp. 487-535.

Long. M. H. (ed) (2005). *Second Language Needs Analysis.* Cambridge: Cambridge University Press.

Long. M. H. and G. Crookes (1987). "Intervention Points in Second Language Classroom Processes." In Das, P. (ed). *Patterns of Classroom Interaction.* Singapore: SEAMEO Regional Language Centre.

Long, M. H. and G. Crookes (1992). "Three Approaches to Task-Based Syllabus Design." *TESOL Quarterly*, *26*(1), pp. 27-56.

Long, M. H. and J. Norris (2000). "Task-Based Teaching and Assessment." In Byram, M. (ed). *Encyclopedia of Language Teaching*. London: Routledge, pp. 597-602.

Mansouri, F. and L. Duffy (2005). "The Pedagogic Effectiveness of Developmental Readiness in ESL Grammer Instruction." *Australian Review of Applied Linguistics*, *28*(1), pp. 81-99.

Mayer, M. (1969). *Frog, Where Are You?* New York: Puffin Books.

Mason, T. (2010)

http://www.timothyjpmason.com/WebPages/LangTeach/Capes/Ep-Dossier/HistLectures/Lesson1.htm

McGroarty, M. (2001). "Bilingual Approaches to Language Learning." In Celce-Murcia, M. (ed). *Teaching English as a Second or Foreign Language*. 3rd edition. Boston, MA: Heinle, pp. 345-356.

McLaughlin, B. (1987). *Theories of Second Language Learning*. London: Edward Arnold.

McNamara, T. F. (2007). *Language Testing*. Oxford: Oxford University Press.

Michalska, B. (2010). Interface between language testing and SLA research: Investigating correlations between proficiency rating scales of the common European Framework and developmental Stages of Rapid Profile. Unpublished Thesis, Newcastle, University 2010.

Multhaup, U. (2002). "A Processing View of English Grammar." In Finkbeiner, C. (ed). *Wholeheartedly English: A Life of Learning*. Berlin: Cornelsen Verlag, pp. 176-195.

Müller-Hartmann, A. and M. Schocker-v. Ditfurth (2004). *Introduction to English Language Teaching*. Stuttgart: Klett.

Müller-Hartmann, A. and M. Schocker-v. Ditfurth (eds) (2005). *Aufgabenorientierung im Fremdsprachenunterricht. Task-Based Language Learning and Teaching. Festschrift für Michael K. Legutke*. Tübingen: Narr.

Müller-Hartmann, A. and M. Schocker-v. Ditfurth (2011). *Teaching English: Task-Supported Language Learning*. Paderborn: Schöning/UTB.

Norris, J. and L. Ortega (2001). "Does Type of Instruction Make a Difference? Substantive Findings from a Meta-Analytic Review." In Ellis, R. (ed). *Form-Focused Instruction and Second Language Learning*. Malden, MA: Blackwell, pp. 157-213.

North, B. (1992). "European Language Portfolio: Some Options for a Working Approach to Design Scales of Proficiency." In *Council of Europe 1992*, pp. 158–174.

North, B. (2000). *The Development of a Common Framework Scale of Language Proficiency*. New York: Peter Lang.

Nunan, D. (1989). *Designing Tasks for the Communicative Classroom*. Cambridge: Cambridge University Press.

Nunan, D. (2004). *Task-Based Language Teaching*. Cambridge: Cambridge University Press.

Odlin, T. (ed) (1994). *Perspectives on Pedagogical Grammar.* Cambridge: Cambridge University Press.

Oliver, R. (1995). Negative Feedback in Child NS_NNS Conversation. *Studies in Second Language Acquisition*, 17, pp. 459-481.

Ortega, L. and M. H. Long (1997). "The Effects of Models and Recasts on the Acquisition of Object Topicalization and Adverb Placement in L2 Spanish." *Spanish Applied Linguistics*, 1(1), pp. 65-86.

Paradis, M. (1994). "Neurolinguistic Aspects of Implicit and Explicit Memory: Implications for Bilingualism and SLA." In Ellis, N. (ed). *Implicit and Explicit Learning of Languages.* London: Academic Press, pp. 393-417.

Pienemann, M. (1984). "Psychological Constraints on the Teachability of Languages." *Studies in Second Language Acquisition*, 6(2), pp. 186-214.

Pienemann, M. (1985). "Learnability and Syllabus Construction." In Hyltenstam, K. and M. Pienemann (eds). *Modelling and Assessing Second Language Acquisition.* Clevedon: Multilingual Matters, pp. 23-75.

Pienemann, M. (1989). "Is Language Teachable? Psycholinguistic Experiments and Hypotheses." *Applied Linguistics*, 10(1), pp. 52-79.

Pienemann, M. (1992). *Assessing Second Language Acquisition Through Rapid Profile*. Manuscript. University of Sydney.

Pienemann, M. (1995). "Second Language Acquisition: A First Introduction." *Australian Studies in Language Acquisition No. 2: Sydney: University of Western Sydney.*

Pienemann, M. (1998). *Language Processing and Second Language Development: Processability Theory.* Amsterdam: John Benjamins.

Pienemann, M., B. DiBiase, S. Kawaguchi (2005). *Cross-linguistic Aspects of Processability Theory.* Amsterdam: John Benjamins.

Pienemann, M. (2006). "Spracherwerb in der Schule. Was in den Köpfen der Kinder vorgeht." In Pienemann, M., J.-U. Keßler and E. Roos (eds). *Englischerwerb in der Grundschule. Ein Studien- und Arbeitsbuch.* Paderborn: Schöningh/UTB, pp. 33-63.

Pienemann, M. (2007). "Processability Theory." In VanPatten, B. and J. Williams (eds). *Theories in Second Language Acquisition. An Introduction.* Mahwah, NJ: Erlbaum. pp. 137-154.

Pienemann, M. (2008). "A Brief Introduction to Processability Theory." In Keßler, J.-U. (ed). *Processability Approaches to Second Language Development and Second Language Learning.* Newcastle upon Tyne: Cambridge Scholars Publishing, pp. 9-29.

Pienemann, M., M. Johnston and G. Brindley (1988). "Constructing an Acquisition-Based Procedure for Second Language Assessment." *Studies in Second Language Acquisition*, 10,2(88), pp. 217-243.

Pienemann, M. and M. Johnston (1987). "Factors Influencing the Development of Language Proficiency." In Nunan, D. (ed). *Applying Second Language Acquisition Research.* Adalaide: National Curriculum Resource Centre, pp. 45-141.

Pienemann, M. and J.-U. Keßler (2007). "Measuring Bilingualism." In Auer, P. and L. Wei (eds). *Handbook of Applied Linguistics. Vol. 5: Multilingualism.* Berlin and New York: Mouton/deGruyter, pp. 247-275.

Pienemann, M. and J.-U. Keßler (in press, a). "Processability Theory." In Gass, S. and A. Mackey (eds). *Handbook of Second Language Acquisition* (chp.13). New York: Routledge/Taylor Francis.

Pienemann, M. and J.-U. Keßler (in press, b): *Studying Processability Theory. An Introductory Textbook.* Amsterdam: John Benjamins.

Pienemann, M., J.-U. Keßler and E. Roos (eds) (2006). *Englischerwerb in der Grundschule. Ein Studien- und Arbeitsbuch.* Paderborn: Schöningh/UTB.

Pienemann, M., J.-U. Keßler and M. Liebner (2006). "Englischerwerb in der Grundschule: Untersuchungsergebnisse im Überblick." In Pienemann, M., J.-U. Keßler and E. Roos (eds). *Englischerwerb in der Grundschule. Ein Studien- und Arbeitsbuch.* Paderborn: Schöningh/UTB, pp. 67-88.

Pinker, S. (1984). *Language Learnability and Language Development.* Cambridge, MA: Harvard University Press.

Piske, T. (2006). "Zur Entwicklung der Englischkenntnisse bei deutschsprachigen Immersionsschülerinnen und –schülern im Grundschulalter." In Schlüter, N. (ed). *Fortschritte im frühen Fremdsprachenunterricht.* Berlin: Cornelsen, pp. 206-212.

Plesser, A. (2008). *Writing and Speaking in ESL: Is Production Steady Across the Production Mode Barrier?* Unpublished thesis at Paderborn University, Germany.

Plesser, A. (in prep.). "Writing and Speaking in SLA: The Mode Steadiness Hypothesis." In Keßler, J.-U. and M. Liebner (eds) (in prep.). *Developing and Assessing Second Language Grammars Across Languages*. Amsterdam: John Benjamins.

Plesser, A. (in prep.). "Stabilisation in Second Language Acquisition: Making a Case for Cross-sectional Data." In Keßler, J.-U. and M. Liebner (eds) (in prep.). *Developing and Assessing Second Language Grammars Across Languages*. Amsterdam: John Benjamins.

Plesser, A. & A. Lenzing (2010). "Challenging the Scope-Precision Dilemma in language Testing: The CEFR & Linguistic Profiling". Paper presented at the *PALA*, September 17th-19th, Sydney, Australia.

Prahbu, N. S. (1987). *Second Language Pedagogy*. Oxford: Oxford University Press.

Pullum, G. K. (2003). "Learnability: Mathematical Aspects." In *The Oxford International Encyclopedia of Linguistics*. 2nd edition. Oxford: Oxford University Press, pp. 431-434.

Purpura, J. E. (2004). *Assessing Grammar.* Cambridge: Cambridge University Press.

Richards, J. C., J. Platt and H. Weber (1985). *Longman Dictionary of Language Teaching and Applied Linguistics*. Harlow, Essex: Longman.

Richards, J. C., J. Platt and H. Weber (1992). *Longman Dictionary of Language Teaching and Applied Linguistics.* Harlow, Essex: Longman.

Richards, J. C. and W. A. Renandya (eds) (2002). *Methodology in Language Teaching: An Anthology of Current Practice.* Cambridge: Cambridge University Press.

Richards J. C. and T. S. Rodgers (2006). *Approaches and Methods in Language Teaching*. 2nd edition. Cambridge: Cambridge University Press.

Rimmer, W. (2006). "Measuring Grammatical Complexity: The Gordian Knot." In *Language Testing*, *23*(4), pp. 497 – 519.

Robinson, P. (1997). "Generalizability *and* Automaticity of Second Language Learning Under Implicit, Incidental, Enhanced *and* Instructed Conditions." *Studies in Second Language Acquisition*, *19*, pp. 223-224.

Rodgers (2009) http://www.cal.org/resources/Digest/rodgers.html

Roos, E. (2006). "Unterrichtskonzeption und Spracherwerb." In Pienemann, M., J.-U. Keßler and E. Roos (eds). *Englischerwerb in der Grundschule. Ein Studien- und Arbeitsbuch*. Paderborn: Schöningh/UTB, pp. 217-235.

Rutherford, W. and M. Sharwood Smith (1985). "Consciousness-Raising and Universal Grammar." *Applied Linguistics*, 6, pp. 274-82.

Rutherford, W. (1987). *Second Language Grammar: Learning and Teaching*. Harlow: Longman.

Rutherford, W. (1988). "Functions of Grammar in Language-Teaching Syllabus." In Rutherford, W. and M. Sharwood Smith (eds). *Grammar and Second Language Teaching. A Book of Readings*. New York: Newbury House, pp. 231-249.

Rutherford, W. and M. Sharwood Smith (eds) (1988). *Grammar and Second Language Teaching. A Book of Readings*. New York: Newbury House.

Schmidt, R. (1994). "Implicit Learning and the Cognitive Unconscious: Of Artificial Grammars and SLA." In Ellis, N. (ed). *Implicit and Explicit Learning of Languages*. London: Academic Press, pp. 165-209.

Schmidt, R. (2001). "Attention." In P. Robinson (ed). *Cognition and Second Language Instruction*. Cambridge: Cambridge University Press, pp. 3-32.

Schmidt, R. F., F. Lang and G. Thews (2005). *Physiologie des Menschen (mit Pathophysiologie)*. 29th edition. Heidelberg: Springer Medizin Verlag.

Schuldt, A. and Y. Schröter (2009). "Textbooks and Grammar Teaching." Paper presented in the Seminar "Teaching Grammar" at Ludwigsburg University of Education. WS 2009/10; 11/11/2009.

Schwarze, Dirk (2005): Meilensteine: 50 Jahre documenta. Kunstwerke und Künster. Berlin:Bostelmann & Siebenhaar.

Selinker, L. (1972). "Interlanguage." International Review of Applied Linguistics, 10, pp. 209-31.

Scott, M. S. (1974). "A Note on the Relationship Between English Proficiency, Years of Language Study and the Medium of Instruction." *Language Learning*, 24, pp. 99-104.

Seedhouse, P. (2005). "'Task' as Research Construct." *Language Learning*, 55(3), pp. 533-570.
Selinker, L. (1972). "Interlanguage." *International Review of Applied Linguistics*, 10, pp. 209-231.
Sharwood Smith, M. (1988). "Applied Linguistics and the Psychology of Instruction: A Case for Transfusion?" In Rutherford, W. and M. Sharwood Smith (eds). *Grammar and Second Language Teaching. A Book of Readings.* New York: Newbury House, pp. 206-223.
Skehan, P. (1996). "Second Language Acquisition Research and Task-Based Instruction." In Willis, J. and D. Willis (eds). *Challenge and Change in Language Teaching*. Oxford: Heinemann, pp. 17-30.
Skehan, P. (1998). *A Cognitive Approach to Language Learning*. Oxford: Oxford University Press.
Slobin, D. (1985). "Crosslinguistic Evidence for the Language-Making Capacity." In D. Slobin (ed). *The Crosslinguistic Study of Language Acquisition. Volume 2: Theoretical Issues*. Hillsdale, NJ: Lawrence Erlbaum, pp. 1157-1256.
Snow, M. A. (2001). "Content-Based and Immersion Models for Second and Foreign Language Teaching." In Celce-Murcia, M. (ed). *Teaching English as a Second or Foreign Language*. 3rd edition. Boston, MA: Heinle, pp. 303-318.
Swain, M. (2005). "The Output Hypothesis: Theory and Research." In Hinkel, E. (ed). *Handbook of Research in Second Language Teaching and Learning.* Hillsdale: Lawrence Erlbaum Associates, pp. 471-483.
Swain, M. and S. Lapkin (1982). *Evaluating Bilingual Education. A Canadian Case Study*. Clevedon: Multilingual Matters.

Tarone, E. (1988). *Variation in Interlanguage*. London: Edward Arnold.
Tonouchi, L. (2001). *Da Word*. Honolulu: Bamboo Ridge Press.
Trim, J. L. M. (2007). *Council for Cultural Co-operation / Modern Languages Division: Gemeinsamer europäischer Referenzrahmen für Sprachen: lernen, lehren, beurteilen*. Berlin: Langenscheidt.
Trudgill, P. and J. Hannah (2002). *International English: A Guide to the Varieties of Standard English*. 4th edition. London: Edward Arnold.

Quirk, R., S. Greenbaum, J. Leech and J. Svartvik (1985). *A Comprehensive Grammar of English*. Harlow: Longman.

Van Avermaet, P., M. Colpin, K. Van Gorp, N. Bogaert and K. Van den Branden (2006). "The Role of the Teacher in Task-Based Language

Teaching." In Van den Branden, K. (ed). *Task-Based Language Teaching. From Theory to Practice.* Cambridge: Cambridge University Press, pp. 175-196.

Van den Branden, K. (ed) (2006). *Task-Based Language Teaching. From Theory to Practice.* Cambridge: Cambridge University Press

Van den Branden, K. (2006). "Introduction: Task-Based Language Teaching in a Nutshell." In Van den Branden, K. (ed). *Task-Based Language Teaching. From Theory to Practice.* Cambridge: Cambridge University Press, pp. 1-16.

Van Gorp, K. and N. Bogaert (2006). "Developing Language Tasks for Primary and Secondary Education." In Van den Branden, K. (ed). *Task-Based Language Teaching. From Theory to Practice.* Cambridge: Cambridge University Press, pp. 76-105.

VanPatten, B. (ed) (2004). *Form-Meaning Connections in Second Language Acquisition.* Mahwah, NJ: Erlbaum.

Van Valin, R. (2001). *An Introduction to Syntax.* Cambridge: Cambridge University Press.

Ward, Jamie (2006). *The Student's Guide to Cognitive Neuroscience.* Hove: Psychology Press.

Weaver, C., C. McNally and S. Moerman (2001). "To Grammar or Not to Grammar: That is Not the Question!" *Voices from the Middle, 8*(3), pp. 17-33.

Weber-Fox, C. M. and Neville, H. J. (1996). "Maturational Constraints on Functional Specializations for Language Processing: ERP and Behavioral Evidence in Bilingual Speakers." *Journal of Cognitive Neuroscience, 8*, pp. 231-256.

Werlen, E. (2007). "Kontexte und Ziele Bilingualen Lehrens und Lernens – Grundzüge einer Didaktik des Bilingualen Lehrens und Lernens." In Schlemminger, G. (ed). *Aspekte Bilingualen Lehrens und Lernens. Schwerpunkt Grundschule.* Balong-term memory-annsweiler: Schneider-Verlag Hohengehren, pp. 199-220.

Wesche, M. B. (1993). "Discipline-Based Approaches to Language Study: Research Issues and Outcomes." In Krueger, M. and F. Ryan (eds). *Language and Content.* Lexington, MA: D. C. Heath; pp. 80-95.

Wesche, M. B. (2002). "Early French Immersion: How Has the Original Canadian Model Stood the Test of Time?" In Burmeister, P., T. Piske and A. Rohde (eds). *An Integrated View of Language Development. Papers in Honor of Henning Wode.* Trier: WVT, pp. 357-379.

Weskamp, R. (2001). *Fachdidaktik: Grundlagen & Konzepte.* Berlin: Cornelsen.

Williams, J. (2004). "Implicit Learning of Form-Meaning Connections." In VanPatten, B. (ed). *Form-Meaning Connections in Second Language Acquisition.* Mahwah, NJ: Erlbaum, pp. 213-230.

Willis, J. and D. Willis (eds) (1996). *Challenge and Change in Language Teaching.* Oxford: Heinemann.

Willis, D. and J. Willis (2007). *Doing Task-Based Teaching.* Oxford: Oxford University Press.

Wimsatt, W. C. (1999). "Generativity, Entrenchment, Evolution, and Innateness: Philosophy, Evolutionary Biology, and Conceptual Foundations of Science." In V. G. Hardcastle (ed). *Where Biology Meets Psychology.* Cambridge, Mass.: MIT Press, pp. 139-179.

Wode, H. (1978). "L1-Erwerb, L2-Erwerb und Fremdsprachenunterricht." In *Die Neueren Sprachen*, 77(5), pp. 452-465.

Wode, H. (1988). *Einführung in die Psycholinguistik. Theorien, Methoden, Ergebnisse.* München: Hueber Verlag.

Wode, Henning (1995). *Lernen in der Fremdsprache. Grundzüge von Immersion und bilingualem Unterricht.* Ismaning: Max Hueber Verlag.

Yule, G. (1997). *Referential Communication Tasks.* Hillsdale: Lawrence Erlbaum.

Yule, G. (2006). *The Study of Language.* 3rd edition. Cambridge: Cambridge University Press.

Zaunbauer, A. C. M. and J. Möller (2007). "Schulleistungen monolingual und immersiv unterrichteter Kinder am Ende des ersten Schuljahres." *Zeitschrift für Entwicklungspsychologie und Pädagogische Psychologie*, 39, pp.141-153.

Ziegésar v., D. and M. v. Ziegésar (2009). *Einführung von Grammatik im Englischunterricht/ Materialien und Modelle.* Nachdruck der 2. Auflage. München: Oldenbourg.

Zydatiß, W. (2000). *Bilingualer Unterricht in der Grundschule: Entwurf eines Spracherwerbskonzeptes für zweisprachige Immersion.* Ismaning: Hueber.

Zydatiß, W. (2007). *Deutsch-Englische Züge in Berlin (DEZIBEL): Eine Evaluation des bilingualen Sachfachunterrichts an Gymnasien – Kontext, Kompetenzen, Konsequenzen.* Frankfurt and New York: Peter Lang.

Acknowledgements

This book would never have been possible without the personal and professional support of many people. Unfortunately, it is impossible to mention each of them here; however, we would like to express our gratitude to all those who were involved in the making of this book in one way or another. First of all, we would like to thank our inspiring students, both in Ludwigsburg and in Paderborn, who were patient enough to try out some of the chapters in various seminars and who provided us with valuable feedback.

We are most grateful to Manfred Pienemann (Paderborn University), who has given us mental and professional support throughout the last five years. He has constantly supported our efforts to apply his psycholinguistic theory to the foreign language classroom. He developed one of the most influential theories in second language acquisition, namely *Processability Theory* (Pienemann 1998 and 2005), which is the underlying theoretical framework of this book. The primary goal of our book is to introduce an *Interlanguage Approach* to grammar teaching that goes beyond teaching the grammar of one target language.

Further, we wish to thank our colleagues, both at Ludwigsburg University of Education and Paderborn University, for their open ears and their advice concerning the manuscript of this book and the work surrounding it. We are most grateful to Vijaya John Kohli, Karina Lammert and Sina Weber (Paderborn University), Peter Fenn (Ludwigsburg), and Angela Hahn (Munich) for their comments on both the first drafts as well as the full manuscript. Special thanks to Peter Fenn, who also supported us by bringing his native speaker competence to bear on the editing of our book. In this regard, we also want to thank Teresa Behr.

Furthermore, we would like to thank particularly Anke Lenzing (Paderborn University) for her valuable support. Not only did she proof-read various chapters of the book, but she has always been open-minded towards our ideas. Special thanks to her for her inspiring and authentic friendship, which has grown even more with personal challenges, and, above all, with conducting promising SLA research with Anja.

Benjamin Ade-Thurow (Ludwigsburg) and Ronny Eckardt (Paderborn) did a great job refining the shape of the manuscript. Many thanks to them for their style editing and most valuable support during the formatting of the manuscript.

The book makes use of some illustrations that were designed to support the learning process while reading the book. Those illustrations were created by Verena Wendel (www.verena.wendel.com), an art student at Ludwigsburg University of Education. She did a great job visualising some of the underlying concepts of our book in the form of wonderful pieces of modern art. We would really like to thank Verena for her contribution to this book. Another important student from Ludwigsburg who spent quite some time proof-reading and style editing is Carolin Reuschel. She also supported our work with contributions to the study section of the book.

Writing a book is always a great and time-consuming adventure. We would like to express our grateful thanks to our families, who not only supported but also encouraged us to sit down and get our work done – even if this meant that we did not have time to spend with them.

Last but not least, we would like to thank Engelbert Thaler (Augsburg) and Diethard Sawicki (Schoeningh Verlag) on behalf of the publishers.

It is quite possible that we have forgotten to name some other important contributors to our project, but this is only the result of our forgetfulness and not because these people did not offer important contributions. This last paragraph is therefore dedicated to all those of our students, colleagues, and friends who also contributed to the making of this book and whom we did not mention here personally as a result of out forgetfulness: Thank you very much!

Ludwigsburg and Paderborn, April 2011
Jörg-U. Keßler & Anja Plesser

Index